Advance praise for *Shi'ite Islam: Polity, Ideology, and Creed:*

"I can't think of any book in English that serves so well as a primer and introduction to Shi'ism and as a brilliant account of revolutionary theory in Iran . . . An original book in various aspects, and unique for the range of coverage."
Professor Ira Lapidus, University of California at Berkeley

"Written in the best tradition of French participatory observation of Islam by one of the world's leading scholars of Shi'ism and Iran, this is unquestionably the most comprehensive account of the historical, religious, and sociological factors that have contributed to the emergence of the 'islamic revolution' in Iran, as well as a most insightful analysis of the dynamics of contemporary ideological and political trends in the islamic world at large. Obviously a very important book."
Professor Hermann Landolt, McGill University

"Yann Richard's *Shi'ite Islam* is an illuminating study of som⌐   significant Muslim communities. Based on a clear exposition of t⌐   from the earliest days of Islam, it sheds a remarkable and ⌐   es in the contemporary world. Richards's knowle⌐   is long personal experience, and the book is a⌐   author is likely to get to a view of Shi'ism from   ⌐ts to understand what Shi'te Islam is about, there is   ⌐an Yann Richard's lucid, deeply knowledgeable and sympathet⌐   ⌐o means uncritical – book."
Dr David Morgan, School of Oriental and   ⌐n Studies, University of London

"The author provides a lively kaleidoscopic picture of modern Shi'ite Islam, focussed on the Islamic Republic of Iran, with a distinct personal touch."
Professor Wilfred Madelung, The Oriental Institute, The University of Oxford

"Well-written, highly readable, and scholarly, *Shi'ite Islam: Polity, Ideology, and Creed* is valuable and informative for students, scholars, and general readers."
Nikki Keddie, *Contention*

"A much-needed introduction to Shi'ism by a leading scholar . . . This book offers a warm and most comprehensive account of a rich and variegated tradition by a distinguished Orientalist attuned to Iran and Shi'ism as the best of insiders."
Dr Chibli Mallat, School of Oriental and African Studies, University of London

"Shi'ism has become a subject of particular interest in the West in the last fifteen years, since its prominent role in the overthrow of the Shah and the formation of the Islamic Republic in Iran. The resulting negative image of Shi'ite Islam and scepticism about the place of religion in political life still persist, and the need for explanation remains. Yann Richard, unusually well equipped to pierce the veil of ignorance, raises and discusses many crucial questions in this personal, elegant, and judicious account of Shi'ite Islam. In doing so, he reveals not only the evolution of the modern face of Shi'ism, but also the cross-currents and tensions below the surface . . . Yann Richard's stimulating book provides many insights for both students of the Middle East and the general reader."
Dr Charles Melville, Faculty of Oriental Studies, University of Cambridge

Studies in Social Discontinuity

General Editor: Charles Tilly, The New School for Social Research

Studies in Social Discontinuity began in 1972 under the imprint of Academic Press. In its first fifteen years 53 titles were published in the series, including important volumes in the areas of historical sociology, political economy, and social history.

Revived in 1989 by Blackwell Publishers, the series will continue to include volumes emphasizing social changes and non-Western historical experience, as well as translations of major works.

Published:

The Perilous Frontier
Nomadic Empires and China
Thomas J. Barfield

Regents and Rebels
The Revolutionary World of an Eighteenth-Century Dutch City
Wayne Ph. te Brake

The Word and the Sword
How Techniques of Information and Violence Have Shaped Our World
Leonard M. Dudley

Coffee, Contention, and Change
in the Making of Modern Brazil
Mauricio Font

Nascent Proletarians
Class Formation in Post-Revolutionary France
Michael P. Hanagan

The Structures of History
Christopher Lloyd

Shi'ite Islam
Polity, Ideology, and Creed
Yann Richard

Social Evolutionism
A Critical History
Stephen K. Sanderson

Coercion, Capital, and European States
AD 990–1990
Charles Tilly

Anti-Semitism in France
A Political History from Léon Blum to the Present
Pierre Birnbaum

In preparation:

Forget the Family
David Levine

Shi'ite Islam

Polity, Ideology, and Creed

Yann Richard

Translated by Antonia Nevill

BLACKWELL
Oxford UK & Cambridge USA

English translation first published 1995

Blackwell Publishers
238 Main Street
Cambridge, Massachusetts 02142
USA

108 Cowley Road
Oxford OX4 1JF
UK

Library of Congress Cataloging-in-Publication Data

Richard, Yann.
    [Islam chi'ite. English]
    Shi'ite Islam: polity, ideology, and creed / Yann Richard.
        p. cm. – (Studies in social discontinuity)
    Includes bibliographical references (p.) and index.
    ISBN 1-55786-469-1. – ISBN 1-55786-470-5 (paperback)
    1. Shi'ah.   I. Title.   II. Series.
BP193.5.R5313   1995
297'.2042–dc20   94–15820
                                                                     CIP

British Library Cataloguing in Publication Data

A CIP catalogue record for this book is available from the British Library.

Typeset in 11 on 13 pt Ehrhardt
by Graphicraft Typesetters Ltd., Hong Kong
Printed in Great Britain by Hartnolls Limited, Bodmin, Cornwall

This book is printed on acid-free paper

Contents

Series Editor's Preface

Studies in Social Discontinuity present historically grounded analyses of important social transformations, ruptures, conflicts, and contradictions. Although we of Blackwell Publishers interpret that mission broadly, leave room for many points of view, and absolve authors of any responsibility for proselytization on behalf of our intellectual program, the series as a whole demonstrates the relevance of well-crafted historical work for the understanding of contemporary social structures and processes. Books in the series pursue one or more of four varieties of historical analysis: (1) using evidence from past times and places systematically to identify regularities in processes and structures that transcend those particular times and places; (2) reconstructing critical episodes in the past for the light they shed on important eras, peoples, or social phenomena; (3) tracing the origins or previous phases of significant social processes that continue into our own time; (4) examining the ways that social action at a given point in time lays down residues that limit the possibilities of subsequent social action.

The fourth theme is at once the least familiar and the most general. Social analysts have trouble seeing that history matters precisely because social interaction takes place in well-defined times and places, and occurs within constraints offered by those times and places, producing social relations and artifacts that are themselves located in space-time and whose existence and distribution constrain subsequent social interaction. The construction of a city in a given place and time affects urban growth in adjacent areas and subsequent times. Where and when industrialization occurs affects how it occurs. Initial visions of victory announce a war's likely outcomes. A person's successive migrations have cumulative effects on his or her subsequent mobility through such simple matters as the presence or absence of information about new opportunities in different places and the presence or absence of social ties to possible destinations. A population's previous experience with wars, Baby Booms, and migrations haunts it in the form of bulging or empty cohorts and unequal numbers of the sexes. All these are profoundly historical matters, even when they occur in the present; time and place are of their essence. They form the essential subject matter of Studies in Social Discontinuity.

Edward Shorter, Stanley Holwitz, and I plotted the Studies in Social Discontinuity in 1970–1; the first book, William Christian's *Person and God in a Spanish Valley*, appeared in 1972. Over the years, Academic Press published more than 50 titles in the series. But during the early 1980s publication slowed, then ceased. In 1988, Basil Blackwell agreed to revive the Studies under my editorship. In 1989, the series resumed under Blackwell's auspices with *The Perilous Frontier*, a study of nomadic empires by Thomas Barfield. *Shi'ite Islam* boldly continues the renewed series.

Although the series began with William Christian's extraordinary religious ethnography, it has never before taken up the general history of a creed. Yann Richard's book therefore marks a splendid departure, or rather series of departures: a survey of religious change over Islam's entire timespan; a sensitive exposition of Shi'ite ideas, practices, and variants; a contemporary geography of Shi'ite adherents; and an interpretation of the faith's political ramifications. Shi'ism attracts outside attention today because of the supposition that it expresses a peculiarly Iranian point of view; Richard shows us both the origin and the error of that identification.

Through Antonia Nevill's elegant translation, Yann Richard's voice comes through as calm, reflective, and sympathetic. I know too little of Islam to say how accurately Richard portrays the Shi'ite faith. Religious, ideological, and political partisans have strong stakes in many of the issues he explores: the historical relations between Sunni and Shi'ite Islam, the Shi'ite approach to women and sexual pleasure, the place of Shi'ism in the politics of Iraq and Lebanon, the place of clerics in the Iranian revolution, and much more. Still, the care he takes to document and qualify his analyses – for example, his luminous presentation of Sufism and its relation to Shi'ism – lends credence to an account only an intimate familiarity with the Islamic world could make possible.

Most likely some readers will claim that no non-Muslim, however learned, can portray this major current of Islam accurately, while others will fault Richard's account of the Iranian Revolution, or at least of its major players. The story he tells necessarily emphasizes ideology, and therefore deemphasizes geopolitics, economics, and class struggle. Since students of revolution and political change commonly treat Iran as a major case of ideological struggle, however, even uncompromising materialists will have much to learn from Yann Richard's portrayal of factions, personalities, beliefs, and practices. If from the faithful's viewpoint he remains an outsider, he travels about as far inside, and as empathetically, as any outsider can do.

Charles Tilly
New York City

Preface

December 1983: France had just lent Iraq, which had attacked Iran in 1980, five Super-Étendard aeroplanes carrying Exocet missiles – a formidable threat to the oil installations in the Persian Gulf. Tehran immediately orchestrated a violent anti-French campaign, in response to an anti-Iranian and anti-Islamic campaign in France.

Having gone to Iran for both family and professional reasons, I found myself at the time in Mashhad, a great place of pilgrimage close to the frontier with Afghanistan. A friend's brother, a prominent cleric in the local theological faculty, insisted on meeting me at the hotel where I was staying, together with my Iranian father-in-law and one of his friends, who had come to make the pilgrimage. In the end I accepted his invitation to lunch, so graciously expressed: "I will send my son to collect you about noon tomorrow."

The meal was delicious and I was sorry that the proprieties did not allow me to thank my host's wife, who made no appearance. We visited the theologian's private library: this stately and smiling mulla was also a lover of old books, manuscripts, and lithographs. He showed us some superb examples of calligraphy and gave me several rare works, including a bibliographic catalogue that he had compiled. Then, as we were about to take our leave, our host looked me full in the eye and inquired in a friendly way: "M. Richard, are you a Christian?"

I must confess I had an instant's hesitation: in Islam, a doctor of law knows very well that the son-in-law of a Muslim can only be Muslim. The Islamic Republic is not the place in which to flout the proprieties of religious law. The simplest answer would have been a little white lie, which the Lord in his mercy would have forgiven me. (This is actually the situation in Islamic countries: one is born a Muslim – or possibly becomes so – without the need for any baptism to sanction one's entry into the faith, even symbolically. All men *are* potential Muslims, and those who have the good fortune to be born or to enter into the community of the chosen cannot under any circumstance leave it. In Iran, by virtue of a special freedom belonging to that nation, popular culture knows no religious pressure, and Iranians have never asked me to make a public profession of faith. Why, therefore, did my host ask the question?)

As he had shown me such warm hospitality, the idea of shying away from his question did not cross my mind. He knew my answer in advance. His reaction, simple yet sublime, made me weep with emotion: he offered me an old edition of the New Testament, in Persian, in an antique binding with a golden clasp, explaining that he possessed a complete version of the Bible. My father-in-law, at first embarrassed because I had dared to flout the conventions in his presence, backed me up by remarking on the common origin of monotheistic religions.

Recognition of my "otherness" by a guardian of the rigid dogma of Islam makes me profoundly indebted and grateful to that open-minded mulla, to my father-in-law who stood up for me, and to all those who, when the Iranian Shi'ites were going through such a troubled time, did not lose their head but kept alive in their heart the fragile flame of faith and tolerance in the face of every tempest. It is also the purpose of this book to acknowledge that the Shi'ites, who believe in God in their own way, are people like any others, with fears, hopes and desires.

I have chosen to describe the "beliefs and ideologies" rather than the dogmas, and thus to emphasize the way in which religion is connected with contemporary societies, to describe political and ethical concerns rather than "objective" history. The danger of subjectivity is obvious . . . How can one remain a passive and indifferent observer in the face of such an important phenomenon, above all in its revolutionary extension, of which the media have sometimes shown us such a terrifying picture? By listening to the words of the actors on the scene, for example the ayatollahs or the militants, I obviously run the risk of increasing the value of what they say and turning it into a statement of a truth, while the many circumstances that might contribute to diminishing its value would remain obscured . . . Orientalists and political scientists are sometimes accused of paying too much attention to those cultural logics that claim to throw light on events by means of pre-existing ideological structures: societies would seem in some way predestined to a certain type of state, and the events that occur – however unfortunate they may be – seem ineluctable . . . All these arguments are open to debate: they make us listen with wariness to what the ayatollahs have to say, but may they not prevent us from listening![1]

I extend my thanks to all those who have contributed to the completion of this book: my French and Iranian friends and colleagues, those who by their critical appraisal have helped me to improve the English version, notably Patricia Crone, Andrew Newman, and especially Antonia Nevill, my patient translator.

I dedicate this book to my son, Émile-Rouzbehan, and to all those who suffer from the debasement of religion into the ideology of power or a means of oppression. *Zirā yaqin midānam ke dard-hā-ye zamān-e hāzer, nesbat be-ān jalāli-ke dar mā zāher khāhad shod, hich hast* (the sufferings of this present time are not worthy to be compared with the glory which shall be revealed in us; Rom. 8: 18).

---

1   See F. KHOSROKHAVAR, P. VIEILLE et al. "L'Orientalisme: Interrogation," *Peuples méditerranéens*, 50 (January–March 1990), and all the debates about E. Said's *Orientalism*, New York, Vintage Books, 1979.

1
A Few Words about Shi'ism

Islam embraces two principal branches, Sunnism – the majority faith – and Shi'ism (*shi'a, tashayyo'*). Within Shi'ism the most important group is Imamism or "Twelver" (in Arabic, *esnā 'ashari*) Shi'ism, so named because of the cult of the Twelve Imams who in turn succeeded the Prophet. It has been the official religion in Iran since 1501, the year of the Safavid dynasty's accession. Other branches of Shi'ism, such as Ismailism and Zeydism, share common origins with Twelver Imamism, but Zeydism emerged from the Twelvers' list of Imams after the fourth, and Ismailism after the sixth, having then a different list of successors and adopting different rules, notably with regard to political power. The 'Alavites, the Druzes and other marginal groups have historical links with Shi'ism; their adherents are relatively few in number. This book deals chiefly with Imamism.

Arabic is certainly the original tongue of the revelation and the only authorized language of worship, and a knowledge of it is compulsory for Islamic studies, but Islam is no more an Arab religion than Christianity is a Jewish religion. The largest number of Muslims today are to be found in Asia, Indonesia, and the Indo-Pakistan peninsula. One of the oldest civilizations in the world, the Iranian nation today represents the great centre of Shi'ite Islam.

The Iranians are Aryans, interbred for centuries (before Islam) with Semitic populations and, since the tenth century AD, with peoples of Turco-Mongol origin from central Asia. They have preserved their culture and their Indo-European language, Persian (*fārsi*), but have always used Semitic alphabets (once Aramaic, now Arabic) to write their tongue. Modern Persian has developed very little over the last ten centuries or so, despite the contribution of Arabic (50 percent of the words in literary language) and Turkish vocabulary. Iran and *Persia* are really the same: in 1935 Rezā

Shah forbade foreign diplomatic missions to use the traditional name, until then the only one known to westerners, and enjoined them to replace it with *Iran*, a name used from ancient times by Iranians to designate their country (rather as if the Germans were suddenly to urge us to call their country Deutschland). Before Islam the dominant religion in Iran was Zoroastrianism (the cult of Ahura Mazda). Judaism has been present there since earliest antiquity (after the captivity in Babylon), and Christianity since the first centuries AD. Islamization was swift, but did not wear away the culture or destroy the language. Today there are 98 percent Muslims in Iran, of whom about 84 percent are Shi'ites.

SOME STATISTICS ON SHI'ISM

No Muslim country publishes reliable statistics on the proportions of minority Muslim groups within its frontiers. The distinction between Sunnis and Shi'ites still bears too many seeds of violence, and to represent it in terms of majority/minority would provoke some intense reactions. Nevertheless, by means of calculation and cross-checking, it is possible to arrive at proportions whose credibility is generally accepted by specialists: out of some 800 to 900 million Muslims in the world, about 11 percent (or over 80 million) are Shi'ites.[1]

Iran, with at least 43 million believers (out of a total population of 52 million in 1990), possesses the strongest and certainly the most homogeneous Shi'ite community. It is not a matter of ethnic homogeneity: only about half the Iranian Shi'ites are Persian-speaking. Twenty percent of the Kurds, most of the Arabic-speaking tribes of Khuzistan and most of the Turkish-speaking tribes (including almost all the Azerbaijanis) are Shi'ites. Iranian Sunnis are generally to be found on the geographical margins: the Baluchis on the frontier with Pakistan, the Turkomans on the old Soviet frontier, the Kurds and certain Arab tribes on the Iraqi frontier. Non-Muslim minorities, all of whom have existed in the country for longer than Islam (Zoroastrians, Jews, Christians), represent no more than 1 or 2 percent of the population *in toto*. The Bahā'is, whose religion stemmed from Shi'ism in the nineteenth century, represented up to 1 percent of the population

---

1 I am using mainly the figures put forward by Md-R. DJALILI, *Religion et révolution*, Paris, Economica, 1981, pp. 23ff, and M. MOMEN, *An Introduction to Shi'i Islam*, New Haven and London, Yale University Press, 1985, pp. 264ff.

before the Revolution (they were not counted in the statistics as they were not recognized by the Iranian state).

In Iraq, the Shi'ites are in the majority, with about 55 percent of the total population (about 18 million). Chiefly grouped toward the south of the country, notably around the Shi'ite holy places of Najaf and Karbalā, they were at the centre of an old rivalry between the Ottoman Empire and the Iranian monarchy for control over Shi'ite pilgrimages. Regarded by Ottoman officials, up till 1918, as a turbulent minority, the Shi'ites have latterly enjoyed more equitable treatment but still lack integration in the Sunni-dominated nation, where they are sometimes perceived as Iranian agents.

In the Arabian peninsula, Shi'ism on the whole occupies an uncomfortable position because of the small number of its followers and the theological hostility of the fundamentalist Wahhābis of Saudi Arabia: Imamism – in their eyes – mingles polytheistic beliefs and idolatrous practices with original Islam.[2] The Shi'ites are in the majority only in the islands of Bahrain (70 percent, or about 170,000 Shi'ite believers), which were formerly Persian possessions and were claimed by Iran until 1971 (a new short-lived claim was immediately denied by Tehran in 1979), but there the state is in the hands of Sunnis. In Kuwait, which has a strong Persian colony, there is a minority of about 137,000 Shi'ites, or 24 percent of Kuwaiti citizens, but only 10 percent of the population (which includes many foreigners). Large Shi'ite communities also live in Qatar (20 percent of the population, about 50,000 Shi'ites) and in the United Arab Emirates (6 percent, or 60,000 believers). In Saudi Arabia there appear to be about 440,000 Shi'ites, or 7 percent of the Saudi population and 5 percent of the total number of residents in the country.

In Lebanon Shi'ites, traditionally called *motāwila* (pl. of *mutawāli*), with about a million faithful, form upwards of a third of the population. They are spread among South Lebanon (Jabal 'Āmil) and the Biqa' plain, along the Syrian frontier, but also fairly recently in the suburbs of Beirut. Many are in exile in black Africa, where they are prospering in trade, without severing their links with their homeland.

India, which today is the second largest Muslim country in the world, contains about 80 million Muslims (12 percent of the total population). Out of that community it is estimated that between 15 and 20 percent are

2   J. A. BILL, "Islam, Politics and Shi'ism in the Gulf," *Middle East Insight*, 3, 3 (January –February 1984), pp. 3–12; *idem*, "Resurgent Islam in the Persian Gulf," *Foreign Affairs*, 63, 1 (Fall 1984), pp. 108–27, quoted by J. KOSTINER, "Shi'a Unrest in the Gulf", in M. Kramer, ed., *Shi'ism, Resistance and Revolution*, Boulder, Colo., Westview Press, and London, Mansell, 1987, p. 173.

Shi'ites, both Imamis and Ismailis. In actual fact, the distinction between Shi'ites and Sunnis is sometimes difficult to establish because of the inter-community violence that moves many Indian Shi'ites to disguise their differences. In Pakistan the number of Shi'ites is put at 12 million, centred mainly in the Punjab, in the Lahore region.

The Shi'ites of Afghanistan are about 15 percent of the total population, or 2.5 million. They are to be found in the Hazara ethnic group and among the Qezelbāsh, who appear to be the descendants of the soldiers and officials installed in the country by the Iranian sovereign Nāder Shah in the eighteenth century, and by various Persian-speaking groups. They are generally despised by the Sunni majority which has always ruled the country and did not legally recognize the legitimacy of Shi'ism and Ja'farite jurisprudence until 1963. The Iranian Revolution and the role of Islamist groups in the resistance to Soviet troops' occupation of Afghanistan gave the Shi'ites new importance, but failed to combine them with the Sunnis in an overall national design.[3]

Among the several hundred million Muslims in the ex-Soviet Union, there is a large Shi'ite community in Azerbaijan (4.5 million) who, through the ability of radio and television to cross frontiers, and a sense of shared ethnic identity, are deeply interested in what is happening on the Iranian side; Shi'ite groups in central Asia are submerged in a mass of Sunnis who look rather toward Pakistan and Saudi Arabia for a religious renewal, even though they still often regard Iran as representing the refinement of language and culture.

To these figures would be added those of Syria and Turkey if one could consider the 'Alavites of these countries (respectively 4 million and 900,000) as Shi'ites.[4] But that would be a misconception. This Turkish heterodox Islam, whose faithful adopted certain Shi'ite practices in the sixteenth century, such as the cult of the twelve Imams, mental dissimulation (*taqiya*) and the Moharram celebrations commemorating the death of Imam Hoseyn, does not really conform to established Shi'ite rites: their meetings are not held in mosques, and there are no clergy to lead the prayers. In some-

---

3 O. ROY, *Islam and Resistance in Afghanistan*, Cambridge, Cambridge University Press, 1986 (French text, pp. 68ff).

4 My thanks to Thierry Zarcone for allowing me to use his unpublished notes here on Shi'ism in Turkey. See C. CAHEN, "Le Problème du shī'isme dans l'Asie mineure turque préottomane," in *Le Shī'isme imāmite* (Strasbourg Symposium, May 6–9, 1968), Paris, PUF, 1970, pp. 115–29. Also: M. KRAMER, "Syria's Alawis and Shi'ism," in *idem, Shi'ism, Resistance and Revolution*, pp. 237–54; M. SEURAT, *L'État de barbarie*, Paris, Le Seuil, 1989.

aspects the 'Alavites resemble the Ismailis, with their secret ritual, free interpretation of the Koran, etc. But a large number of 'Alavite beliefs have a pre-Islamic origin (animism and shamanism) disguised under an appearance of Islam.

There are however Turkish Shi'ite communities, totalling 1,500,000 people, living on the one hand in the north-east, among the Azeris of the Kars district, and on the other in Istanbul, among the Iranians who have been settled there since the nineteenth century. The Turkish Azeris attend their mosques and have themselves buried in their cemetery, unlike the 'Alavites.

In Syria, since President Hafiz al-Asad took power in 1971, the 'Alavite minority, which represents 10 percent of the Muslim community in the country, has controlled all the central political organs, much to the detriment of the militant Sunnis, notably the Muslim Brotherhood. There are also about 50,000 Twelver Shi'ites in Syria.

DOCTRINAL CHARACTERISTICS

Since the Iranian Revolution everyone knows that Shi'ites are Muslims, like the Sunnis respecting the central dogma of the oneness of God (*towhid*, "There is no other god but God"), the same sacred writing (the Koran), the same prophet Mohammad, the same belief in the resurrection followed by the last Judgement (*ma'ād*) and the same fundamental obligations, prayer, fasting, pilgrimage, almsgiving, and *jehād* (holy war).[5] These common points are more important than the differences: there is no longer any theoretical objection to a Shi'ite performing his prayers with a Sunni, or vice versa although many difficulties have existed in the past and in practice still remain.

To the essential beliefs of Islam, the uniqueness of God, the prophecy of

---

5   Most Shi'ites accept the edition of the Koran carried out by the caliph 'Osmān (644–56); cf. for example Sh. SANGALAJI, *Kelid-e fahm-e Qor'ān* (Key to the Understanding of the Koran) 3rd edn, Tehran, 1345/1966, pp. 9–16; See E. KOHLBERG, "Some Notes on the Imamite Attitude to the Qur'an," in S. M. Stern et al., eds, *Islamic Philosophy and the Classical Tradition: Essays presented . . . to Richard Walzer*, Oxford, 1972, pp. 209–24; H. LÖSCHNER, *Die dogmatischen Grundlagen des ši'itischen Rechts*, Erlangen and Nuremberg, Carl Heyrnans, 1971, pp. 70ff; J. ELIASH, "The Ši'ite Qur'ān: A Reconsideration of Golziher's Interpretation," *Arabica*, 16 (1969). Recently, Md-A. AMIR-MOEZZI has shown that early Shi'ism taught that the Imams possessed a fuller Koran: *The Divine Guide in Original Shi'ism*, Albany, SUNY Press, 1994, ch. 3.3.

Mohammad and the resurrection of the dead, Shi'ites add belief in God's justice (*'adl*) and the Imamate. Unlike certain tendencies in Sunnism which insist on the arbitrary will of God (Ash'arism rejects the use of reason to illuminate faith), Shi'ism proclaims, in agreement with a more rationalizing theology (that of the Mo'tazelites), that God can act only within the bounds of justice, which implies a certain rationality in creation, and above all that man is free to choose his own actions. If that were not so, God would be punishing man for a disobedience for which he would not have been responsible.

The Imamate (*emāma*) is to some extent the consequence and the application of the principle of justice to the guidance of humankind. God, who created men, could not let them go to their perdition. That is why He sent them the Prophets, the last of whom was Mohammad, to guide them along the path of justice and truth. But after the death of the last Prophet it was unthinkable that God in His wisdom should leave men to their own devices without there being, in every era, a spiritual guarantor, proof of the truth of the revelation, to direct the community: this is the Imam, the "Guide." As he plays a fundamental role in the relations between God and men, the Imam cannot be chosen by fallible men and left to the vicissitudes of history: he must fulfill certain conditions of principle, be perfectly learned in religious matters, be absolutely just and equitable, be perfect, free from any fault (*ma'sum*), be the most perfect man (*afzal*) of his time; it is inconceivable that someone more perfect should obey another less perfect. He must be part of what Henry Corbin calls the "Immaculate Pleroma" of the Shi'ite gnosis, which includes the Very Pure Fourteen, that is to say, Mohammad, his daughter Fatima and the Twelve Imams, created for all eternity. The Imam is designated by a supernatural investiture (*nass*) coming from God by the intermediary of the Prophet or the Imam who has preceded him: he receives his authority from on high. Thus the infallible Imam links the human community with the invisible world.

Since the year 874 of the Christian era the Shi'ites have been living in the age of the Twelfth Imam. The twelfth of Mohammad's successors was supposedly hidden from the eyes of his followers at that date; the Twelver Shi'ites (who recognize twelve Imams) believe that the last Imam is still alive and will return at the end of time to establish a reign of justice and truth.[6]

Shi'ite doctrines are based on collections of traditions quite distinct from those of the Sunnis, the Four Books, with their evocative titles: "What

6 On all these points, see below, ch. 2.

Suffices in the Knowledge of Religion" (*al-Kāfi 'elm od-din*), by Mohammad Koleyni (d. 941); "He Who Has No Jurist at His Disposal" (*Man lā yahzoroho 'l-faqih*), by Sheikh Saduq b. Bābuya (d. 991); "The Correction of Doctrines" (*Tahzib al-ahkām*) of Sheikh Mohammad at-Tusi (d. 1067); and lastly, "The Clear-Sighted View of the Divergences of Tradition" (*al-Estebsār fi mā-khtolefa fihe men al-akhbār*), a résumé of the foregoing by the same Sheikh Tusi.

To these collections were added more recent books, less reliable from the point of view of the authenticity of the traditions formed therein, such as the numerous volumes of the "Ocean of Lights" (*Behār ol-anvār*) of Mohammad-Bāqer Majlesi, a theologian of the Safavid period (d. 1699), loudly decried by modern reformers. They blame him for having cluttered religion with all sorts of secondary beliefs, some of which – notably the directives concerning sexual behavior – cause amusement among today's mocking free-thinkers.

Shi'ite doctrine varies noticeably from the Sunni juridical schools as regards inheritance and marriage: the better place allotted to women has probably emerged from the important role of Fatima in the genesis of Shi'ism. But Islam is primarily a religion for men, and Shi'ism, by recognizing the legitimacy of the temporary marriage "of pleasure," has certainly sought to acknowledge more rights for males, whatever may be said about it by today's apologists who, on the contrary, claim there is more flexibility and a greater realism in morality.

PRACTICES

Strict Sunni Muslims, such as the Wahhābi sect dominating Saudi Arabia, go out of their way to scorn the cult of the dead, explicitly condemned by the Prophet. They refuse to raise tombstones and build mausoleums. Quite different is the custom of the Shi'ites, who not only honor their dead, erect the most sumptuous monuments to their saints, organize pilgrimages to the tombs of the Imams and their descendants (the *emāmzāda*), but also turn death and martyrdom into the focal point of their devotions. The living memory of the departed and the intercession of the Imams is a protection felt to be very efficacious by this community, who bear the memory of having been persecuted for centuries by the Sunni majority.

The Shi'ites regroup the five obligatory prayers into three points in the day: the midday and afternoon prayers are performed together, as are those of the evening and night. A tradition affirms that the Prophet considered this practice permissible.

The summons to prayer is the same as for the Sunnis, with the exception of the invitation to perform a good action (*hayya 'alā kheyr ol-'amal*), added twice after the invitation to salvation (*hayya 'alā'l-falāh*), as well as the phrase "I attest that 'Ali is close – *vali*, friend and possessor of the power – to God" (*ashhado anna 'Alian vali'ol-Lāh*), repeated twice after the profession of faith. In this way one can distinguish a Shi'ite from a Sunni mosque.

Like all Muslims, Shi'ites perform their prayers after ritual ablutions (slightly different for them) on a little prayer mat unsullied by impurities. Customarily they place a tiny tablet of clay brought from a holy place (Mashhad, Karbalā, or Najaf) on the spot where their forehead will touch the ground. They keep alive a particular spirituality through prayers connected with the Imams, such as the prayer that the First Imam, 'Ali, taught his disciple Komeyl ebn Ziyād. Supererogatory recitation of this very beautiful incantatory prayer, usually prescribed for the traditional anniversary of the Twelfth Imam, the 15th of the month of Sha'bān in the lunar calendar, is performed on Thursday evenings. In Iran it is known as *Do'ā-ye Komeyl*, Komeyl's prayer.

Like all Muslims, Shi'ites also are under the ritual obligation to accomplish the pilgrimage to Mecca (*hajj*) at least once in their lifetime. The troubles that have arisen during the *hajj* since the Iranian Revolution, and notably on July 31, 1987 (402 dead, 275 of whom were Iranian), are not due to a politicization exclusively imputable to the Shi'ites: all Islamist militants, Sunni or Shi'ite, look on the annual pilgrimage as an international gathering that is both political and religious. Numerous Shi'ites (the majority?) disapprove of this improper politicization of the *hajj*.

Another specifically Shi'ite devotion is the importance given to visiting the tombs of the saints (*ziyāra*), recommended by theologians. It applies principally to the tombs of the Imams, who are like intermediaries or intercessors between man and the unapproachable God of Islam. Shi'ites accord equal honor to the descendants of the Imams (in Iran, *emāmzāda*, *sayyed*) who through their spiritual knowledge and their lives have been a *sign* of the divinity on this earth. They belong to the Family of the Prophet.

In Iraq the great centers of Shi'ite pilgrimage are Karbalā (the tomb of Imam Hoseyn, visiting which cleanses all sins), Najaf (the mausoleum of Imam 'Ali built, according to some traditions, on the site of the tomb of Adam and Noah), Samarra (the mausoleum of Imam 'Ali-Naqi) and Kazemeyn (the mausoleums of Imams Musā Kazem and Mohammad-Taqi). These places are called the "*atabāt*," the sacred "Thresholds." The rites of pilgrimage include processions circling the tomb of the holy one (anti-clockwise), similar to the circumambulation around the Ka'ba temple of Mecca, the reading of pilgrims' prayers (*ziyārat-nāma*) and touching the grille surrounding the tomb. An ancient belief has it that those who are buried at Najaf do not undergo the torments of the afterlife, in particular the terrifying interrogation by the Angels Monker and Nakir. That is why many Shi'ites were in the habit of having themselves buried in the vicinity of these sacred places, and not so long ago their bodies were transported by mule from great distances, in defiance of all the prophylactic regulations in times of epidemics, a custom denounced by secular reformers.

For numerous Shi'ites in Iran, above all in a period of hostile relations between Iraq and the government in Tehran, the only pilgrimage that counts is to Mashhad. In former times it was necessary to cross inhospitable regions, infested with Turkoman brigands (described by the French orientalist Gobineau in the *Nouvelles asiatiques*), endure the hardships of the desert, or perhaps travel by boat and the "modern" routes that passed through central Asia under Russian domination, in order to arrive at that oasis of coolness where lies the immense sanctuary of the Eighth Imam, Rezā, with its gilded dome and shimmering ceramic cupolas dating from the Timurid epoch (fifteenth century) dominating the whole town. Mashhad, the great provincial market place and crossroads of central Asia, offers far more than a simple sanctuary, and one never tires of discovering in it the human and intellectual treasures of a metropolis. Today, with the reopening of frontiers between Iran and the former Soviet Muslim Republics, Mashhad is again an international capital city.

Another important Iranian pilgrimage takes place to the tomb of the Imam Rezā's sister, the holy Fatima the Pure (*Hazrat-e Fātema-ye Ma'suma*), at Qom, 120 km south of Tehran. Whereas Mashhad is luxurious and grand, Qom has a provincial air, even after the Islamic Revolution turned it into a second capital: the water is brackish, the women there are cramped in hideous black sack-like garments, the bazaar is tiny, mullas invade all the little town so that there is no alleyway, cul-de-sac, or market stall where one can escape the sour smell of the scent with which they scrupulously smear themselves. Religious knick-knacks are on sale everywhere, clay tablets for the forehead during prayer, rosaries, Korans, and books of popular devotions, but also those cakes of *sowhān*, fatty, pungent, and sickeningly sweet. And the river, beside which one would like to be able to stroll in the evenings to get rid of the all-invading dust, is desperately dried-up in any season.

This reputation does not detract from any of the charm of Qom and,

French Christian that I am, I have always felt at ease there. Never, in Qom, have I been asked who I am, why I have come, what I think about Islam or the government: courteous tactfulness spares the newcomer any need to justify his incongruous presence, which is accepted along with all the other incongruities in this town. Bookshops as well as librarians know what a researcher is, in this place that is entirely devoted to study and the publishing of books. There have always been plenty of foreigners in Qom and, even before the Islamic Revolution, European, American, or Japanese converts were frequently to be seen there, not to mention Lebanese, Iraqi, Indo-Pakistani, and African students.

One day in 1981 at Oxford a renowned Iranian mulla confided in me: Qom and Oxford were the two towns in the world where he felt good, because there teaching and study were truly the central activity. In these two cities of ancient traditions, he loved the international exchanges and the total indifference to the judgements of the outside world. The biography (only slightly novelized) of this very mulla, written by an American academic, gives a very vivid picture of the world of clerical studies in Qom, and of the many trends of thought which come face to face there.[7] At the beginning of the 1970s a daring Englishwoman, disguised as a man, penetrated the sanctuary of Qom and its theological schools: her irreverent but enthralling account reveals to what extent the young mullas in this reputedly inhospitable town gave her their confidence and opened up a dialogue of surprising sharpness with her.[8]

It would be tedious to list all the places of Shi'ite pilgrimage, either inside or outside Iran, as each has its own special features, for example that of Shah 'Abd ol-'Azim, south of Tehran, or the Master of the Lamp (*Shāh Cherāq*), at Shiraz. Since the war with Iraq the Iranians have occupied the mausoleum of Saint Zeynab, Hoseyn's sister, near Damascus in Syria, where they have been making pious "tours" organized for the families of war victims. It was there in 1977 that the pre-revolutionary writer 'Ali Shari'ati was buried: to hold his funeral in Iran at that time would have provoked riots, and the Shah's police would not authorize it. A burial place

7   R. MOTTAHEDEH, *The Mantle of the Prophet*, New York, Simon & Schuster, 1985; London, Chatto & Windus, 1986.

8   Sarah HOBSON, *Through Persia in Disguise*, London, John Murray, 1973. On Qom, see also M. FISCHER (an American ethnologist who lived at Qom for a year prior to the Revolution), *Iran: From Religious Dispute to Revolution*, Cambridge, Mass. and London, Harvard University Press, 1980; J. CALMARD, "Kum," *Encyclopedia of Islam*, 2nd edn; M. BAZIN, "Qom, ville de pèlerinage et centre régional," *Revue géographique de l'Est*, 13, 1–2 (1973), pp. 77–136.

was therefore made for him near the ancient capital of the Omayyads, and the Imam Musā Sadr, an Iranian holy man who had for a long time been settled in Lebanon, pronounced the ritual prayers. More recently, the tomb of Imam Khomeyni near Tehran has since 1989 started to become one of the great sites of Shi'ite pilgrimage. Will it be razed to the ground one day, like the mausoleum of Rezā Shah ten years earlier? Or transformed into the dispenser of miraculous cures for centuries to come?

IN THE PARADISE OF THE "RADIANT ONE"

Shi'ism makes a cult of death and martyrdom. There is no better illustration of Shi'ites' beliefs and conception of the sacred than their devotion to the great symbolic figures of the past who serve as a reflection of their community, who are honored for having been tortured, for having borne witness to the faith. The gratitude owed to them can be fulfilled through an initiatory journey. The merit gained from this pilgrimage visit comes from the fact that one has torn oneself away from the daily round and traveled a long road to come and share in their pains, weep with them and together with them wage a symbolic battle against the forces of evil.

How is a pilgrimage created, how can a dead man come to possess such merit for the believers who pray at his tomb? How do miracles – real or imagined – happen? These are questions that may be answered since a great Shi'ite saint who died among his people in 1989 and was buried amid collective hysteria has become the object of an unprecedented cult. The sanctuary of Imam Khomeyni (d. June 3, 1989) lies beside the Tehran cemetery: it is the "Paradise of the Radiant Daughter of the Prophet" (*Behesht-e Zahrā*), close to the ancient village of Rey (Rages in the Bible) where the holy 'Abd ol-'Azim, a theologian contemporary with the Eleventh and Twelfth Imams, has lain for centuries in his mausoleum, near which the remains of the Qājār rulers were also interred.

The sanctuary, at first erected with whatever was to hand, then enlarged and constructed in more noble, lasting materials, is already surrounded by the complete infrastructure of a great centre of pilgrimage – hotels, a place for private prayer, parking space, toilets, rooms for rest and listening to sermons, gardens with a pool for ablutions, telephone exhange, displays of devotional objects, beggars' quarters teeming with the poor, the maimed, and the sick, etc. As Iranians were banned between 1987 and 1991 from making the pilgrimage to Mecca, and the pilgrimage to the "Sacred Thresholds" in Iraq (Najaf and Karbalā) has been closed for even longer, it would seem that Qom and Mashhad were not enough to quench Iranians' thirst for the sacred, as they rushed to the ayatollah's tomb even before the stone slab had been firmly sealed to implore his intercession, the forgiveness of their sins, and the curing of their illnesses. What an apotheosis for a man whose first words, on his return from exile in 1979, had been to render homage in that very cemetery to those who had suffered under the Shah's regime! These people so fascinated by sacredness and martyrdom are rewarded with a hero who died in his old age at the summit of power and now sleeps forever alongside those – all too numerous – who were killed in their youth for his sake.

It was in this immense necropolis, in fact, that Khomeyni made his first speech after alighting from the plane bringing him back from Paris. He denounced the Shah's regime as a regime of death. History will compare and judge: the fate of the "martyrs" of the Iran–Iraq war, the fate of the tortured, victims of terrorist attacks . . . Behesht-e Zahrā has become the rallying point of the great sorrowing processions of victims of the new regime, and no one is fooled any longer about the consequences of the Revolution or the war, seeing the recent spread of the necropolis. Yet Khomeyni was buried in this very spot, in his own country, surrounded by an innumerable and fervent crowd.

Opponents complained of manipulation. They did not understand. They said, quite rightly, that the state exerted a great deal of pressure to force local communitites to pay up in order to make the sanctuary more attractive, to provide it with sumptuous carpets and many services. However, they cannot deny that Khomeyni was the first Iranian head of state since Mozaffaroddin Shah (1907) not to die in exile and held in contempt by his people. That victory is also one of the Iranian people over the powers that took turns manipulating the last Iranian monarchs, Qājār and Pahlavi.

The vastness of the monument, begun only a few years ago on this desert plain, surpasses imagination. From afar there are golden glimpses of the cupola and minarets through the dusty haze that envelops the Tehran–Qom motorway. At night, everything is bathed in brilliance thanks to a forest of floodlights that never experience the daily breakdowns of the national electricity grid. The lights set at the summit of the building can be seen, so it is said, from at least 25 km away in all directions. Despite the brilliance of the gold leaf, the edifice appears less smart as one draws near because of the works in progress that will transform it into a monumental centre of pilgrimage and Islamic teaching, even larger than those at Qom or Mashhad. Inside, it is already possible to get some idea of the splendor and immensity to come: a square hall with sides about 120 m long

(14,400 m^2!), under what is doubtless still temporary roofing supported by a rigid metal framework and simple columns, also of metal. The floor – on two levels, a raised gallery and the prayer hall, with the shrine at its centre from which the tomb itself can be seen – is covered with flawless marble, which teams of cleaners are permanently engaged in polishing. Surrounding the gallery and around the shrine are new Persian carpets, which some people use as recliners, so thick is the wool and so comfortable the ambience. One certainly feels at ease in this spotless place, pleasantly heated on a winter's morning and, so it is said, equally pleasantly air-conditioned and cool in the torpid heat of summer. The distribution of various foodstuffs, dates, cakes, fruit, and other sweetmeats, offered to all and sundry when vows have been fulfilled, gives the place an extremely convivial air.

It is true that the aim of pilgrimage is not to gorge oneself, or recline on carpets, or merely to admire the grandeur of the building: it is to visit the Imam, the intercessor for the anguish of his people. This anguish, to judge by the tears shed and the large banknotes slipped between the grille and the glass of the cenotaph, is not just a material distress. Of course, the simplicity of clothing and faces shows that the affluent do not resort to the same intercessor to make their voices heard. Provincials who have come from several hundred kilometers away, or Tehranis accomplishing by a visit to the Imam one due to their own dead – there they are with their beard or their chador (large veil covering head and body) and the children, and they are overwhelmed: this luxury, recalling the mosques and other places of pilgrimage, in no way intimidates them; they know how to take advantage of it. They draw near to someone who in his lifetime was approached only by a privileged few, and they revere him as they revere the Shi'ite Imams or their descendants whom they ask to intercede for them.

Such veneration for a head of state who has just died might pass for a rite of "civil religion," in the way that the Russians long revered the remains of Lenin, the Turks those of Mustafa Kemal, or the Chinese those of Mao, a sort of official duty one fulfills when obliged to visit the capital. Here the difference is patent: not only is there no need to stand in line to enter but one can even settle down in the mausoleum to share a few hours of intimacy with the departed. Everyone knows what to do, whether it is the hour for prayer or whether, around the shrine, one passes a hand over the lattice encaging him, or over the glass, in order to plug into that spiritual energy, to touch the charisma of the deceased and profit from his grace.

All these good folk coming to pray by the tomb, tying ribbons to a grille, attaching votive padlocks to the chains of the gate . . . These gestures, which belong to a visit to a sacred tomb, remind us that Khomeyni was not solely a statesman. His death, which was the occasion of such an outpouring of tears, was not the death of just any great person. It was the death of a *saint*. I am not talking about the challenge to the West and its conception of holiness that Khomeyni represented in his lifetime, or of the revulsion inspired in the majority of westerners by the thought that this person could be numbered among saints like Joan of Arc, Francis of Assisi or Thérèse of Lisieux. By "saintliness" I mean that religious value venerated in people who have demonstrated an exemplary zeal for religion, an asceticism, and undivided absolutism. For Shi'ites, holiness or saintliness is associated with martyrdom, tragedy, death. Khomeyni, a descendant of the Prophet who suffered repression and exile, who fought against all hope to overthrow a regime reputed to be unshakable, and who died without changing the slightest intonation in his obstinate language in the defense of Islam, deserves to be linked with the ancestors or the faith who were persecuted for preserving intact the heritage of the Prophet Mohammad. That eminently saintly quality, which earned him access to the honor of a mausoleum that immediately became a place of pilgrimage, is further emphasized by the Shi'ite tradition which denies equality between men and ever seeks the guidance (*ershād*) of great spiritual leaders.

Having become a saint, Khomeyni is no longer a problem for anyone, but himself resolves all problems. He has left the realms of politics, of what is hateful, violence, and lies, to become the Other, the divine friend to whom one turns to prepare one's place in the immortal city. He is already part of the Holy Family.

2
A Holy Family

Every community has its sacred history, a store of foundational deeds and myths allowing the collective consciousness to protect itself against oblivion and adversity. To complement the Koranic revelation, Muslims have therefore admitted a corpus of traditions, the *sunna*, on which their theologians can draw when they want to lay down precise commandments, to follow the example of the Prophet Mohammad more closely, or to convey their faith in a more lively and impressive manner. This corpus is made up of chains of information ("I heard this from so-and-so, who had it from such-and-such . . . who recounts that . . .") and of "sayings" (Arabic, *hadith*) recounting the words, actions and deeds of the Prophet.

For the Shi'ites, these traditions, which are often the same as those of the Sunnis, are transmitted along different "chains" and gathered into special corpora. They come to them through the intermediary of the Imams, who are the "transmitters" *par excellence*, because they are in possession of the esoteric secrets and themselves belong to the Prophet's family. For the Shi'ites, the sacred history is first and foremost the life of the Prophet and his Community, but it is extended by the history of the Imams, which allows one to understand equally the mystic and esoteric doctrine and their political attitude as a minority, a situation they endured for several centuries.

'ALI, BETWEEN GLORY AND FAILURE

The first tradition in which the Shi'ites take pride, and which the Sunnis do not totally reject, is the legitimacy of the right of 'Ali, Mohammad's cousin and son-in-law, to succeed him as head of the Muslim Community.

After the death of Mohammad in 632, the majority of the faithful rallied around Abu Bakr, whom they recognized as caliph or "successor to God's Messenger" (*khalifat rasul Allāh*), and who was followed as leader of the Community by 'Omar and 'Osmān. But some of the Companions had misgivings about these nominations. The first caliph, Abu Bakr, had been appointed while Mohammad's close relatives were busy with the preparations for his funeral.[1] Among the latter was 'Ali, the Prophet's son-in-law and cousin, who only learned of the election from somebody else and, finding himself unable to intervene, had to accept it: his turn would come later.

Only a few weeks before his death the Prophet, returning from a final pilgrimage to Mecca, had stopped at Ghadir Khomm, an oasis on the Medina road. Taking 'Ali's hand in his right hand, Mohammad had asked the crowd of faithful accompanying him if he was not the supreme authority (*owlā*). With their unanimous approbation, he had then declared; "Whomsoever I protect (*mowlā*), 'Ali is likewise his protector. O God, be a friend to [or 'be close to,' *vali*] whoever is his friend and an enemy to whoever is his enemy!" According to the Sunnis, the Prophet wanted only to support 'Ali in some internal conflicts and had no intention of giving him precedence over other senior men from his phratry or clan.

Who was this young man of 32, aspiring to lead the Community in the face of a respectable elderly man like Abu Bakr, who was nearly twice his age? Apart from being the Prophet's cousin and foster brother, 'Ali had been his adoptive brother (Abu Tāleb, 'Ali's father, had taken in the orphan Mohammad), his boon companion, and had been one of the first to believe in his mission. Some people even say that on the day in September 622 when Mohammad left Mecca for Medina, 'Ali slept in his bed so that the polytheistic Meccans should not immediately discover the flight (or Hegira, *Hejra*) of the Muslims. Later, 'Ali was a valiant fighter and served the Prophet as secretary and diplomat. Moreover, he had married Fatima (Fātema), one of the daughters that his holy cousin had produced with his first wife Khadija, and she had given him two sons, Hasan and Hoseyn, who were regarded as Mohammad's only male descendants in the absence of any surviving son: from them issued the line of Shi'ite Imams, and through them all the lines of *sayyed*, notably those of the Hashemite sherifs (princes) who descended from the Imam Hasan and reigned uninterruptedly over Mecca from the tenth century until they were supplanted by the Saudis in 1924.

---

1 See the account as reconstructed by M. RODINSON, *Mohammed*, New York, Pantheon, 1971 (French text, pp. 323ff).

Although, according to the Shi'ites, 'Ali was the Prophet's appointed successor, he was at first kept from the caliphate. He resigned himself to waiting for years before he could take his turn at leading the new Muslim Empire, and his trusting wait is today still considered the very model of the Shi'ite virtue of patience. It was in fact useless to shed blood in order to hasten an event willed by God. But at a deeper level, the fact of having been set aside caused 'Ali to internalize and idealize the succession he thought he deserved to hold.

A Shi'ite tradition, echoed in the seventeenth century by the Iranian theosopher Qāzi Sa'id Qommi, tells that the Apostle of God (Mohammad) had the choice between the status of servant and king, but chose to be a Prophet Servant (*'abd nabi*) rather than a Prophet King. So his succession could be neither that of an exoteric sovereignty (*saltanat zāhera*, that is, according to political laws), nor despotic. It had to be of a purely religious nature (*khelāfat diniya*), that same spiritual sovereignty (*saltanat ruhāniya*) of which only beings who shared the soul of the Prophet could be worthy, as Mohammad himself said of 'Ali and 'Ali's sons, Hasan and Hoseyn.[2]

'Ali Shari'ati, a thinker and sociologist who died in 1977 and who was at the origin of the revival of Islam among young Iranian intellectuals before the Revolution, gave another interpretation of 'Ali's withdrawal.[3] He stressed 'Ali's heroism and sense of priorities in a period when any overt opposition would certainly have been fatal for Islam:

> 'Ali held his peace for the sake of the unity of Islam and gave his support to the government of those people. Throughout his 25 years' wait, this hero who had cut down his enemies with his sword . . . had to keep silent and remain inactive. He saw his house attacked and his wife insulted, but maintained a silence which he described succinctly when he said that for nearly 25 years he had had "dust in his eyes and thorns in his mouth."[4]

'Ali thus waited 25 years: after Abu Bakr, who survived his son-in-law Mohammad by only two years, the caliphate came to 'Omar. 'Ali apparently gave up all military or political office. Nevertheless, on the election of 'Othmān his opposition became more forthright. In fact, the third caliph

---

2 H. CORBIN, *En Islam iranien: Aspects spirituels et philosophiques*, Paris, Gallimard, 1971, vol. I, p. 80; H. ENAYAT, *Modern Islamic Political Thought*, Austin, University of Texas Press, and London and Basingstoke, Macmillan, 1982, pp. 25ff.
3 On Shari'ati, see below, ch. 4.
4 'A. SHARI'ATI, *'Ali* (Collected Works, vol. XXVI), Tehran, Nilufar, 1361/1982, p. 146.

represented the rich Meccan bourgeoisie and his reign prefigured what the Omayyad caliphate at Damascus would become: nepotism supplanted social justice and the splendor of festivals, allegedly borrowed from the Byzantines, replaced the ascetic piety of the first Muslims. 'Ali, so it is said, was linked with the conspiracy responsible for the assassination of 'Othmān in 656.

Then at last came 'Ali's election and the golden age of Islam, if we are to believe the Shi'ites who turn the five years of his reign into the period when divine justice was realized on earth. Islamic militants take 'Ali as an example, as if he were still, even in the twentieth century, the best illustration of Islamic political order. Although no one doubts 'Ali's uprightness and virtue, chiefly for having so patiently awaited his turn to exercise power, it was nevertheless under the fourth caliph that the great divisions between Muslims became irreversible.

'Ali had to confront two rebellions: the first was led by 'Aysha, the daughter of Abu Bakr and favorite wife of the Prophet; she wanted to avenge the murder of 'Othmān, supported by close companions of Mohammad, who by seceding were threatening to break away the provinces of Iraq and Iran. 'Ali, backed by partisans from the Iraqi town of Kufa, won a victory near Basra in 656 in a battle watched by 'Aysha mounted on a camel (hence the name, Battle of the Camel).[5] The insurgents were executed and 'Aysha, who was later reconciled with 'Ali, sent back to Medina. But another revolt came from Damascus, where Mo'āwiya, head of the Omayyad clan to which 'Othmān had belonged, profited from his 20 years of military experience in fighting against the Byzantine Empire. The Bedouins supporting 'Ali had the worst of it: the battle of Seffin in Iraq appeared likely to go on *ad infinitum*, when the two sides agreed to submit to human arbitration, which the Omayyads had demanded by spiking leaves of the Koran on the end of their lances. The judgement, given in 658, was unfavorable to 'Ali: it rejected his argument against the punishment of the assassins of 'Othmān, the caliph, who in his view had been guilty of prevarication. Taking advantage of the problems that 'Ali was having with dissidents, Mo'āwiya consolidated his positions in Syria and occupied Egypt.

'Ali subsequently had to contend with further dissidence. Certain purists considered that "judgement belongs to God alone," and so rejected the legitimacy of using human arbitration to settle so grave a question as the differences between 'Ali and the Omayyads over the caliphate. These

5   See the French translation by M. ROUHANI from the text of Sheikh Moufid, *La Victoire de Bassora ou Al-Jamal*, Paris, 1974.

dissidents were the "Kharijites" (*khawarij*) of Kufa, "those who *go out*" (for holy war). They also called themselves "those who give their life in payment for the cause of God." They were exterminated by 'Ali at the battle of Nahravān, which was a massacre. According to tradition, ten Kharijites survived and went off to publicize their cause, taking advantage of their persecuted state. Going to the very extreme of Islam's egalitarian principles and henceforward placing 'Ali among the enemies of God, they spread fear by committing terrorist-type assassinations. Today the last of the Kharijites are the Ibadites, who live in the sultanate of Oman and North Africa.

In 661 'Ali was to succumb to blows from a poisoned sword delivered by a Kharejite, Ibn Moljam, in front of the door of the mosque in Kufa. His tomb at Najaf (Iraq) is one of the principal places of pilgrimage for the Shi'ites, and since the Middle Ages its environs have housed an important centre of theological studies. 'Ali's death is often presented by Shi'ites as a model of freely accepted martyrdom. "It was because he had reached that very highest dwelling-place that the Lord 'Ali − peace be on him! − at the moment when the sword's blade began to pierce the centre of his skull, declared: '*By the God of the Ka'ba! I swear it, I am saved and victorious.*' " This can be read in a religious instruction manual of the Islamic Republic of Iran during the Iran–Iraq war: its intention was to encourage the young to imitate the first Imam and go to meet martyrdom in the war against Iraq.

The failure of 'Ali's caliphate, which was unable to maintain the cohesion of the Community, is one of the most disturbing paradoxes in Muslim history: do the Shi'ites not look upon it as the supreme model of all Islamic government? It is true that 'Ali's sayings, sermons and letters, gathered nearly 300 years after his death into a collection, the *Nahj ol-balāgha* (The Path of Eloquence), bear witness to an admirable code of ethics. Its style, according to certain Arab authors, makes this anthology of virtuous and noble counsels one of the jewels of ethical literature. The fact that the *Nahj ol-balāgha* arouses equal admiration in both Sunnis and Shi'ites does not however conceal its philosophical banality, and in any case the attribution to 'Ali is not certain (ancient Greek and Persian sources cannot be ruled out).[6] A famous extract from the collection is a letter addressed by 'Ali to one Mālek al-Ashtar, whom he appointed governor of Egypt: the Shi'ites readily see this letter as a model of "Islamic constitution," in which the principles of modern democracy are already prefigured . . .[7]

6   See Ch.-H. de FOUCHECOUR, *Moralia*, Paris, ADPF, 1986, pp. 118ff; K.-H. GÖBEL, *Moderne schiitische Politik und Staatsidee*, Opladen, Leske and Budrich, 1984, pp. 42ff.
7   See 'ALI B. ABI TĀLEB, *Nahjul Balagha: Peak of Eloquence*, Elmhurst, NY, Tahrike Tarsile Qur'an, 1984, pp. 534ff; GÖBEL, *Moderne schiitische Politik*, pp. 40ff.

In the religion of the people, 'Ali is actually the supreme model of an enlightened and inspired sovereign: he would seem to have held that role already as chancellor (*vazir*) in Mohammad's government. Strong as a lion, armed with the sword called Zu-l'feqār (which had, as its name indicates, two points or two blades), he is held up as a model for fighters. An unfortunate politician, 'Ali has been transformed by militant ideology into a martyr for justice. He could of course have rebelled against the appointment of the first three caliphs and the complete isolation to which 'Othmān reduced him; he could have used cunning to render Mo'āwiya powerless, flattering him at first and then neutralizing him by surprise; he could have carried on regardless of the stratagem of the leaves from the Koran at the battle of Seffin and used his military advantage. But, according to Shari'ati, he opposed all temptation to violence with a categoric "no:"

> He laid out a path, a permanent model for humankind, he has shown man once and for all the perfect example of a man . . . That is how he became an Imam, otherwise he would have been nothing but a failed governor, rejected by all, and both he and his line would have been annihilated. For an Imam is one who goes ahead, to show man the direction to take, at all times. That is why he refused the rank of victorious leader, which would have been extinguished at his death, and preferred instead the role of Imam, which led him to retreat, after refusing any compromise, but which extended his life beyond death. We see that every day he is more alive, that we have ever greater need of him, and hearts that are vibrant for humanism, liberty, justice, and purity . . . turn ever more towards him and his Imamate.[8]

The author of this pre-Islamic Revolution glorification is an intellectual, but he is rediscovering and justifying a profound tendency of Shi'ite religiosity. As an Imam, 'Ali is vested with powers that make him, so to speak, the equal of the Prophet (certain sects, such as the "Faithful to the Truth" of Kurdistan, or the 'Alavites of Syria and Turkey, would even say that 'Ali outranks Mohammad, that he is the "essence of God"). The pious public resorts in droves to 'Ali as intercessor, as he is closer to humble believers than Mohammad and a real intermediary between this world and heaven. With the Prophet, 'Ali has participated in the sublimest mystical experiences but, like ordinary mortals, he has endured unjust suffering. In the words of a young provincial to a foreigner asking him about his beliefs,

> When the Prophet set out for his ascent to heaven [*mi'rāj*], Hazrat-i 'Ali wanted to be taken along, but Mohammad refused . . . The Prophet left, but

8 'A. SHARI'ATI, *'Ali*, Tehran, Nilufar, 1361/1982 (Collected Works, vol. XXVI), pp. 108–9.

on his journey he was stopped by a lion who requested his ring for letting him pass. And when he was dining near the throne of God, a hand appeared from behind a partition and joined him in the meal. And while Mohammad was eating half an apple, the hand took the other half. The next morning Hazrat-i 'Ali asked the Prophet what had happened. The Prophet told him and showed him the half apple from heaven. Hazrat-i 'Ali took the other half from his pocket and Mohammad saw that it was the matching piece . . . Then Hazrat-i 'Ali gave him back the ring which the lion had taken. That is, Hazrat-i 'Ali had been the lion and was near the throne at the same time as the Prophet. Thereupon the Prophet said, "I don't know 'Ali as God, but neither do I know him to be separate from God."[9]

The golden legend of 'Ali is preserved in schools through religious manuals that rival one another with tales of miracles and prodigies to make children dream. Thus during his caliphate 'Ali bought two shirts and offered the finer one to his servant – to set an example. Elsewhere one reads that 'Ali, at the height of his power, discovers a coat of mail that had been stolen from him to be in the possession of a Christian merchant. The judge before whom both present themselves rises in front of the caliph, the Ruler of the Faithful, who in no uncertain terms reprimands the magistrate for treating plaintiffs according to rank and not with perfect fairness. In the end, 'Ali does not manage to produce sufficient witnesses, the Christian departs with the goods . . . and begs to become a Muslim!

This popular glory merely amplifies the learned tradition that elevates the First Imam to a quasi-divine rank. In current hagiography, 'Ali, conceived for all eternity in the light of Mohammad, was born in the Ka'ba (sacred temple) of Mecca.[10] Gnostic texts, certainly apocryphal although accepted and commented upon by great classical theosophers, even have the First Imam say that he is the Perfect Man, the celestial Anthropos, as witnessed by the "Sermon of the Declaration" (*khotbat al-bayān*) sometimes included in the *Nahj ol-Balāgha*. 'Ali said:

I am the Sign of the All-Powerful. I am the First and the Last. I am the Manifest and the Hidden. I am the Face of God. I am the Hand of God. I am the Side of God. I am He who in the Gospel is called Elijah. I am he who keeps the secret of God's Messenger . . .[11]

9   R. LOEFFLER, *Islam in Practice: Religious Beliefs in a Persian Village*, Albany, SUNY Press, 1988, p. 52.
10   'EMĀDZĀDA, *Majmu'a-ye zendegāni-e Tchahārdah-e ma'sum* (The Fourteen Immaculate Ones), [Tehran], Maktab-e Qor'an, [1340/1961], vol. I, p. 362.
11   H. CORBIN, *En Islam iranien*, vol. I, p. 96.

THE CLAN OF THE 'ALIDS

Was there a Shi'ite Community organized around the descendants of the Prophet who might aspire to power? For a better understanding of the belief in which today's Shi'ites live, let us recall the historical facts and the way in which they have been transformed by tradition.

Contrary to current Shi'ite belief, the politico-religious movement that we know these days under the name of Imami Shi'ism seems to have emerged at the end of the ninth century, after the disappearance of the Twelfth Imam in 874, and not immediately following the death of the Prophet. A British scholar of Islam has suggested the name "proto-Shi'ites" for the first partisans of the Prophet's family (before 874): unhappy with the Omayyads, they had not yet bluntly pledged their allegiance to a particular line of the Imams and were still hesitating between all the descendants of 'Ali (or 'Alids) and those of his son Hoseyn alone.[12] Some attached themselves to the line of a certain Mohammad, the son of 'Ali and a woman known as the Hanafiya (woman of the Hanifi tribe) whom he had wed after Fatima's death; others opted for other aspirants who were more activist than the descendants of Hasan or Hoseyn. This presentation of the facts shows up the qualitative difference between a Shi'ism of malcontents who were simply seeking the best candidate to defend their cause, and a more speculative Shi'ism which renounced the conquest of power.

The principle of dynastic succession, which comes from neither Mohammad nor the Koran, already existed in the south of Arabia. It is therefore useless to look for a trace of some Iranian imperial tradition here. What matters is the respect for the "family" of the Prophet, in this instance the Hashemite clan among whom traditional Arabs hoped to rediscover the eminent qualities of Mohammad. Iranian tradition may of course have come into it, but rather in the alliance of temporal power (claimed rather than realized) with the sacred charisma of a king by divine right, similar to the glory which (if only in the memory of Persians) surrounded the semi-legendary sovereigns of the Parthian and Sassanid dynasties. Later on the Shi'ites attributed a divinely granted infallibility to the Imam, a spiritual mark passed on like an initiatory secret. The political and military failure of the Shi'ites accentuated the sacred dimension, the belief in the Occultation (state of being hidden) of the Imam, that is to say, both the supreme value set on his mystic power and the implicit acknowledgement of another

---

12   W. M. WATT, *The Formative Period of Islamic Thought*, Edinburgh, Edinburgh University Press, 1973, pp. 38ff.

temporal power, established *de facto* over society; in short, for the Shi'ites the hope of the Imam's eschatological return became all the keener as their almost permanent persecution made life difficult for them in this world below.

Although the first "partisans of 'Ali" (the literal meaning of "Shi'ites," from the Arabic *shi'at 'Ali*, "the party of 'Ali") were Arabs, many Shi'ite militants were also recruited from non-Arab "clients" (or *mavāli*) who lived in the central towns of the empire, notably Medina or Kufa, impatiently awaiting the application of the new religion's egalitarian rules. These *mavāli*, former prisoners of war who had been freed, and converted foreigners who had placed themselves under the "protection" of an Arab notable, often came from Iran, but also from Syria or Egypt.[13] For them, Shi'ism was generally thought of as a demand for justice, in the face of the corruption of the Omayyads. In the middle of the eighth century, before their total integration into Muslim society, they were mobilized by the 'Abbāsid movement which aimed to restore power to a "legitimate" branch of the Prophet's family, the Hashemites, and to shift the political centre from Damascus towards Mesopotamia, where Baghdad was to be founded. Iranian influence was a determining factor in its location near the previous capital of the Sassanids and in the new imperial culture of the caliphate.

Abu Zarr al-Ghefāri, whose role has been highlighted by recent revolutionary discourse in the Islamic Republic, is a typical representative of the proto-Shi'ite hero. Tradition has it that this ascetic experienced a prophetic premonition of monotheism before being influenced by the Koranic revelation, to which he was one of the first to adhere. Because he advocated the redistribution of land, he was exiled to Syria in the time of the caliph 'Othmān, then sent to Arabia by Mo'āwiya, dying there in isolation in 652. Legend describes him as gentle and intransigent as Jesus. But the image of him given these days by Islamists, including the Sunni Muslim Brothers, approaches that of a socialist militant, inveighing against the corruption of the rich and preaching the sharing of wealth.[14]

---

13   C. CAHEN, *L'Islam des origines au début de l'Empire ottoman*, Paris, Bordas, 1970, p. 38.
14   M. RODINSON, *Islam and Capitalism*, trans. B. Pearce, Austin, University of Texas Press, 1978 (French text, p. 171). For sources, see I. GOLDZIHER, *Le Dogme et la loi d'Islam*, Paris, Geuthner, 1973, pp. 115ff; H. ALGAR, "Social Justice in the Ideology and Legislation of the Islamic Revolution of Iran," in L. O. Michalak and J. W. Salacuse, eds, *Social Legislation in the Contemporary Middle East*, Berkeley, University of California Press, 1986, p. 28.

Even if this modern interpretation is rather forced, it flourishes in ideo-logical discourse. 'Ali Shari'ati, for example, devoted numerous lectures, today published in one volume, to this "precursor" of the Islamic Revolu-tion. For Shari'ati, Abu Zarr is a hero battling against inequality and social discrimination, and his entire life has value as a testimony:

> This is why Abu Zarr gave up individualistic material comfort for "revolu-tionary piety," that is to say Islamic asceticism, the asceticism of 'Ali – and not the [mystic] Sufi asceticism of Jesus or Buddha: he did so in order to obtain material comfort and economic equality for men. For whoever fights against the hunger of others must accept hunger himself, and only he who gives up liberty can make a gift of it to society. Such was this revolutionary religion: "both God and bread;" not the religion of weakness, of monasticism, of privation, of going against nature in the misleading expectation of another world, but a religion that deifies man within nature , that makes him God's "caliph" in the material world.[15]

Although Shari'ati draws Abu Zarr toward a socialism that "outshines Proudhon's," he does not overlook the man's mystic dimension. Of course the environment of primitive Shi'ism is perceived in retrospect as an anti-establishment world, but also as the repository of the secrets of Mohammadan revelation. Alongside 'Ali, two central figures illustrate this tendency to over-glorification: Fatima (Fātema), his wife, and Salmān the Pure. Shari'ati's work also bears witness to the importance of these two people in the modern Shi'ite pantheon.

Fatima, born shortly before the beginning of the Koranic revelation, gave her father the Prophet the only male descendants to survive him. The worship rendered to Fatima by pious Shi'ite people somewhat resembles that of Christians for the Virgin Mary: she too is the All-Pure (and certain sects have gone as far as to affirm that she remained a virgin in spite of her motherhood), the mother of a line of "saviours" (the Imams). It was re-vealed to her, we are told, that her last direct male descendant to bear this sacred title, the Twelfth Imam, would be called Mohammad like her fa-ther, and so she was nicknamed "Mother of her father" (*Omm abihā*); Mary is similarly "the daughter of her son," mother of Jesus who is one with God the Father. Fatima is still called the Radiant One (*Zahrā*).

15 'A. SHARI'ATI, *Abu Zarr*, Tehran, Hoseyniya Ershād, 1357/1978, (Collected Works, vol. III), p. 221. Most of the text is a translation by Shari'ati of a book in Arabic by 'Abd ol-Hamid Jowdat al-Sahar.

Fatima is the central figure of the founding nucleus of Islam's Holy Family formed by the "Five of the Mantle" or "Cloak:" this is the name given to the group composed of Fatima and her father Mohammad, 'Ali her husband and her two children Hasan and Hoseyn, gathered together by the Prophet for an ordeal he proposed between himself and the Christians of Najran (the affirmation of Islam as a constituted religion in the face of the other great Abrahamic religion).[16] Mohammad gave his daughter in a monogamous marriage to his adoptive brother and cousin, 'Ali. He made an exception for her by raising the ban on going to pray on the tombs, which gave her a special status and no doubt explains the importance of tombs – disapproved of by rigorous Muslims like the Wahhābis – in Shi'ite worship. Fatima died 75 days after her father while giving birth to a stillborn infant, Mohsen.

The orientalists Lammens and Massignon have given differing interpretations of Fatima.[17] The former perpetuates the rather unflattering portrait of the mother of the Imams left by their Omayyad enemies – an awkward, stubborn, sickly woman, always moaning and devoid of any attraction. For Massignon the mystic orientalist who takes up the Shi'ite tradition, Fatima is on the contrary "the hostess who receives those emancipated by her father," she who welcomes foreigners (Mariam the Copt and Salmān the Persian) and whose descendants "will always be the champions of equality between Arab and non-Arab believers," she who stood up to Abu Bakr and his daughter 'Aysha, "the intercessor for the dead" whose prayer is perpetual, as she is exempt from the periodic uncleanness that keeps women from prayer . . . But without dwelling on what Massignon calls the *hyperdulia* (excessive adulation) of Fatima, mention must be made once again of a modern militant interpretation, that of Shari'ati, who himself acknowledges his debt to the French orientalist in the editing of the lectures he devoted to the Lady of Shi'ism.

'Ali Shari'ati begins by criticizing the role allotted to women in traditional Muslim society and the false ideal of superficially emancipated women frequently adopted by westernized Iranian bourgeois as a reaction to the old model. Fatima will provide the true model: Shari'ati describes her by dramatizing her role, the daughter and confidante of the Prophet, the

---

16 L. MASSIGNON, "La Mubāhala de Médine et l'hyperdulie de Fatima," in Y. Moubarac, ed., *Opera minora*, vol. I, Paris, PUF, 1969, pp. 550–72; 'Der gnostiche Kult der Fatima im schiitschen Islam,' *ibid.*, pp. 514ff.
17 H. LAMMENS, *Fatima et les filles de Mohammad*, Rome, Scripta Pontificii Instituti Biblici, 1912. For Massignon, see the articles quoted in the preceding note.

perfect spouse in a household that was not free from material worries, the mother entrusted with bringing up two future leaders of the Community. But we are not speaking here of some prefabricated mold, says our author: when Fatima asked Mohammad for material help, Mohammad taught her to recite prayers of praise . . . A surprising response, which in reality would teach her to become herself! Shari'ati has used this as title for his lecture, "Fatima is (becomes) *Fatima*."[18] To become oneself is not an empty act if one understands here the militant will no longer to depend on others in order magically to overcome adverse situations, as we are invited to do by the traditional religion criticized by Shari'ati, but on the contrary to rely on one's own strengths. Spiritually fulfilling one's own identity is a matter of acquiring not an unmerited and "unworthy salvation," but the "dignity of salvation" and the disposition needed to attain it.

Salmān, the last great figure of the first generation of mythical Shi'ism, is an Iranian who came to Islam at the end of a mystic quest and who, before becoming Fatima's protégé, seems to have been to some extent her counselor and confidant. Even more than for Fatima, here we enter religious legend, but a particularly fertile legend. Iranian by birth, his religion was doubtless Zoroastrianism; he bears the Persian name of Ruzbeh (Felix).

Having become a Christian, Salmān adopted an ascetic way of life (notably abstaining from wine), set off on a journey to Palestine and Syria where he was reduced to slavery, and is said to have heard from a monk the news that a new prophet had appeared. Having reached Medina, he recognized God's messenger in Mohammad, and was set free by him. Converted to Islam, although not an Arab, he lived on intimate terms with the Prophet, who said some surprising things about him: "Salmān is one of us, us, the people of the House;" "May he be to you like Loghman the wise; he knows the first knowledge and the second, and Paradise sighs for him five times a day." Salmān appears to have been an open supporter of 'Ali for the caliphate, which he expressed in two words recorded in Persian: *Kardēd o-nakardēd*, that is (according to old interpretations) "You have done [well] [to elect a leader], but you have not done [well] [to deviate from the legitimate source of authority]," or (according to a more polemical interpretation of the Imamis), "You have kept to the infamous example of the

---

18 'A. SHARI'ATI, "Fātema, Fatema'ast," *Zan* (Collected Works, vol. XXI), Tehran, Sabz, 1360/1981, pp. 141, 145. See also M. K. HERMANCEN, "Fatimeh as a Role Model in the Works of 'Ali Shari'ati," in G. Nashat, ed., *Women and Revolution in Iran*, Boulder, Colo., Westview Press, 1983, pp. 87ff.

Israelites [who rebelled against Aaron] and have removed yourselves from the exemplary authority of your Prophet by taking it from his family."[19]

Whichever version is chosen, Salmān is considered one of 'Ali's first and most ardent supporters. Dying at Madā'in (in present-day Iraq) between 641 and 649, he had an extremely rich posthumous destiny, and was chiefly revered as the spiritual ancestor of craft guilds and mystic orders. For Shi'ites, he is above all an initiate, one of those friends of the Prophet who were swift to pledge allegiance to 'Ali, bearing witness at the same time to the universal nature of Islam: Salmān is the supreme expatriate, the first of the non-Arabs to acknowledge the prophecy about Mohammad. In this sense, he foreshadows the words of the Sixth Imam, "Islam began as an expatriate and will once again become expatriate as at the beginning. Blessed are those among the community of Mohammad who leave their own country."

THE BATTLE OF KARBALĀ

'Ali had two sons by Fatima, his first and, until her death, only wife: Hasan and Hoseyn. Both were indulged by their grandfather the Prophet, but they hardly had the time to get to know him well since the elder was seven when Mohammad died. Hasan, surnamed Mojtabā (the Chosen), had a tranquil life: on 'Ali's assassination, after apparently taking up arms again, he chose instead to establish a pact with the Omayyads and, richly rewarded, withdrew to Medina. According to the Shi'ites, Mo'āwiya also made concessions, notably accepting that after his death a council should appoint the caliph to succeed him. Imam Hasan had numerous wives, some say as many as 90, and several hundred concubines, hence his nickname of "Repudiator" (*metlāq*). He died in 670, poisoned by one of his wives at the instigation of the Omayyads, according to later Shi'ite tradition, which also credits him with numerous miracles. In the view of the Sunnis, Hasan's pact undermines the subsequent claims of the Imams. It also gives a solemn example of non-resistance to tyranny, with the aim of safeguarding the general interests of the Community. After the 1979 Iranian Revolution, ayatollah Shari'at-madāri, suspected because he had been conciliatory toward the imperial regime, also claimed the right to be different, invoking

---

19 L. MASSIGNON, "Salmān Pāk et les prémices spirituelles de l'Islam iranien," *Opera minora*, vol. I, pp. 443–82.

the reformism of Imam Hasan against the revolutionaries: "The revolutionaries," he said in self-defence, "boast of Che Guevara and other third-
world militant Marxists; for myself, I have chosen the Second Imam. The
criterion of political action should be neither Marxism nor socialism, but
Islam."[20]

The death of Hasan, removed from power, 38 years after Mohammad,
following the military and political failure of 'Ali, did not seem to predict
a brilliant future for Fatima's line. But paradoxically the gilded and shame-
ful failure of Hasan was to be replaced very swiftly by a victory for his
brother Hoseyn, the Prince of Martyrs.

Kufa, a small town that has vanished today, was originally the encamp-
ment of the Arab armies engaged in the conquest of Iran. Situated on the
Euphrates, not far from Madā'in, the ancient capital of the Sassanids, it
remained central to the young Muslim Empire, being quite close to Arabia
and Iran without in any way being part of them. 'Ali, having set up his
capital at Kufa for a time, enjoyed great popularity there which carried on
to his descendants.[21]

The situation bequeathed by Imam Hasan to the Family of 'Ali was not
enviable. Hoseyn, born in 626, had looked on, powerless to act, at the pact
of his brother Hasan with Mo'āwiya. But on the latter's death in May 680,
he refused to pledge allegiance to his son Yazid, whose overt impiety and
taste for feasting and wine are described by historical sources. Hoseyn, who
was at Damascus, took refuge in Medina where he received an appeal from
the inhabitants of Kufa urging him to head a rebellion. Ill-informed of the
real danger, and especially of the countermeasures taken by Yazid, Hoseyn
sent his cousin Moslem b. 'Aqil as a scout and set off after he had completed
the "little pilgrimage" (*'omra*). To the objections of his supporters who
were frightened to see him run headlong into so senseless an enterprise,
Hoseyn answered: "God does as He pleases . . . I leave Him to choose what
is best . . . He is not inimical to the man who proposes what is right and
good (*al-haqq*)."[22]

Prevented from getting to Kufa by Omayyad troops sent to head him
off, on October 2, 680 (2 Moharram 61) Hoseyn found himself obliged to
bivouac at Karbalā, a tiny spot in the desert. Access to the water of the

20   Y. RICHARD, "Seyyed Kazem Shari'at-Madāri, 1904–1986," *Universalia*, 1986; *Encyclopaedia Universalis*, 1987, pp. 608–9.
21   See S. H. M. JAFRI, *Origins and Early Development of Shi'a Islam*, New York, Longman,
1976, pp. 101–29.
22   L. VECCIA VAGLIERI, "(al-)Husayn b. 'Ali b. Abi Talib," *Encyclopedia of Islam*,
2nd edn, s.v.

Euphrates was cut off by the enemy. 'Abbās, Hoseyn's half-brother, managed to fill a few pitiful goatskins to give a sip to the 72 companions who had camped for several days in the torrid heat. Among them was Zeynab, the Imam's sister, and 'Ali, his son, who was still a child and the future Fourth Imam, both of whom would survive.

Having refused invitations to surrender, the Imam prepared for the final battle and warned his friends of the dangers of staying with him: "I praise God who has honoured us with the Prophecy and has taught us the Koran and religion . . . I know of no companions more worthy . . . than mine, or any family more pious than mine . . . May God reward you all. I think tomorrow will be the end of us . . . Go, all of you. I will not keep you. The night will cover you. Use it as your steed . . ." After a final vigil of prayer came the last combat and massacre: on the morning of 10 Moharram, Hoseyn addressed his enemies to ask them to reflect before attacking the one whom the Prophet had cherished and to let him depart with dignity. But others demanded submission. Hesitant assailants, held back by last-minute scruples, set fire to the tents and tried to seize the women. Among the first victims that the Imam gathered in his arms were his son 'Ali-Akbar, Qāsem the son of Hasan, and Abo'l-Fazl al-'Abbās his brother. Heart-rending scenes are recorded by tradition and magnified by the mournful piety of the Shi'ites. Thus, when Hoseyn was holding a newborn baby in his arms, an arrow pierced the baby's neck and the Imam shed the blood on the ground invoking God against the wicked.

Shemr b. Sa'd (known to the Sunnis as Shamer) advanced at the head of a group and attacked Hoseyn, who was decapitated. His head would be taken to Kufa, then to Damascus. His body, trampled by horses, was buried on the spot, where today there is a great mausoleum.

FROM THE MASSACRE TO THE MYTH

The impact of the massacre of Karbalā is out of all proportion to the event itself, a small battle between rival clans which lasted only a day and resulted in no more than a few dozen dead. But Muslim consciousness was shaken by the tragic fate of the grandson of the Prophet Mohammad and his determination to fight to the very end a government that held up to ridicule the ethics and principles of earliest Islam. The martyrdom of Hoseyn has become the prototype of every struggle for justice, every suffering. That is where the heart of Shi'ism lies, in this agony which is at one and the same time a revolt and a sign of hope.

A whole body of contradictory interpretations attempts to throw light on this tragedy and offer some keys to an understanding of Shi'ism. Just to keep to current trends, in the contemporary era, I will pause over two principal directions. On the one hand, the debate that has divided the Shi'ite clergy over the question of Hoseyn's foreknowledge: did he know what dark destiny awaited him at Karbalā and , if so, why did he go there? On the other hand, was Hoseyn a revolutionary hero seeking to overthrow an impious regime, or did he rather symbolize the failure of the ideal in the face of violence, leaving the memory to solace helpless believers confronted with a political system of which they disapprove?

In 1971 there appeared in Tehran a little book in a new style, "The Eternal Martyr," in which the author, a cleric named Sālehi-Najafābādi from the region of Isfahan, gave an exhaustive account of the dramatic adventure of Hoseyn's martyrdom drawn from all the existing sources.[23] Besides the very direct style and an almost academic concern for precision, which it is not customary to find coming from a clerical pen, what was striking about the book was that it confronted head-on the problem posed by the Karbalā massacre to traditional doctrine: if Hoseyn was really the Third Imam, vested with the supernatural powers that make him the Prophet's legitimate successor, he ought, according to the Shi'ites, to possess total knowledge of the world's happenings, because if not, his ability to guide Muslims would be no better than that of other men. If Hoseyn knew beforehand that he would suffer a failure at Yazid's hands, how can it be explained that he threw himself wholeheartedly into the battle, endangering not only his own life but that of his family and friends and the cause he was defending? This classic aporia about predestination does not disconcert the author of "The Eternal Martyr" for whom, on the contrary, the Imam's behavior proves that he did all in his power to win the battle: if he found himself vanquished, it was only through lack of information on the attitude of the inhabitants of Kufa, and because of his adversary's cynical determination to have done with the Shi'ite rebellion (something that the respect due to Mohammad's grandson would not have led one to expect).

Lured by the subversive nature of this unlucky hero, the progressive clerics of the pre-revolutionary era gave their support to Sālehi-Najafābādi's arguments, which were heading in the same direction as the interpretation presented at that time by 'Ali Shari'ati, and which were disturbing the lugubrious torpor of traditional Shi'ites. A fierce polemic against the book

23 SĀLEHI NAJAFĀBĀDI, *Shahid-e jāvid*, 12th edn, enlarged, Tehran, Resā, 1361/ 1982.

conducted in the theological schools of Qom by the clerical rearguard split the Shi'ite clergy. By a stroke of bad luck the Shah's political police immediately got wind of the affair and took advantage of it to isolate in the religious camp those clerics in favor of "The Eternal Martyr" who, as if by chance, happened also to be fervent supporters of ayatollah Khomeyni, then in exile in Najaf. Among those who were the most committed was an important theologian who was to play a leading role in the Revolution, ayatollah Montazeri.

The controversy over this book actually recalled a double fundamental aspect of the Karbalā myth. I use the word "myth" here to denote the formative nature of the event, whose proportions have been greatly exaggerated by the Shi'ites. In fact, if the massacre of the Imam gained such a place in the religious sensibilities of those Muslims who were placed in a minority, then persecuted by the Sunnis and forced for centuries – apart from a few intervals – to live their lives clandestinely, it was because it corresponded so aptly with the attitude of failure that was so much their own. If the Imam had been vanquished in his earthly life, his struggle could therefore result in victory only at the End of Time. And if *he* had been defeated, then all Shi'ites could accept a situation in which they were disadvantaged and dominated, while keeping alive the feeling of a revenge that must be awaited until the next world. In modern times, in a society ruled by an impious regime, where religion has no right of predominance, to weep for Hoseyn is to weep for an invisible victory and sublimate the humiliations of the present as just so many necessary sufferings in order to hasten the long-awaited realization of the eschatological reign of justice and truth, that of the Imam of Time. An anthropologist has shown how the "two images" of Hoseyn can be in competition during the revolutionary phase, notably at the time of the Moharram celebrations which are always an occasion for intense and fervent activity.[24]

The first aspect of Hoseyn is that of an intercessor who must be pleased in order to attract his benevolent attention. By virtue of his martyrdom he enjoys special favor with God, so his intercession will probably be more effective than that of any other saint. Hoseyn can forgive sins and guarantee entry to Paradise. In order to please him, one shares in the pain of his martyrdom on the occasion of the mourning period of Moharram by

24   On the mourning rites of Moharram, see below, ch. 4; M. HEGLAND, "Two Images of Hussain: Accommodation and Revolution in an Iranian Village," in N. R. Keddie, ed., *Religion and Politics in Iran*, New Haven and London, Yale University Press, 1983, pp. 218–35.

weeping and offering votive meals and refreshments. He can also be asked
for recovery from illness, release from prison or other favors. Here the
connection becomes apparent between Hoseyn the intercessor and the social or political authority to which one must render homage and pledge
allegiance in a thousand and one ways in order to derive advantage, protection or assistance from it . Homage is rendered to whoever is in command.
The attitude of dependence governing social order is projected on to the
Imam. Hoseyn is simultaneously Imam and martyr, something which
imbues his worship with the value of a particularly praiseworthy commitment. Mournful lamentations added to the acceptance of a relationship of
passive dependence turn this first aspect of Hoseyn into a sort of social
regulator allowing frustration to be lulled.

The second aspect is that of Hoseyn fighting for justice, against the
iniquitous power of the Omayyads. According to Shari'ati, who devoted
several lectures to the revolutionary hero of Karbalā, the martyrdom is
what is ordinarily honored in dead heroes, sacrificed during battles against
the enemy, and is a misfortune that arouses compassion. In the Shi'ism of
his time Shari'ati sees that during the commemoration of Karbalā, on the
day of 'Ashura (tenth day of Moharram), people weep copiously without
knowing exactly why; and at the same time, he says, corruption turned
Islam (described by allusion as if the author were speaking of the Omayyads'
Islam) into a corrupt religion meant to tranquillize the affluent and consolidate the power of the government. Sālehi-Najafābādi's book, he continues,
marks a step forward against the distortion of tradition, but still describes
Karbalā as no more than an operation in a holy war that did not succeed.
Hoseyn undertook his campaign against Yazid at a crucial period when the
"holy war" (*jehād*) was itself vain and pointless. He was not going to a
military operation, but was committing himself to making a heroic statement which went beyond all wars: his was an outstanding presence, tran-
scending the pettiness of the caliph's power and affirming, beyond the
gates of death, those intangible values against which violence is powerless,
Martyrdom is the only means to recall those values that have been passed
over in silence, and to lay bare what has been hidden.

In Karbalā, the enemies of Hoseyn conquered only the bodies of the martyrs, but the ideology of the martyrs condemned these enemies and their
regime. With their blood, the martyrs canceled their enemies' grand conspiracy forever . . . With *shahādat* [i.e. "martyrdom"] Hoseyn did what the
miraculous hand of Moses did. From the blood of the martyrs he created
something like the breath of Jesus, which gives sight to the blind and life to

the dead and . . . this was not exclusive merely to his own time and land. *Shahādat* is not war – it is mission. It is not a weapon – it is a message. It is a word pronounced in blood.[25]

THE RENUNCIATION AND THE "MARTYRDOM" OF THE IMAMS

After the political failure and murder of 'Ali, the renunciation of the caliphate by his first son Hasan and the suppression of Hoseyn's revolt, the Shi'ite cause was, to say the least, in a poor position. However, the scandalous excesses of the Omayyads during the century of their dynasty's existence (661–750) constantly aroused a desire for change. For the time being, a group of inhabitants of Kufa, the *Tavvābun*, who "repented" having abandoned Hoseyn without defending him, rebelled against the Omayyads and were crushed in 684: almost exclusively Arab, they were not really sure of the cause for which they were fighting, most likely for Hoseyn's son, Imam Sajjād. Another group of Shi'ites, among whom were many Iranian followers (*mavāli*), rebelled in the same period for motives as much social as religious, seeking to promote the cause of Mohammad, the son of Imam 'Ali and the Hanafiya. The survivors of the Tavvābun joined them, with their leader Mokhtār, who was killed in 686 or 687.

Devotion to the son of the Hanafiya did not stop with the death of Mokhtār; the latter had given Shi'ism its esoteric color and eschatological dimension by insisting on the role of the Imam as *Mahdi*, "he who is guided," that is , "he who listens to the absolute Guide, God." This term, applied later to the Twelfth Imam, would take on a very powerful meaning for Shi'ites, that of Saviour. Only the political effacement of Hoseyn's son had been able temporarily to divert supporters of the descendants of 'Ali toward another candidate; they returned in the end to the last few of the Twelve Imams.

Among the adversaries of the Omayyads, partisans of the "'Abbāsid Revolution," many Shi'ites dreamed of putting one of 'Ali's descendants back on the caliph's throne. Although such an aim ran into violent opposition from the sovereigns of Damascus, and then Baghdad, there is nothing to show that it constituted a danger for the Sunni order. Nevertheless, because of their beliefs and half-hearted allegiance to the authority *in situ*,

25   'A. SHARI'ATI, "Shahādat" (Martyrdom) in *Hoseyn, vāres-e Adam*, (Collected Works, vol. XIX), Tehran, Qalam, 1360/1981, pp.188ff, trans. in M. Taleqani, M. Mutahhari, and A. Shari'ati, *Jihād and Shahādat: Struggle and Martrydom in Islam*, ed. M. Abedi and G. Legenhausen, Houston, Iris, 1986, pp. 208ff.

the Shi'ites provided a refuge for two kinds of malcontents: political and mystical.

FROM HOSEYN TO THE HIDDEN IMAM

If Shi'ite tradition is to be believed, Hoseyn's descendants all came to a tragic end and were in general poisoned on orders from the caliph. Of these persecuted martyrs, only the Twelfth escaped his enemies, in a supernatural manner.

According to Shi'ite tradition, the succession of the Imams seems to have carried on automatically from father to son, starting from the Fourth. Theoretically, however, dynastic inheritance has no legitimate validity and it is the living Imam who on his own authority (*nass*) appoints his successor as being the most worthy, both spiritually and physically, to carry out the duties of commander. He passes on to him personally the esoteric secrets that he himself inherited, and that come down to him from the Prophet.

The Fourth Imam, 'Ali, son of Hoseyn, who escaped the Karbalā massacre, was called Zeyn al-'Ābedin, "Ornament of the devout," or Sajjād, "He who prostrates himself in adoration:" prayers attributed to him are in current use by Shi'ites today, and are collected in a popular devotional anthology, the *Sahifa sajjādiya*.

A pious legend recorded by the historian Tabari has it that the mother of this Imam was Shahrbānu, the daughter of the Sassanid Emperor Yazdegerd III: Imam 'Ali had this captive princess married to his son to avoid her being sold to the highest bidder. Iranian traditions have profitably tapped this rich vein that establishes such a strong link between the humiliated family of the Imams and a nation that was swift to embrace Islam. There is no source that can truly confirm or deny this story, which gives rise to reservations on the part of modern revolutionary Islamists: having fought against the old regime, they reject this aristocratic harnessing of Shi'ism and the old connivance between the imperial system and a certain type of religion.[26] Having withdrawn to Medina, far from all public activity, Imam Sajjād is said to have died by poisoning on the orders of the Omayyad caliph Heshām, in 712 or 713. He is buried at the Baqi' Shi'ite cemetery in Medina.

---

26 See 'A. SHARI'ATI, *Tashayyo'-e 'alavi, tashayyo'-e safavi* (Collected Works, vol. IX), Tehran, Tashayyo', 1359/1980, pp. 88ff, 100. This ancient tradition is equally widespread outside Shi'ism; cf. J. CALMARD, "Le Culte de l'Imam Husayn" (unpublished dissertation), Paris, EPHE, VIth section, 1975, vol. II, p. 183.

Figure 1 Genealogy of the Twelve Imams

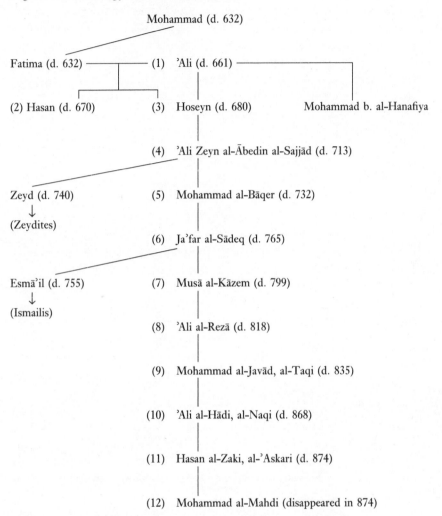

His son, the Fifth Imam, Mohammad, surnamed al-Bāqer "the Over-flowing" (implying "with knowledge"), lived apart from public matters and died, very probably poisoned, in 732. He also is buried in the Baqi' in Medina. Although Imam al-Bāqer was the first to define the principle of appointment on the authority (*nass*) of the Imams, in his lifetime he had to confront the rivalry of his brother Zeyd (killed in battle in 740) who roused the Shi'ites of Kufa. The political posterity of Zeydite Shi'ism, notably in the north of Iran (Tabarestān, or present-day Māzandarān) up till 1033, and above all until 1962 in the Yemen (when Imam Badr was overthrown by a pro-Nasser revolution), is a sign that, within Shi'ism itself, divergent theological options had evolved. For the Zeydites, the principle of appointment by investiture (*nass*) is worthless. Personal merit alone is what matters: they maintain that power comes back by right to any descendant of 'Ali and Fatima who can manage to obtain it. Zeyd himself was only the son of a slave, whereas Imam al-Bāqer's mother was the daughter of Imam Hasan, but the dual legitimacy of their rival in no way impeded the Zeydites in the affirmation of their claims.

The Sixth Imam, Ja'far al-Sādeq ("the Truthful"), son of Mohammad al-Bāqer, was the most brilliant of 'Ali's descendants. He lived in Medina during that tense period when the caliphate was transferred from the Omayyads to the 'Abbāsids. Keeping himself apart from political demands, Imam Ja'far let the Zeydite revolt be crushed in 740 without taking sides, nor did he commit himself to supporting the 'Abbāsids. Later, in 762, he put his family's partisans on their guard against the aspirations of Mohammad al-Nafs al-Zakiya, a descendant of Imam Hasan who enjoyed wide popularity and refused allegiance to the 'Abbāsids. The Sixth Imam's position over all these revolts was one of remarkable severity: the Imam must wait, while passing on his teachings, until the time comes for him to assume power. He holds that power through explicit appointment by his predecessor, but also because of his knowledge, both exoteric and esoteric (positive knowledge and spiritual awareness). It is the duty of every believer to recognize the Imam, who is the link between God and men. "Whosoever dies without having known his Imam dies as an infidel," he is reported as saying. Furthermore, if circumstances are not favourable, one must not tempt fate, and it is preferable, according to Ja'far al-Sādeq, to employ that specifically Shi'ite virtue of "mental dissimulation" (*taqiya*). Poisoned – so says Shi'ite tradition – on the orders of the 'Abbāsid caliph al-Mansur in 765, Ja'far al-Sādeq is buried in Medina.

This Imam stood out clearly from the others for his intellectual radiance. He was first of all a legislator: the school of Imamite jurisprudence, which may be put on the same plane as the four schools of Sunnism, is called the Ja'farite school because of the primordial role played by Imam Ja'far in the codification of Shi'ite religious law. He also attracted learned Sunnis who came to him to glean the traditions of the Prophet, notably Abu Hanifa, the founder of the Hanafite school. But the name of the Sixth Imam is above all associated with the introduction into Islamic culture of the science of alchemy, a "science" according to the criteria of the time, of course. Alchemy and other esoteric disciplines seem to have been developed in his entourage among the "followers" (*mavālī*) of Iranian origin, chiefly Shi'ites from the town of Kufa.

One of them, Jāber b. Hayyān (who died about 815), whose existence is attested by historical sources, was a disciple of the Imam: works on alchemy are attributed to him – the Jāberian *Corpus* – although certain scholars think that they cannot have been written before the end of the ninth century, which renders the attribution suspect.[27] It is nevertheless an established fact that alchemy had penetrated Ja'far al-Sādeq's entourage as early as the eighth century, probably having come from Jewish and Christian circles which had access to Greek sources, and it was then Arabized, Islamized by doctors, pharmacists, and craftsmen seeking the Elixir of Life. Jāber's *Corpus* ascribes a fundamental role to the Imam as part of the Great Work of alchemy: no operation could take place without his recognition . . . These speculations, which no longer contain the slightest element of political or sociological Imamology, show to what an extent, in the space of a few generations, the temporal failure of the Imams had managed to transform the thinking of their supporters and turn Mohammad's descendants into purely spiritual figures.

A major quarrel over the succession to Imam Ja'far was to result in the first important schism in the Shi'ite Community: the Sixth Imam had at first designated his elder son Esmā'il (whose mother was descended from Imam Hasan) to be his heir, but Esmā'il predeceased him, which perturbed the Shi'ites. 'Abdullah, Esmā'il's brother by the same mother, disappeared shortly after his father. The majority of Shi'ites then turned to Musā, the son of a slave, in whom some had recognized Ja'far's successor from the outset, or so tradition tells us.

The death of Esmā'il b. Ja'far (shortly after 754) worried many partisans of the Imams, for the omniscience attributed to 'Ali's successors should have apprised the Sixth Imam of the fate of his son and heir.[28] Many

---

27   See T. FAHD, "Ga'far as-Sādiq et la tradition scientifique arabe," *Le Shī'isme imāmite* (Strasbourg Symposium), Paris, PUF, 1970, pp. 131–42; P. LORY, *Alchimie et mystique en terre d'Islam*, Lagrasse, Verdier, 1989.

28   For everything regarding Ismailism, see F. DAFTARY (preface by W. Madelung), *The Ismā'īlīs: Their History and Doctrines*, Cambridge and New York, Cambridge University Press, 1990, pp. 93ff; M. G. S. HODGSON, *The Order of Assassins: The Struggle of the Early Nizari Ismā'īlīs against the Islamic World*, The Hague, Mouton, 1955; idem, "The Ismā'īlī State," in J. A. Boyle, ed., *The Cambridge History of Iran*, vol. V: *The Saljuq and Mongol Periods*, Cambridge, Cambridge University Press, 1968, pp. 422–82; C. JAMBET, *La Grande Résurrection d'Alamūt: Les Formes de la liberté dans le shi'isme ismaélien*, Lagrasse, Verdier, 1990; B. LEWIS, *The Assassins: A Radical Sect in Islam*, London, 1967. On the Ismailis of India, see below, ch. 5.

believed the latter was not dead, but prudently concealed by his father to protect him from enemies. Others, known as the Mobārakiya (after Esmāʾil's surname, al-Mobārak, the "blessed"), turned to his son, Mohammad b. Esmāʾil, claiming that the Imamate had been passed on to Esmāʾil before the death of Imam Jaʾfar.

Esmāʾil had been connected with radical circles, hostile to the passiveness of Imam Jaʾfar, among whom some had gone as far as deifying the Imams. The Shiʾites who rallied to him, commonly called Ismailis (*Esmā ʾili*), were generally spurned by Sunni historians and even Twelver Shiʾites, who gave them the name *bāteni*, "Esoterists," or Qarmati, from the name of a community settled in the Bahrain peninsula in the tenth century. They themselves preferred to call their movement *al-daʾvat al-hādiya*, "the well guided mission," a title recalling their duty to preach that all Muslims should join their cause. They played an important historical role: in Egypt, the Ismaili Imams ruled under the name of Fatimid caliphs between 969 and 1171; in Iran and Syria the "Nizarites," who claimed the legitimacy of the Fatimids through Nezār, a son of caliph Mostanser (d. 1094) founded Ismaili princedoms that were vanquished only by Mongol conquest in 1257 and 1273. The Nizarites were known under the name *Assassins*, arising from the legends spread about them by the Sunnis and the terror they inspired in their enemies; they developed a learned speculative doctrine that greatly influenced Persian Sufism; the present Imam of the Nizarite Ismailis, Shāh Karim al-Hoseyni Mahallati, Aga Khan IV, whose reign began in 1957, is the forty-ninth in the Nizarite line of Imams (the first being Ali b. Abi Tāleb). Nizarite Ismailis are known in India as Khojas. Another of Mostanser's sons, Ahmad al-Mostaʾli-be-Llāh, had less radical supporters, whose descendants are the Bohras (or Bohoras) of India.

The Seventh Imam of the Imamite Shiʾites, Musā, surnamed al-Kāzem ("he who is self-controlled, keeps silent"), was faced with a political system hostile to Shiʾites and arrested on the orders of the ʾAbbāsid caliph Hārun al-Rashid. He is said to have died in his Baghdad prison, poisoned, in 799 and is buried at Kāzemeyn, near Baghdad, where his mausoleum has become a great pilgrimage centre.

His son, ʾAli b. Musā, the Eighth Imam, surnamed al-Rezā – also transcribed Ridā or Ridhā – is one of the great figures of Shiʾism, very popular in Iran, where he has his mausoleum. Imam Rezā, to give him the name customary in Iran, was the son of a Nubian slave girl, a fact which illustrates, as for several other Imams, that Shiʾism reposes on a surprising combination of aristocratic legitimacy, through the purely Arab blood of the Prophet, and an ethnic and social intermingling.

The 'Abbāsid Empire had been divided into two by Hārun al-Rashid, the western half coming to his first son, Amin, and the other to the second, Ma'mun, born of an Iranian mother. In 816, on the death of his brother, Ma'mun wanted the Eighth Imam, then fifty-one years old, to be his heir and conferred on him the title of "al-Redhā," "al-Rezā," "he who pleases" either God or men, a probable allusion to one of the titles of the 'Abbāsid pretenders to the caliphate – *al-rezā men āl Mohammad*, "he of the family of Mohammad with whom we are in agreement." At first reluctant, the Imam went to Marv (in the Khorasan, today Mary in Turkmenistan) where the 'Abbāsid princes swore allegiance to him. In reality, he was nominated not on the basis of Shi'ite claims to legitimacy, but according to political criteria, without concern for the possible rights of his heirs to the succession. Ma'mun gave his daughter to be al-Rezā's wife and had coinage struck bearing his name. The black standard of the 'Abbāsids was exchanged for the green of the 'Alids. But the inhabitants of Iraq rebelled against these changes and the dropping of Baghdad as capital. Ma'mun had to reinstate Mesopotamia, and Imam 'Ali al-Rezā, who was accompanying him, died on the journey in the small town of Tus: the Shi'ites think he was sacrificed for reasons of state, poisoned by fruit (grapes or pomegranates) in 818. He is buried in the heart of the present-day Iranian town of Mashhad (whose name means "place of martyrdom"), near the tomb of Hārun al-Rashid.

Imam Rezā was in fact more attracted by the practice of medicine, or intellectual and theological debate – tradition recounts enthralling discussions in which he argues with learned Christians, Jews, and Zoroastrians – than by political problems. The brief interlude of his appointment as heir to power gives an insight into the general misunderstanding that hangs over the Shi'ite conception of power: the demand for legitimacy does not seem intended really to guide the historic government of men, but to gather Muslims together in a religious plan where politics become secondary. This dialectic between a theoretical claim to political power and a quietist attitude will become explicit only with the hidden Imam.

The sanctuary of Imam Rezā has become a center of Shi'ite piety, above all since the fourteenth century, with the conversion to Shi'ism of the Mongol ruler Oljaytu (surnamed Khodābanda, the Persian equivalent of 'Abdullāh, "Servant of God," 1304–16). Under the Safavids, starting from the sixteenth century, pilgrimage to this shrine offered an alternative to the pilgrimage to Mecca, or those to Najaf and Karbalā, situated in enemy Sunni territory. Another figure in the Holy Family also came to Iran: this was the sister of the Eighth Imam, Fatima Ma'suma (Fatima the Pure), who died at Qom, a small Shi'ite town as early as that era, while trying to rejoin 'Ali al-Rezā in Khorasan. From the Middle Ages onward a centre of teaching the traditions of Shi'ism grew up around her tomb, and has been given new life since 1922.

The Ninth Imam, Mohammad, surnamed al-Javād, "the magnanimous," or al-Taqi, "the pious," according to Shi'ite tradition, was poisoned in 835, at the age of 24, by his wife, the daughter of the caliph Ma'mun. He is buried at Kāzemeyn. The son of a Moroccan slave girl, the Tenth Imam, 'Ali al-Hādi, "the guide," or al-Naqi, "the pure," lived in a period of anti-Shi'ite repression, and appears to have been poisoned in 868, at the age of 40, in the military city of Samarra (Iraq) where he is buried.

His son, the Eleventh Imam, Hasan al-Zaki, "the upright," or al-'Askari, "he who is kept in the camp," also appears to have been poisoned by the caliph in 874, after living in semi-hiding, and then under close political surveillance in Samarra. The caliph al-Mo'tamed is said to have ensured that the Imam had no heir and that none of his wives was pregnant. It was in fact on his possible descendants that the legitimacy of Shi'ite claims depended. As may be seen, the climate was not favourable towards the Imams, even if the tales told by Shi'ites about the martyrdom of each of them have no certain historical value.

THE OCCULTATION OF THE IMAM

Whatever the truth may be about the poisonings of which the Imams were victims, it is quite certain that they were confronted by a difficult political situation: theoretical claimants to power, politically impotent, backed by discontented supporters of the Omayyad and 'Abbāsid caliphs, taking refuge in an esoteric justification of their quietism, the Imams were an embarrassment to everyone. When they were physically present, they gave the lie to certain of the allegations made about them by the Shi'ites. When they were absent, their eschatological "efficacy" could no longer be questioned and the desire for a return of their reign of justice became almost a reality.

The Occultation is therefore a convenient solution. Because of a succession about which there are doubts in the community, or when there is a premature disappearance, it is decided, against all evidence, that the Imam is present; in other words his disappearance is denied. The theological necessity for such a dogma is proved by the fact that, even before the Twelfth Imam, several figures revered by the Shi'ites were declared "occulted:" their death could not be real, since they were the saviours "guided by God." The first, it seems, was Mohammad, the son of 'Ali and the Hanafiya, whom Shi'ite extremists had adopted as their leader: hidden during the present time, he would at the last return "to fill the world with justice and equity, whereas it is full of injustice and oppression" according to the eschatological definition of the Mahdi's role at the end of the world.[29] The same belief in his power of salvation developed for Mohammad al-Nafs al-Zakiya (an 'Alid contemporary with the Sixth Imam), as well as for the Fifth, Sixth and Seventh Imams and for Esma'il, who gave birth to Ismailism.

It was after the failure of the political experiment of the Eighth Imam, 'Ali al-Rezā, that the need to find an alternative to the unendurable situation imposed by the 'Abbāsids prompted the Imamites to turn to new practices: dissimulation (*taqiya*) to escape persecution, the delegation of the Imam's powers (*vekāla*) in order to justify allegiance to an imprisoned Imam represented by an agent (*vakil*), and lastly the Occultation, until the end of the world, of the Saviour in whom hopes of liberation are centred.

The mother of the Twelfth Imam, according to Imami tradition, was a Byzantine slave: some people even say that her name was Narjes (Narcissus) and that she was the daughter of the Byzantine emperor, therefore a descendant of Simon Peter, the first head of the Christian Church: her son thus linked the two cycles of spiritual succession, of Jesus Christ and Mohammad. Born in 869 (the 15 Sha'bān 255 of the Hegira) at Samarra, where his father was a prisoner, the Imam was named Abo'l-Qāsem Mohammad, like the Prophet. His most common surnames are Hojja or Hojjat Allāh ("guarantor/proof of God"), Qā'em Āl Mohammad ("he who rises, who revives or who is raised up, of the family of Mohammad"), Qā'em be-amr Allāh ("he who is risen by God's command, or who carries out God's command"), Mahdi ("he who is guided"), Montazar ("awaited"), Sāheb oz-Zamān ("master of Time or the End of Time"). According to a Shi'ite tradition, the Prophet foretold that after Hoseyn there would be only nine Imams: "The Ninth will be the Resurrector; he will fill the earth with peace and justice as today it is filled with violence and tyranny. He will fight to bring back [the revelation] in the spiritual sense [*ta'vil*] as I myself fought for the revelation in the literal sense."[30] The Mahdi must, besides, have the same name as the Prophet . . .

29   See A. A. SACHEDINA, *Islamic Messianism: The Idea of the Mahdi in Twelver Shi'ism*, Albany, SUNY Press, 1981, pp. 10ff.
30   See CORBIN, *En Islam iranien*, vol. IV, pp. 304–5.

Almost nothing is known about the life of this Imam. Some cast doubt on whether he ever existed. A researcher has counted at least thirteen historical variations within the earliest Shi'ite family on the subject of his life.[31] For the Twelver Shi'ites, he disappeared miraculously at the age of no more than eight, and communicated with this world only through four agents, delegates or mediators (*vakil, nā'eb, safir*). It was only on the death of the last of these agents of the invisible Imam, in 941, that the Great Occultation began (*al-Gheybat al-kobrā*), a new era that would not finish until the End of Time: the Imam is alive, but hidden from our eyes. Tradition recounts that in his last message the Imam warned believers:

> I shall no longer reveal myself to anyone, until the divine permission is granted. But that will happen only after a very long lapse of time. Hearts will become inaccessible to compassion. The earth will be filled with tyranny and violence. People will rise up among my Shi'ites claiming to have seen me in the flesh. Beware! Anyone who claims to have seen me in the flesh before the final happenings is a liar and an impostor. There is no help and no strength except in God the Most-High, the Sublime.[32]

The doctrine of the Occultation has existed, at least in this form, since the time of Koleyni. This Shi'ite traditionist, having died in the same year as the disappearance of the Imam's last agent, was unable to make a distinction between the two types of occultation: the minor occultation, during which the Imam's agents could communicate his messages to believers, and the major occultation after their death. Apart from the fact that it places belief in a purely irrational domain, this doctrine very soon ran up against obvious objections. Thus, in the era when the Baghdad caliphate was under the dominance of the Buyid viziers (945–1055) whose adherence to Shi'ism was well known, the Shi'ites were asked why the Imam remained in Occultation as he was no longer in any danger. They replied that the Imam's enemies were still about; hence, no doubt, the idea that the End of Time, at the Imam's reappearance, would be the era when Shi'ite doctrine would have spread throughout the entire world.

There is another tradition linked with the Occultation of the Mahdi, which Shi'ites probably inherited from Zoroastrian beliefs: that of the appearance on the earth of the Twelfth Imam shortly before the Resurrection at the same time as the "return," or reincarnation (*raj'a*), of "those

31   See SACHEDINA, *Islamic Messianism*, pp. 42–55.
32   From CORBIN, *En Islam iranien*, vol. IV, p. 234.

whose faith is of a high degree and whose good works are numerous," and of those who, by contrast, "will have reached the depths of corruption and oppressed countless friends of God." The first will be rewarded by seeing the kingdom of truth and will receive "all the worldly goods they ever wanted." As for the rest, "God will be master over those who have rebelled against Him before they died and will obliterate their offence with acts of vengeance that He will make them suffer."[33] As expressed by the Sheikh al-Mofid (d. 1022), we are thus present at a veritable act of divine retribution, before everyone dies once more and goes before the court of eternal justice.

It is understandable that modern minds are shocked by this too human dogma, doubtless intended to allay the wrath of those who felt that the impious were enjoying the good things of this world with impunity while the just were oppressed and poverty-stricken. About 1930 a reformist Iranian theologian, Shari'at Sangalaji, purely and simply rejected belief in the "Return," and was consequently the victim of almost general anathema, despite a courageous stand by Sheik 'Abdolkarim Hā'eri, who at the time was director of theological studies in the schools at Qom, affirming that one could be a Shi'ite without necessarily believing in the "Return."[34] The secondary polemic which then developed, and which resurfaces sporadically, illustrates the Shi'ites' difficulty in distinguishing between the fundamental traditions of their belief and those which are perhaps no more than additions due to circumstance.

We have seen how the idea of the Occultation of the Imam was imposed on the Shi'ite community by a necessity that was both political and metaphysical. Because the line of the 'Alids vanished as a result of repression, it was necessary to maintain the spiritual force – the very justification of Shi'ism – which believes that God can never, at any moment, leave the Earth without an "apodictic proof" (*hojjat*, an argument that is essential, beyond contradiction) to guide men towards Him. That is the meaning of the Imamate (Imam means "guide"), the central doctrine of Shi'ism.

---

33   D. SOURDEL, "L'Imamisme vu par le Cheikh al-Mufīd," *Revue des études islamiques*, 40 (1972), pp. 217–96; here pp. 8 and 53. See also SACHEDINA, *Islamic Messianism*, pp. 166ff.

34   See Y. RICHARD, "Shari'at Sangalaji: A Reformist Theologian of the Ridā Shāh Period," in S. A. Arjomand, ed., *Authority and Political Culture in Shi'ism*, Albany, SUNY Press, 1988, pp. 159–77.

For further reference to the problem of the Imam's "return," and a spiritual interpretation of this subject in early Shi'ism, see Mohammad Ali AMIR-MOEZZI, *The Divine Guide in Original Shi'ism*, Albany, SUNY Press, 1994, ch. 4.3.

THE IMAMATE AND COMMUNITY ORGANIZATION

As he recognizes no authority on earth except that of an Imam, to whom, by definition, no one can claim to be related, the Shi'ite believer is free as regards the government of the time, chiefly as far as his religion is concerned. Whoever the sultan, Shah, caliph or (Muslim) President of the Community may be, a Sunni Muslim is bound by obedience to those in authority (*ulu'l-amr*) who preserve the cohesion of the Community. There is nothing like that in Shi'ism, since the fully legitimate sovereign is absolutely out of reach. Hence the idea that *ulema* (learned men) must meet theological needs without aspiring to take the Imam's place. Moreover, as the Imam is supposedly alive, legal doctrines are not frozen in immutable positions, but can produce new answers in response to new situations: the "gate of interpretation" (*bāb al-ejtehād*) is open.

The criterion required to exercise that interpretation is theological "learning" (*'elm*). Here one comes back to the principle according to which the eligibility of an Imam depends on the exoteric knowledge (understanding of the phenomena of the visible world) and esoteric knowledge (understanding of invisible realities) that he has acquired. In theory, this double knowledge conditions every rule of succession of spiritual authority. Thus the *ulema* are subject to the same type of selection as the Imam; they must possess theological and practical knowledge to allow them to implement the Law and the spiritual charisma to give them authority over the believers; at their own level they similarly claim the same kind of legislative function, the teaching of the Law and spiritual guidance, for even in the absence of the Imam justice must still be dispensed and the faith must still be taught.

If knowledge allows the function of the Imam to be perpetuated, simple believers, those who are aware of their own ignorance, must practice imitation (*taqlid*) in order to keep to the precepts of those who have knowledge. And they must have available an easy criterion for identifying those *ulema* who can be taken as a model. In fact, there is nothing more harmful or dangerous than usurped spiritual guidance, and the perils of servile imitation are denounced from one generation to the next. That is why theological treatises and manuals "on resolving problems" provide criteria which turn the theologian into a "guide to imitate" (*marja' al-taqlid*): he must be a *mojtahed* (theologian recognized by his teachers as fit to carry out the effort of interpreting the Law), that is to say, a mature, reasonable,

Twelver Shi'ite, of legitimate birth, lively, and impartial.[35] As there is certainly more than one individual who can match this catalogue of virtues, the most learned must be chosen, that is, the one who could outstrip all the others in matters of legal interpretation. If the believer is not capable himself of judging the degree of theological knowledge, he can refer to trustworthy people if they are in agreement in designating the same person as "the most learned *mojtahed*."

Here is an area where the Shi'ite believer is directed to his own conscience and where freedom is complete. Let us add that if the *material* vision of the hidden Imam is impossible or forbidden, *spiritual* vision is common practice. Firstly, every Shi'ite, in every period, must know the Imam of the time, otherwise he will die without knowing God (the Imam being the incontrovertible proof of God). Thus a knowledge of the hidden Imam is required, in one way or another. It can be achieved by way of dreams or visionary happenings of which it would be vain to seek tangible traces. Shi'ite literature and popular piety are rich in tales of appearances, in which the faithful believer meets his Imam at a time of great distress, in a sacred place, during a pilgrimage, at the moment of an important decision . . .[36]

Here we are not on the plane of an externalized religion that is sure of itself, but of a personal faith. What makes it even more difficult to grasp is the fragility of Shi'ism's social status, which accustomed believers, before their religion gained belated official recognition, to dissimulate their convictions out of prudence (*taqiya*). Spiritualized, this practice leads to what Corbin called the "discipline of the arcane," which consists in not divulging secrets in order to avoid causing them to lose their mystical flavour and become mere formulas: they are unveiled only to the initiated.

I shall deal in another chapter with the different historical arguments over the legitimacy of the civil authority and the numerous dissensions of the Shi'ites as regards religious authority, but we must understand straight away the fundamental consequences of the doctrine of the Occultation on the Shi'ite conception of Community organization.

The fact that the Imam is "present," though hidden, renders illegitimate any absolute claim to authority over men, as the sovereign who assumes a position of command is usurping the only existing authority. Such a

---

35 See the first pages of the "practical treatises" currently used in Iran. For example that of ayatollah Shari'at-madāri (d. 1986).

36 CORBIN, *En Islam iranien*, vol. IV, p. 330.

situation is disturbing and the argument of the authority of the hidden Imam has rarely been upheld in any systematic manner. In fact the absence of authority would give rise to disorder, and allow violence to win the day over justice. The Muslim Community would be the first to suffer from any weakening that might somehow stem from itself: better to have an imperfect ruler (from the point of view of Shi'ism) than no ruler at all. Since the Imam is absent-present and no one is fit to set himself up as the representative of his will, it must be accepted that political authority is subject to a certain relativity.

According to some traditions, the Imam will not return to Earth to begin the cycle of the End of Time until the era's tribulations have become unendurable and apocalyptic chaos has sealed humanity's fate. The First Imam is said to have made this prophecy: "I dreamed of a child of my flesh, the eleventh of my descendants. He is the *Mahdi* who will fill the world with justice and fairness when the height of injustice and tyranny in this world has been reached." But Koleyni, relating this tradition in the tenth century, also relates others according to which no one will ever be able to predict the day of the Mahdi's coming. An uncertainty that allows Shi'ites to be put to the test in order to distinguish the faithful from the rest.

This belief poses the problem of participation in political institutions. To take part fully would seem to be ruled out by the consideration of allegiance which will always hold a Shi'ite back. We shall see how one can get round that difficulty in contexts where the civil authority itself boasts of Imamite legitimacy and neutralizes the arguments making all authority dependent on that of the Imam, as has happened in Iran since the sixteenth century. Matters are more serious when the civil power is held by militant Sunnis, enemies of the Family of the Imams: should the case arise, is it necessary to refuse to take part in institutions at the risk of leaving the Muslim Community defenceless in the face of government's oppressive demands? The theologians' reply will often be pragmatic, motivated by the need to salve the conscience of Shi'ites who, in one way or another, collaborate with the current authorities. This was the case notably in the Buyid period (945–1055), when the caliphate was dominated by Shi'ite viziers.[37] In reality, the possibility of collaborating arises from the fact that any government is fundamentally acceptable, and that it is better to contribute to peace than to disorder. But this in no way settles the question, for Islam closely intermingles the religious and the political: acknowledgement

---

37   W. MADELUNG, "A Treatise of the Sharif al-Mortadā on the Legality of Working for the Government (*mas'ala fī'l-amal ma'a'l-sultān*)," *BSOAS*, 43, 1 (1980), pp. 18–31.

of the government brings with it the obligation to obey, to pay ritual taxes, to declaim the Friday sermon in its name, to take part in the military operations of the holy war, etc. It will be seen that Shi'ites have been reluctant about many of those points, even when political power was wielded by their co-religionists.

The hidden Imam must reappear, and believers wait for that day. Their waiting often gives rise to a passive attitude, far removed from the dynamic and revolutionary spirit that Shari'ati saw in Imam Hoseyn's rebellion. There are indeed two ways of waiting: in resignation and submission, or on the other hand, in dissatisfaction and rejection of the present situation. In the first instance, one accepts anything without aspiring to change; in the second, one rebels and reacts out of a desire for radical alteration.[38] This distinction made by Shari'ati about 'Ali awaiting his moment to rule applies perfectly to the eschatological expectation:

The social and political problem is nullified, responsibilities are limited to the individual ethical sphere, the Occultation is no more than a cycle of submission and passive waiting; as society is not likely to be saved, everyone must think first of his own survival; it is accepted as inevitable that society, faith, social order, culture, and public morality slide into decadence until the reappearance of the Imam is rendered inescapable. From this perspective the Occultation is only the price of liberation from all the powers of this world; it is the legalized acceptance of everything that happens and exists, the suppression of all collective responsibility: henceforward everyone can crawl in his own individualism, and all the hopes, beliefs, and feelings of the Shi'ites can be summed up in two principles: dolorism and the execration of the Sunnis, nothing more!

This gloomy picture of Shi'ism fossilized in the acceptance of established disorder is, for Shari'ati, in contrast with a Shi'ism modeled on the example of Imam 'Ali, in which the period of the Occultation is one when man must, on the contrary, shoulder the prophetic responsibilities of the Imam:

These are the men who must henceforward teach about Islam, administer justice, organize an Islamic society, govern themselves, defend Islam and Muslims against the powers of this world, and Islamic unity against Jews, Christians, and other enemies . . . and choose from amongst themselves those who specialize in a genuine knowledge of Islam, of Islamic law, and the

38 SHARI'ATI, *'Ali*, p. 159.

affairs of the society of their time . . . to compel them to guide the destiny
of men and to take for their leader the most educated and most upright man
among them to take the "Imam's place," which is the place of the Prophet
of Islam![39]

SHI'ISM AND THE HOLY FAMILY

The reinterpretation of traditional dogmas by Shari'ati's revolutionary ideology allows us briefly to take stock of the foundation of Shi'ism. Two
opposing ideas are revealed: that of absolute guide of the human kind,
intermediary between God and man, intercessor, apodictic guarantee, a
perfect man who demands blind and unfailing allegiance; and that of an
openness resulting from the absence of any material power structure, a
message of liberation based on the rejection of oppression.

For Shi'ites, the Imamate is linked to a conception of justice extended to
God: He who at the resurrection will judge men according to their actions
is *obliged* to provide them constantly with the means of salvation. And there
cannot be a void which, by hypothesis, would leave men in their ignorance:
the Prophets, the Imams, the hidden Imam are guarantees of the divine
order into which man is invited to reinstate himself. A society without an
Imam is anarchic, that is to say, it is vulnerable, swiftly dominated by the
forces of oppression. That is why, as Shari'ati says, when the Imam is not
accepted as head of the Community, it is not the rights of the Imam that
are harmed, but those of the people who have no one to guide them.

The millenarist anticipation of the Imam's reappearance makes Shi'ism
a doctrine turned, far more than Sunnism, towards meta–history, towards
an idealistic anticipation of the End of Time. Theosophical speculation is
overt, well-founded, legitimate. Man seeks to understand what stage he
has reached in the divine cycle. Despite the fundamental idealism of this
vision of the world, the Occultation of the Imam is not an obstacle to a
social dimension, since Shi'ism was born of a political stand and remains
basically inspired by a search for fairness and justice. There is no political
barrier, as the Imam demands only that men shall stay faithful to the directives of the revelation which liberate the "weak" (*mostaz'afin*) from the
yoke of the "arrogant" (*mostakbarin*). Revolutionary ideological discourse
immersed itself in this message, which is noble but sufficiently vague to
adapt itself to the most diverse situations.

39 SHARI'ATI, *Tashayyo'-e safavi*, p. 223.

3
A Mystic Theology

For the French, Rosny-sous-Bois, an urban junction in the suburbs of Paris, is more likely to bring road travel to mind than Shi'ite mysticism. Nevertheless, that is where I have an appointment, in a house that is spacious and modern, though not excessively luxurious, set in flower-planted grounds. Happy to have reached this haven after the labyrinth of freeway interchanges, I discover the sign written in large letters, in both French and Persian, that intrigues the uninitiated passers-by: House of the Sufis, *Khāneqāh-e Ne'matollāhi*.

I have to present my credentials. I am shown into a vestibule where I notice more than one sign of Iranian culture, chiefly carpets and *kilims* on the floor. Shoes as well, lined up before the door, inviting me to remove mine out of respect for sacred ritual and customs. Ahead of me is a large room, bathed in a profusion of electric lights: the windows are shut off by curtains of printed cotton from Isfahan. At the far end, under an enormous photograph of himself, is the master. The scene evokes Persian miniatures, in which the prince gives audience, seated on his throne . . . "Man's condition is obscure. And some show signs of excellence. In the evenings when there was great drought in the land, I heard you spoken about on this side of the world, and the praise was unstinting. Your name was the shade of a great tree. I spoke of it to the dusty men on the roads; and they found themselves refreshed." These lines by Saint-John Perse are indeed well suited to the particular encounter awaiting me.

Dr Javād Nurbakhsh is the man. Wearing loose-fitting garments and a sort of indoor coat, with the traditional headgear, he has a craggy face punctuated by an abundant moustache, and his eye is keen; he invites me to draw near, holds out his hand without getting up, makes a pleasantry to put me at my ease and resumes the pipe of his narghileh, its bubbling noise when he inhales the smoke refreshing us all. There are several Iranians of some renown in the company: a former minister of Shapour Bakhtiar; a celebrated lady radio personality from the Shah's era; the wife of an old-regime general and her daughter who plays the *tār* (the ancestor of our guitar) splendidly; a poet-musician who not long ago was a militant in the Tudeh (Iranian Communist Party), and a well-known academic who has come from Iran and will soon return there, unlike the others, whose fate is to ruminate nostalgically in exile. In the background, there are also young people whose nationality is not clear to me; either they do not speak Persian, or speak it with a British or perhaps even a French accent; they look after the guests with the servile and solemn obsequiousness of lackeys without livery.

This evening is not a ritual session: tonight the master, passing through Paris, is receiving initiates' friends and answering their questions. We are also invited to share a simple meal, for which the table is set with a special rite, the salt being served first. After this convivial feast and listening to music, the former radio celebrity reads poems by the master, chosen by himself from his *Divān* (anthology of poetry); he will generously bestow copies on those guests whom he wishes to honor.

This generosity is not inspired by proselytism: he has enough disciples, says Nurbakhsh. We shall not be invited to attend on Thursday and Sunday evenings for the rites reserved for the initiated, including the commemoration of the divine name (*zekr*) with prayer, preaching, concerted meditation, litanies, and trances. These rites are well known today.[1] The most moving defies description, and is the rhythmic repetition of a vigorous invocation embracing the profession of faith ("There is no god but God," *Lā elāha ella' Llāh*) declaimed in unison, with all lights extinguished, to the point of oblivion of time and self. Only experience can convey some idea of it. The specifically Shi'ite part of the ritual is the frequent repetition of the phrase *yā 'Ali*, an invocation to the First Imam. Certain rites, generally kept secret, are reserved for initiates, like the "feast of supplication" (*majles-e niyāz*) or other ritual meals.

There are certainly many neophytes in the house of the Sufis, for Dr Nurbakhsh's success, at any rate outside Iran, is spectacular. The magazine

---

1 See R. GRAMLICH, *Die schiitischen Derwischorden Persiens*, Wiesbaden, Franz Steiner, 3 vols, 1965, 1976, 1981, vol. III: *Customs and Rites*; N. POURJAVADY and P. L. WILSON (Preface by Sd H. Nasr), *Kings of Love: The Poetry and History of the Ni'matullāhi Sufi Order*, Tehran, Iranian Academy of Philosophy, Boulder, Colo., Great Eastern Book Co., and London, Thames & Hudson, 1978, pp. 168ff.

Sufi, published in London in two editions, Persian and English, gives the addresses of fourteen "centers of the Ne'matollāhi Sufi order" in western Europe and the United States: three *khāneqāh* in California alone! In France, the second Sufi House was opened in Lyon in 1990. It is difficult to know whether this success is due to the personality of the founder, the bewilderment of exiled Iranians at the brutal form adopted by Shi'ism, or the disarray of the West which is turning avidly towards all the ecstatic formulas of the East.

Born in 1926 at Kermān, in the south-east of Iran, Javād Nurbakhsh is a psychiatric doctor, who ran the faculty of psychiatry of Tehran University, and also spent a year working at the Sainte-Anne hospital in Paris (1962–3). But his spiritual career is more important than his professional career. At the age of twenty-two Nurbakhsh became the favorite disciple of Munes-'Ali Shah Zu'r-Riyasateyn, a Sufi master of the Ne'matollāhi order, and married one of his daughters, succeeding him in 1952. He was the first Sufi head, or "Pole" (*qotb*) to have an active professional life and, apart from Sufi meetings, to abandon the ritual garments (coat and headgear).

His intellectual activity is unbounded: he has written and published numerous treatises on Sufism intended to place the mystical path within the reach of all. He is also the author of commentaries on the surahs (chapters) of the Koran and two collections of poems. Furthermore, Nurbakhsh has published critical editions of numerous classical Sufi texts, such as the "Rose Garden of Mystery" (*Golshan-e rāz*), a fourteenth-century treatise by Shabestari, the "Jasmine of the Faithful Lovers" ('*Abhar ol-'āsheqin*) by Ruzbehān of Shiraz, and chiefly the works of Shah Ne'matollāh Vali of Kermān, the great holy man who gave his name to the order, and died in 1431.

Nurbakhsh presents Sufism as a path of love entrenched in Islam and freed from philosophical jargon. He tries to help everyone whose heart's desire is to devote himself to a quest for the infinite. A learned and studious man, a powerful charismatic personality, a formidable leader of men, Dr Nurbakhsh has imparted new vitality to his order, which today represents the most coherent group in Iranian Sufism. At present he lives in exile, but has not completely given up the idea of returning to Iran, where he has numerous disciples or adepts. After the Revolution, the Islamic authorities invited him to pledge allegiance to Imam Khomeyni in order to demonstrate that there was no political ambiguity between the Ne'matollāhi order and the new government. The insistence of the authorities led Nurbakhsh, who was anxious above all things to preserve his freedom, to go into exile. Several invitations from the leaders of the Islamic Republic asking him to

come back to Iran have met with an irrevocable ironic reply: "I will return
on the day when you can guarantee that I can insult Khomeyni with
impunity, if I wish to do so."

For Nurbakhsh, the man who laughs at God because he feels close to
God, and makes fun of clerical religion, the mullas are nothing more than
charlatans who are shut off from genuine spiritual life. Not that Nurbakhsh
is opposed to the religion practised in the mosques: on the contrary, he
declares himself filled with the mission of protecting the mosque against
irreligion.[2] Temporarily, the *khāneqāh* in Iran, although not closed authori-
tatively by the government, felt threatened and would not put up with the
controls it wished to impose on them. They prudently put their activities
"on hold" and placed their libraries in crates in safe places while waiting for
better days to come. But in order to understand the reasons which pushed
Nurbakhsh into exile, we must return to the very complicated relationship
between Sufism and Shi'ism.

THE CLERICAL ORDER AND THE DISORDER OF THE MYSTICS

Sufism was born of a need to express the mystical love of the one and only
God within the rigid precepts of Islam. The Mystic Path (*tariqat*) followed
by the "dervishes" (a Persian word meaning "poor") is in opposition to the
Law (*shari'at*) imposed on Muslims, as the esoteric (interiority, innerness)
is in opposition to the exoteric (exteriority, outward appearance). *Mutatis
mutandis*, between Sufism and juridical Islam there are the same kinds of
argument as those which stirred the first Christians to ask whether the
grace of the Resurrection gave them dispensation from strict observance of
the Jewish Law.

Originally, Sufism was an essentially Sunni phenomenon: in Shi'ism, the
interior aspect of Islam was already eminently developed thanks to imamology
and the theology of "divine friendship" (*valāyat*), and Shi'ites feel less
need for charismatic and spiritual leadership, or the theosophical speculations which draw Sunnis towards Sufism. Passionate love for the Imams,
and above all the hidden Imam, Guide of the believers, replaces the devotion of the Sufis for their charismatic head, "Pole," or Sheikh.

The historical gestation of a Shi'ite Sufism was a long procedure. Until
the fifteenth century, in Anatolia and Iran, Sufi congregations, while still
attached to Sunnism, developed a cult of 'Ali and the Twelve Imams which

2   POURJAVADY and WILSON, *Kings of Love*, p. 177.

drew them very close to the Shi'ites. This was notably the case with the order of the Kobraviya[3] and certain Shi'ite thinkers, like Heydar Āmoli, who had explicitly incorporated the heritage of Sufism. But in the sixteenth century the rise of the Safavid dynasty in Iran profoundly upset relations between Sufism and Shi'ism: around the middle of the fifteenth century, before acceding to the monarchy (1501), the clan which led a great Sufi movement in the north of Iran, the Qezelbāsh (in Turkish, the "Red-heads," because of the colour of their headgear), had gone the whole way in crossing over to the Shi'ite denomination.

In order to impose Shi'ism as the official religion and to set up the legal and administrative apparatus, the Safavids had to call upon the Imamite *ulema*. Conflict was inevitable. The most learned theologians in the service of the Safavids hounded the Sufi orders which had a large following and were calling into question both their clerical authority and the power of the Safavids themselves. The influential head of the mullas, Mohammad-Bāqer Majlesi (d. 1699), the author of the great encyclopedia of Shi'ite theology, "The Ocean of Lights" (*Behār ol-anvār*), did not spare the powerful Qezelbāsh in the repression of Sufism. At the beginning of the eighteenth century most of the Iranian Sufi orders had ceased to exist: at the end of the century the *Ne'matollāhi* (of which Javād Nurbakhsh is today the Pole of the main branch) established themselves again in Iran thanks to Ma'sum-'Ali Shah, who came from India. But the violent attack of a powerful cleric, Mohammad-'Ali Behbahāni (d. 1803), who had him killed, left a deep trauma in the history of Iranian Sufism.[4] Under the Qājār dynasty (1779–1925) manipulation of the Sufis by the political power or the exploitation of the orders as a springboard for social success and a means of escaping the influence of the clergy made the situation even more complicated.

The most striking example of the political return of the dervishes is that of Mohammad Shah (1834–48), the third ruler of the Qājār dynasty, who has been described as superstitious and weak. After having his Prime Minister assassinated, Mohammad Shah appointed as head of the government a Ne'matollāhi dervish, Hājj Mirzā Āqāsi, who had been his private tutor and exercised great influence over him. This man, often represented

---

3   See M. MOLÉ, "Les Kubrawiya entre sunnisme et shi'isme aux huitième et neuvième siècles de l'Hégire," *Revue des études islamiques* (1961), pp. 61–142.
4   The father of Mohammad-'Ali, Āqā Mohammad-Bāqer, had hounded the *akhbāri* Shi'ites. On them, see 'A. DAVĀNI, *Āqā Mohammad Bāqer b. Md Akmal Esfahāni ma'ruf be Vahid Behbahāni*, Tehran, Amir Kabir, 1362. On the repression of the Sufis, see notably H. ALGAR, *Religion and State in Iran 1785–1906: The Role of the Ulama in the Qajar Period*, Berkeley and Los Angeles, University of California Press, 1969, pp. 36ff.

as rapacious and ignorant, but recently rehabilitated by an Iranian historian who regards him as a patriot filled with self-sacrifice, distinguished himself chiefly by neutralizing the clergy and favoring the activities of the dervishes.[5] Reestablished at court and in several specific places of pilgrimage, Sufism was to preserve until the present day that aspect of religious counter-institution in which allegiance to the leader supplants that which the clergy expects to receive exclusively from the faithful. The mystical orders are an alternative – tolerated as long as they remain marginal – to the severity of literalist religion.

An Iranian Sufi order created in the 1950s by Mohammad Anqā nevertheless rejects any domination by a leader: it is that of the Oveysi, for whom the link to the master is purely spiritual and invisible.[6] Another mystical order, also recently created (1899), the Brotherhood Association (*Anjoman-e okhovvat*) refuses to give itself a permanent master, but obeys a council of ten members who co-opt their president; high-ranking Freemason politicians of the Pahlavi period (1925–79) were members of this council. By founding the Brotherhood Association, the Qājār Prince Zahiroddowla (d. 1924), also a Freemason, was doubtless trying less to create a Sufi fraternity than a "lodge," but avoiding the nefarious Masonic label. The association's headquarters, in the Ferdowsi Avenue in Tehran, was used up till the Revolution as a meeting place for various Masonic lodges, whose insignia were discreetly concealed for the dervish ceremonies. Although the rationalist and secular inspiration of the Freemasons apparently has nothing to do with Sufi mysticism, there is certainly some kinship between the two doctrines: mistrust, if not downright hostility, *vis-à-vis* the clergy, elitism, a certain taste for secrecy and ritual as well as a very great fraternal solidarity.

Despite keeping their distance with regard to the clerical apparatus and literalist religion, Iranian Sufis share in that "parasitical" culture denounced, in Iran as elsewhere, by rationalists eager for progress. Sufi associations are nevertheless well adapted to modern ways of life and do their recruiting chiefly among the liberal professions; it is more stylish to be a Sufi than to attend the mosque. Today Sufism is in the main an urban movement, threatened less by industrial growth than by the power of the clergy who regard it as nothing more than an illegitimate competitor in the market of religious values. Its reestablishment in Iran was not accomplished without tension, and matters may still develop further.

---

5   See H. NĀTEQ, *Irān dar rāh-yābi-e farhangi: 1834–1848* (Iran on the Path of Cultural Development), London, Payam, 1988.
6   GRAMLICH, *Die schiitischen Derwischorden Persiens*, vol. II: *The Doctrine*, p. 235.

SUFISM AND SHI'ISM

Sufism is a mystical outpouring within Islam. As such it upsets the *ulema*, the guardians of dogma in both Sunnism and Shi'ism. Not that Islam is without a mystical element: it is enough to read the Koran to be convinced that this is where Sufism finds its principal and inexhaustible source of inspiration. But the Community naturally protects itself against innovation and spontaneity, which disturb social order. Sufism, which claims to establish what might be called a person-to-person loving relationship with God, infringes several of Islam's doctrinal bounds: the obligations of worship (prayers, fasting, pilgrimage, ritual alms) are not abolished, but become secondary in relation to a different kind of worship, warmer, freer, reserved for the initiated. The monotheistic doctrine is the same, but enriched by an ardent literature that cares little for cold doctrinal definitions.

Several common theological characteristics unite Sufism and Shi'ism.[7] First, veneration for the Imam 'Ali, whose "spiritual caliphate" is a central belief for the Sufis. Among both Shi'ites and Sunnite Sufis, these words of the Prophet are often quoted, alluding to gnostic wisdom: "I am the city of knowledge and 'Ali is its portal." Among the symbols recalling this common reference, there is the mantle or cloak with which the Prophet, according to tradition, covered his daughter Fatima, 'Ali and their two sons: it symbolizes the passing on of the prophetic charisma to the Imams descended from 'Ali and Fatima, down to the hidden Imam. The sign of the mantle is taken up in Sufi tradition: to put it on is to be filled with the spiritual power imparted by knowledge of divine secrets, and when the Sufi master hands over the symbolic mantle (*kherqa*) to his disciple he is acknowledging his worthiness to be initiated into the esoteric teaching, to the Mohammadan Light (*nur mohammadiya*) – or Truth – (*haqiqat*). "Transmission" or initiation implies a chain of transmission (*selsela*) in order to ensure the preservation of the doctrine's integrality. In the same way that each Imam transmitted his secret and spiritual function to his successor, each Sufi order proudly guards the spiritual genealogy of its masters, whose source usually goes back as far as 'Ali.

This obsession with using the Mohammadan revelation as a foundation for the persistence of a legitimate spiritual accompaniment for men in every era is a feature common to Sufism and Shi'ism alike. Both doctrines require an apodictic Guide, "mystical Pole" (*qotb*) or Imam, whom it is the

---

7 See S. H. NASR, "Le Shī'isme et le soufisme: Leurs Relations principielles et historiques," *Le Shī'isme imāmite* (Strasbourg Symposium), Paris, PUF, 1970, pp. 215–33.

believer's duty to discover: it has nothing to do with political or human authority, but the seeking, by each man, for "the Imam of his being," the perfect Man (*ensān-e kāmel*). In both groups, this spiritual authority is designated by a term in which ideas of divine love and spiritual guidance are combined: *valāyat*.

The convergence of Shi'ism and Sufism was perceived by certain Imamite theosophists influenced by the doctrine of the Andalusian master Ibn 'Arabi (who died in Damascus in 1240). One of them, Heydar Āmoli, a Shi'ite theologian from the north of Iran, who died ca. 1385, tried to integrate Sufism with Shi'ism, to show that both were saying the same thing:

> Among all the branches of Islam and the various Mohammadan groups, there is none which has vilified the Sufis as much as the Shi'ites have done: in return, no group has railed against the Shi'ites as much as the Sufis. And that despite the fact that both groups have one and the same origin; that they drink from the same fount; that the end to which they refer is one and the same.[8]

In parallel with Heydar Āmoli's theological *rapprochement*, other Sufi orders went over to Shi'ism before the advent of the Safavids. Notably the Kobraviya, an order founded in the thirteenth century by Najmoddin Kobrā, in the heart of which blossomed some of the greatest mystics in Persian literature. Even more than his predecessors, Mohammad Nurbakhsh, in the middle of the fifteenth century, caused the Kobravi to swing toward devotion for the descendants of Imam 'Ali, and went as far as proclaiming himself the Mahdi, the awaited Imam.[9]

MYSTICISM IN EARLY SHI'ISM

There are two differing interpretations of primitive or early Shi'ism. According to the first and most common, Shi'ism came to life around a political conception, but after serious setbacks was forced to fall back on the doctrine of the Occultation: as the Community could not be governed by the ideal Guide, who was not present, Shi'ism continued to develop on the fringe, so to speak, of the norms of the Sunni majority, by abandoning – except periodically – its original political claims. Mystical aspirations served

8 *Jāme' ol-asrār* (Collection of Mysteries), quoted by H. CORBIN, *En Islam rianien*, vol. III: *Les Fidèles d'amour: Shi'isme et soufisme*, Paris, Gallimard, 1972, p. 179.
9 Cf. S. A. ARJOMAND, *The Shadow of God and the Hidden Imam*, Chicago and London, University of Chicago Press, 1984, pp. 74ff.

to compensate for political failure. A second interpretation, relying on the texts of ancient Imamite tradition, rejects the misconception regarding political pretensions: the authority of the Imams is purely spiritual, they are the guardians of divine secrets which certain people – quite naturally – have sought to misappropriate in order to usurp temporal power.[10] Far from wishing to socialize their authority, the Imams seek to transmit the secret that they have received to those who are capable of upholding it without betraying it. By this esotericism the Imams and their disciples are close to Sufism.

Under the Safavids, the to-ing and fro-ing between mystical and political was continuous: without recourse to mysticism, the charisma of the Safavid rulers was incomprehensible; but clerical legalism intervened at every level to meet a specific demand of the new regime, to manage the state, and condemned the charismatic impression; the theosophers, coming on the scene in their turn, neglected political tasks to adopt the most speculative theories which dispossessed the clergy of their spiritual monopoly.

The mystical tendency developed very soon in early Shi'ism. Without a doubt, questions of political succession and power within the Muslim Community were at the origins of the Shi'ites' separation from the Sunni majority. But there is too much inclination to view ancient Shi'ism through the distorting prism of its Sunni detractors, whereas the Imams themselves, whose words are brought down to us through the collections of Shi'ite traditions (*akhbār, hadith*), gave up all hope of a political restoration after Imam Hoseyn's defeat at Karbalā. They defined themselves not as the "partisans (*shi'a*) of 'Ali," but as the "Friends of God." The divine love (*valāyat*) of the Imams is the very perfection of love.

The Imam is the supreme Friend of God and the faithful Imamite is he who finds the Love of God in an act of love for his Imam, the latter being the epiphany of the Divine Attributes. "The first thing about which the believer will be questioned after his death," declares Imam Ja'far, "is his *valāya*, that is, his love (*mahabba*) for us, the Imams. If he has truly professed that love until his dying day, then his prayers, fasting, alms, and pilgrimages will be acceptable. If he has not professed that love, not one of his apparently pious works will be acceptable to God." "God has made us His Thresholds," says the First Imam (sayings recorded by Imam Ja'far), "His Path, His Face towards which all must turn. So anyone who turns away from our *valāya*,

10 See Md A. AMIR-MOEZZI, *The Divine Guide in Original Shi'ism*, Albany, SUNY Press, 1994, chs 2.3: "Vision by the Heart," and 3.4 "Sacred Power."

our love, or vows his devotion to others than ourselves, is turning away from the Path . . . in contrast, he who turns towards us, turns towards springs that are pure, flowing, and inexhaustible by the Lord's Command."[11]

The Koranic prophecy has been unveiled for all men, but its secret, esoteric aspect can be known only through the Imams, who are its guardians. "We the Imams," said the Fifth Imam, "are the Treasuries and the Treasurers of the hidden Secret of God in this world and the next. Our faithful [the Shi'ites] are the treasuries and treasurers for us, the Imams."

The existence of a secret doctrine in Shi'ism had two ethical consequences: access to the holy Imams is not dependent on the will of each person, but on an initiation coming from on high, and that restriction brings with it a certain elitism; on the other hand, in order to safeguard the integrity of the Secret, mental dissimulation or limitation may be demanded of believers. This "discipline of secrecy" is not to be taken here in the purely political sense of prudence in stating one's faith when danger threatens: it affirms the superiority of faith in the divine Love (*valāyat*) over exoteric "submission" (*Islam* in the literal sense).

Islam, replies the Imam Ja'far when questioned about the difference between Islam and the [Shi'ite] faith in the *valāyat*, is the belief in the uniqueness of God and the recognition of the prophetic mission of Mohammad. Thanks to Islam, the Law prevents crimes and regulates dealings between people, marriage, or inheritance, according to rules that all must respect, and prayer and pilgrimage are ritually organized. But the true faith is an esoteric (spiritual) guide for the heart . . . Belonging to the faith involves Islam, but not the other way round, in the same way that one cannot approach the Ka'ba without entering the Great Mosque in Mecca, but one can enter the Great Mosque without going near the Ka'ba.[12]

CLERICAL SHI'ISM VERSUS SUFISM

These mystical meditations that give meaning to Shi'ite spirituality would seem to predispose the Shi'ites to understand the Sufis, and to share with them certain preoccupations orientated towards the supernatural. But

11 M. A. MOEZZI, "Le Shi'isme doctrinal et le fait politique," in M. Kotobi, ed., *Le Grand Satan et la Tulipe: Iran, une première république*, Paris, Institut supérieur de gestion, 1983, p. 71.
12 *Hadith* taken from Koleyni's collection, *al-Osul men al-Kāfi*, chapter "On Faith and Impiety;" cf. MOEZZI, "Le Shi'isme doctrinal," pp. 87–8.

despite peacemaking attempts at reconciliation between Shi'ism and Sufism by certain modern Shi'ite thinkers, such as Sayyed Hossein Nasr, Imamite theologians raise objections of principle against Sufism. It is hard to say whether it is the competition in which they are engaged with the Sufis in the market of religious values which has provoked their criticisms, or whether it is the criticisms that have given rise to the violent opposition in the past, to which I alluded earlier. The theologians of Qom, as Corbin points out, prefer to talk of "gnosis" (*erfān*) rather than Sufism (*tasavvof*), even if by that they refer to the same reality.[13] An outstanding example is given to us by ayatollah Khomeyni himself, who taught mysticism and philosophy at Qom until the beginning of the 1950s and sometimes drew inspiration from the doctrine of the Andalusian Sufi Ibn 'Arabi, but showed total indifference in allowing the closure of Sufi order houses (*khāneqāh*) in Iran after the Revolution.

The arguments of official Islam against the mystic orders were rarely developed, as if by attacking their rivals too plainly the *ulema* were afraid to be seen to take them seriously, or turn them into victims who would attract sympathy. A few modern polemical writings are to be found, however, and notably a series of extremely interesting systematic refutations from the pen of a "turned" former Sufi leader, Keyvān Qazvini, who describes in detail all the ceremonials and the internal organization of his order. This curious figure, who died in 1939, the author of a score or so of books that are mostly polemics against the Sufis, does not entirely renounce what he calls the "true" (*haqiqi*) Sufism as opposed to the "formalist" (*rasmi, marsum*) Sufism.[14] He did not gain widespread acceptance for his attempt at reform, but his books are often cited by the *ulema* who wish to demonstrate the danger of the restrictive ideological framework of the Sufi orders.

To illustrate the point of view of contemporary Shi'ite *ulema*, here are a few pages from a clerical historian seeking to justify the ferocious repression of Mohammad-'Ali Behbahāni against the Sufis at the end of the eighteenth and beginning of the nineteenth century.

There are several explanations of the term "Sufi" [writes 'Ali Davāni in substance] and the Sufis themselves are unable to make sense of them. The first to claim it were heretics, then schismatics influenced by the Brahmans

13   CORBIN, *En islam iranien*, vol. I, p. 11; vol. III, p. 153, etc. Corbin tends to reconcile the divergent trends of mysticism.

14   See R. GRAMLICH, *Die schiitischen Derwischorden*, vol. I, pp. 68–9.

of India. In the Islamic world, those people were enemies of the Family of
the Prophet, like Hasan Basri and others. Keyvān Qazvini dwelt for 40 years
on the plain of Sufism, even becoming one of the heads of the order: he
denounced the Indian origin of Sufism and showed that the terms "Sufi,"
"Sufism" (*sufiya, tasavvof*) are meaningless. The Sufis are people who wear
wool (according to one of the etymologies of the term "Sufi"), and disguise
themselves in the attributes of ascetics and Christian monks in order to
attract the esteem of Muslims and to realize their evil designs . . .[15]

The beliefs of Sufis come down to two basic dogmas: incarnation and
monism (*holul va ettehād*) . . . The incarnationists say that God is one with
the perfect Man, a belief they have borrowed from the Sabeans (a gnostic
community which still exists in Mesopotamia) and the Christians. From this
brief summary we draw the conclusion that the branches of Sufism are all
false, erroneous, and deviant, and differ totally from the religion of Islam,
above all from the road to salvation of Twelver Shi'ism. Sufism conceals its
kinship with Christian monasticism by a verbal loyalty to Islam: they regard
the doctors of the Shi'ite faith as purely superficial people, considering their
own mystic leaders as the only ones to represent the substance of Islam.
They insult the *ulema* in their writings. They attribute an apocryphal *hadith*
to the Prophet, taken up by the Sunnis, in which Muslims are divided into
two groups, those who follow the Law and those who follow the mystic Path
(*shari'at, tariqat*). Their spiritual leaders, Hasan Basri, Ma'ruf Karkhi, Shaqiq
Balkhi, Bāyazid Bastāmi, Mansur al-Hallāj . . . were all Sunnis and enemies
of the Imams, uneducated, unbalanced people, who had no contact with our
Imams while none the less regarding them as guardians of supernatural
secrets . . . As for their claims to ecstasies and visions, these are the result of
hashish or cannabis, drugs forbidden by religion, which some admit to using
regularly. They impose excessive privations on themselves and practice an
asceticism that upsets their temperaments . . . It is very astonishing that
despite all the warnings which have come down to us through tradition and
the teaching of the most important *ulema* – those through whom religion has
been maintained during the course of the centuries – there are still people
who are victims of these charlatans and seek to reach God through their
mediation, abandoning any spirit of criticism.[16]

. . . AND PHILOSOPHY

In the face of the contempt evinced by this contemporary theologian, it is
hard to deny that there are serious disputes between the Shi'ite *ulema* and

---

15   See DAVĀNI, *Āqā Mohammad-Bāqer*, pp. 289ff.
16   Ibid., pp. 290–4.

the Sufis. But the latter are not alone in threatening the clerical monopoly of legitimate teachings on salvation: philosophers as well have sometimes been included in condemnation of the Sufis. Today, however, one of the originalities of Shi'ite Islam is to recognize that metaphysical speculation and philosophical discourse have a certain place in religious knowledge. The Center for Theological Studies at Qom is certainly the only place of Islamic studies in the world where one dare comment on the philosophical treatises of Aristotle or Avicenna, and where the post-Platonic philosophical tradition has remained alive. Ayatollah Khomeyni was known at Qom up till the beginning of the 1950s for his philosophy course and, after the 1979 Islamic Revolution, he continued to quote in his speeches texts by Mollā Sadrā (one of the most brilliant representatives of the Iranian tradition of Islamic philosophy).

To clear up the misunderstandings that are too widespread in the West, we must here consider all these terms: even today, histories of philosophy speak of *Arab* or *Muslim* philosophy, two terms that are inappropriate to designate a tradition both Aristotelian and neo-Platonic that came to a halt with the death of Averroës in Andalusia in 1198. Until that period, by and large, Europe received, by way of Spain, part of the Greek heritage passed on by the Arabs. The upheavals in the Islamic world and the evolution of Christianity ended by casting a veil over later developments, notably those which took place in the Iranian world, above all when Iran, which became Shi'ite in the sixteenth century, cut itself off from the Mediterranean Muslim world with which Europe had more connections.

The first misunderstanding therefore concerns its ethnic name: even at its origin, this philosophy was Arab, at the very most, only through its language. Avicenna (Ibn Sinā), to name but one of the best-known among the great forerunners, was an Iranian, and it is in his wake that Iranian philosophy has blossomed to this very day, with one foot in visionary mysticism and the other in the severity of Aristotelian logic. The second misunderstanding concerns the underlying presupposition of orthodoxy in the adjective "Muslim" (philosophy): as Henry Corbin remarks, there is a connotation of *adherence to the faith* in the fact of being *Muslim*, whereas the *Islamic* culture or philosophy belongs intrinsically to Islam, without any presumption of loyalty or disloyalty to the faith, according to the same idea that would, for example, distinguish between a centre for studies "on Christianity" and a centre for "Christian studies."[17]

---

17 See for instance H. CORBIN, *La Philosophie iranienne islamique*... Paris, Buchet-Chastel, 1981, p. 11.

In reality, the term "philosophy" itself is perhaps inappropriate: two words are used by Islamic tradition, *falsafa*, a simplified transcription of the Greek term *philosophia*, and *hekmat elāhi*, literally "divine wisdom," which Corbin proposes to translate as "theosophy." This word at once indicates to us how philosophers are no longer mere speculators on metaphysical values: they undertake the spiritual adventure of the knowledge of God, and for that make use of other means than revelation and tradition. Philosophical reflection, by seeking to establish the whole truth – including that about faith – through proof and certainty (*borhān va yaqin*), undermined the principle of imitation (*taqlid*) on which the Shi'ite *ulema* based their authority. In the seventeenth century Mollā Sadrā was anathematized, and banned for ten years from teaching, because of his attempts to reconcile religious law, metaphysical speculation and mystic gnosis (*'erfān*, that is, Sufism, with explicit reference to Ibn 'Arabi). He inaugurated meditation, continued among his disciples, on the harmony between the esoteric path and the exoteric path, in other words, the concordance between a knowledge of God obtained by the enlightenment of the heart and mystical inspiration, and that obtained by revelation and putting the religious Law into practice.

Sohravardi

The rebirth of philosophy in Iranian Shi'ism in the sixteenth century was influenced by the work of someone who is difficult to classify, Shehaboddin Yahyā Sohravardi, often called Sheikh ol-Eshrāq, the "Master of illuminant wisdom" or "of oriental Wisdom." Born in 1155, a century after Avicenna's death, Sohravardi was neither a Sufi nor a philosopher properly speaking; he was a Sunni, but sometimes very close to Shi'ism; a Muslim, he openly claimed the spiritual heritage of Zoroastrian Persia, as well as that of the Greek philosophers and hermetics. He died in 1191 at Aleppo in Syria, executed by order of the (Sunni) doctors of the Law and at Saladin's insistence, possibly because he was suspected of being a Shi'ite.

For Sohravardi, the conceptual and discursive path of knowledge could have, at the very most, only the value of a negative approach. He nonetheless recommends its study and shows an example by devoting the first part of his treatise on "Oriental Theosophy" to a reform of its logic. In his opinion, only the "illuminant" knowledge, through revelation and initiation, will enable us to apprehend existence as a spiritual light. Genuine knowledge is a presential illumination (*eshrāq hozuri*) which, after revealing itself, renders its object present by illuminating it. Sohravardi makes a distinction between this knowledge and knowledge through representation (*'elm suri*). Mystic cosmology sets an angelic universe of Light and Spirit against a material, opaque, and tenebrous universe, which forms a screen. Between the two there is an "imaginal" world (*'ālam al-mesāl*), where the active Imagination perceives Forms which manifest themselves in "epiphanic places," or "places of sudden revelation" like the image suspended in a mirror.

Against the backround of this between-world are enacted the dramatized accounts of spiritual initiation by which Sohravardi gives us his interpretation of the human condition: becoming aware of his "western exile," the gnostic is led back to his origins, to the symbolic East whence the light flows. The Pole (*qotb*) that allows the return to the spiritual homeland can exist only through the esoteric dimension of the prophetic revelation, which Sohravardi declares is not closed (whereas for Muslims the positive Prophecy is closed in Mohammad). This last proposition, which brought the "master of the Eshrāq" close to Shi'ism, resulted in his execution by the triumphant representatives of Sunnism, at war with the Crusaders. In spite of his tragic end, Sohravardi showed the way ahead for philosophy in Iran and allowed ancient Persia to be linked to Islamic theosophy, Sufism, and the philosophical revival of the sixteenth century.[18]

The Eshrāq discourse in fact stirred a deep echo among some Iranian commentators, such as Shamsoddin Shahrezuri, or the mathematician, astronomer, and philosopher Qotboddin Shirāzi. Some even say that the Shi'ite scholar Nasiroddin Tusi and the Andalusian Sunni mystic Ibn 'Arabi were influenced by Sohravardi. But it was in the fifteenth century that this influence definitively mingled with that of Shi'ism and the reading of Ibn 'Arabi, and left indisputable literary traces.

When Shi'ism finally triumphed in Iran, in the sixteenth century, it formed a sort of clerical authority (or hierocracy) for itself against which thinkers had to win the right to overt discussion. A breed of philosophers burgeoned, chiefly in the towns of Isfahan (the capital from 1596), Shiraz, and Qom, among the *ulema*, men of learning (*'elm*), and religion; thanks to Henry Corbin, they are commonly grouped together under the title of School of Isfahan.[19] Although these thinkers were the direct heirs of the Islamic *falsafa* and the Greek *philosophia*, and were influenced by Sufism,

18   The principal texts of SOHRAVARDI translated into French are collected in *L'Archange empourpré*, Paris, Fayard, 1976, and Ch. Jambet, ed., *Le Livre de la sagesse orientale*, Lagrasse, Verdier, 1986.
19   See A. J. NEWMAN, "Towards a Reconsideration of the Isfahān School of Philosophy: Shaykh Bahā'i and the Role of the Safawid 'Ulamā'," *Studia Iranica*, 15, 2 (1986), pp. 165–99.

they were henceforward careful not to present themselves as such, but rather to place their thinking in more neutral categories, such as "wisdom" (*hekmat*), "theosophy" (*hekmat-e elāhi*), or "mysticism" (*erfān*). They did their best on occasion to show that they were not opposed to systematic theology (*kalām*) or, of course, to the exoteric law of Islam.

Mollā Sadrā

Sadroddin Shirāzi, commonly called "Mollā Sadrā" or "Ākhund" (d. 1641), explicitly refers to Sohravardi, Avicenna, and the Sufism of Ibn 'Arabi, and also to the foundational writings of Imami Shi'ite tradition. His daring resulted in his being forced by the authorities into a long retirement far from centres of philosophical or religious studies. Before him, in the Avicennan tradition commonly accepted by many Islamic thinkers, being was divided into two categories: necessarily existing in itself (like God); or made necessary through another being. Thus any being which has not been necessitated remains inexistent, and all existing beings are, of necessity, the result of a chain of causes. The most original positions adopted by Mollā Sadrā concern the ontological primacy of existence in relation to quiddity, that is to say, not a bold prefiguration of existentialism, which would have made no sense in his times, but an overturning of Avicennan definitions. As the contemporary Iranian commentator J. Āshtiyāni put it, this metaphysical theory is well and truly "revolutionary:" its premise is that nothing can *be* prior to its "act of existing." "By being *what* it is, every essence *is*," Henry Corbin comments in his turn. "This act of being can occur at every degree of the scale of being, from that of mental existence (*vojud zehni*) to all those of extra-mental existence: perceptible, *imaginal*, intelligible."[20]

Mollā Sadrā adds that essence is not unchangeable, but can pass from one degree to another in the act of being, which he describes as a "movement of substance." In correlation with these degrees of being, he systematizes Sohravardi's theory of presential knowledge: a being has no presence, for itself or others, except insofar as it becomes immaterial and separates itself from the world of annihilation, and from its "being-for-death" . . . "The more intense the degree of Presence, the more intense is the act of existing; from then on, too, the more this existing is to exist, the act of being, beyond death . . ."[21]

This metaphysics in fact comes within a perspective of salvation. The

---

20 H. CORBIN, *En Islam iranien*, vol. IV, p. 78.
21 Ibid., p. 80.

chief work of Mollā Sadrā sets out to throw light on a spiritual itinerary: "The Transcendent Wisdom in the Four Noetic Journeys" (or "Journeys of the Intellect"). It is broken down as follows: (1) journey from the creatural world toward God; (2) journey in God and through God; (3) return to the creatural world; (4) journey in the creatural world, but henceforward with the illumination of the divine presence: an initiation into the knowledge of the soul and recognition of the quintessential oneness of God ("God is the one being"). Thus this philosophy, embraced in its entirety in the questioning on the Origin and the Return, conceptualizes a speculation which must be attuned to the main themes of Shi'ite faith. For example, on the subject of the resurrection of the body, which caused problems for the rationalism of the Avicennans, Mollā Sadrā proposed situating the resurrected body in the between-world (*barzakh*) defined by Ibn 'Arabi, where, upon death, the soul carries the "impalpable body" which is an "imaginal" body (*jesm mesāli*) acquired by the soul itself during its terrestrial peregrinations.

In this general presentation of Shi'ite beliefs there is no room to develop in detail the history of a line of thinking in which Henry Corbin was an unparalleled explorer, and which was studied after him by Ch. Jambet, S. H. Nasr, J. Morris and others. What must be remembered above all is that the vigour imparted to Shi'ite thinking in the Safavid era was never extinguished, even if there were periods less propitious to metaphysical speculation, as at the time of the Afghan invasion of 1722, up until the consolidation of the Qājār dynasty in the nineteenth century. Some *ulema* were opposed to philosophy, as to Sufism, considering it heretical because it referred to Greek tradition and appealed to reason, relegating the Revelation to the rank of a secondary source of knowledge. That dogmatic resistance still lives on among Shi'ite clergy, but is compensated for within that clergy itself by a line of brilliant thinkers who have continued to see themselves as the heirs of Mollā Sadrā.[22]

Contemporary Thinkers

That Shi'ite Iranians have a pronounced taste for philosophical speculation we in the West have known since the days of Gobineau, who wrote at

22   See S. H. NASR, "The Metaphysics of Sadr al-Dīn Shīrāzī and Islamic Philosophy in Qājār Iran," in C. E. Bosworth and C. Hillenbrand, eds, *Qajar Iran*, Edinburgh, Edinburgh University Press, 1983, pp. 177–98; on Mollā Sadrā, see also J. W. MORRIS, *The Wisdom of the Throne: An Introduction to the Philosophy of Mulla Sadra*, Princeton, Princeton University Press, 1981.

length in admiration of Mollā Sadrā's successors, some of whom, like the famous Hādi Sabzavāri (d. 1878), were his contemporaries.[23] On the other hand, despite Corbin's immense work, one forgets that present-day Iran is fruitful ground for discursive thought and open to discussion of ideas. Gobineau himself, together with a rabbi of Hamadan, translated Descartes's *Discours de la méthode* into Persian. He opened the way for the invasion of rationalist, secularized, or desacralized thinking. The attraction of western philosophical systems produced in Iran itself several generations of secular thinkers, often of a positivist, Freemasonic, or Marxist tendency. Certain religiously inspired thinkers, clergy or not, profited from this challenge to consolidate Shi'ite philosophical reasoning.

The most traditional of them, who died in 1982, was a cleric who succeeded Khomeyni in the chair of mystical philosophy at Qom at the beginning of the 1950s, 'Allāma Mohammad-Hoseyn Tabātabā'i; there he trained a generation of philosopher mullas and published a vast body of works, including a Koranic commentary in Arabic (*Tafsir al-Mizān*), a weighty commentated edition of the "Four Journeys" (*al-Asfār al-arba'a*, using the abridged title) of Mollā Sadrā, and a general philosophical treatise on "The Principles of Philosophical Realism," in which he goes to the defence of "realism" (in the medieval, Thomist sense) against modern dialectical philosophies, notably Marxist materialism. Tabātabā'i also conversed, before limited audiences, on the philosophy of Sufism, Tao-Te King, the Upanishads, and St John's Gospel. In Qom he met Henry Corbin, the French orientalist, and also some brilliant Iranian academics, such as Sayyed Hossein Nasr and Daryush Shayegan, who had studied in Europe or the United States.

One of Tabātabā'i's disciples, ayatollah Mortazā Motahhari, was professor of philosophy at the Tehran State Faculty of Theology, until his assassination in 1979 by anticlerical Islamic revolutionaries. He was keenly engaged in the cause of Islamic Revolution alongside his fellow professor of philosophy, ayatollah Ruhollāh Khomeyni. A former pupil of Khomeyni, who lives in semi-retirement at Mashhad, also deserves special mention because of his collaboration with Henry Corbin in an "Anthology of Iranian Philosophers from the XVIIth Century to the Present Day:"[24] Jalāloddin Āshtiyāni, whom Corbin sometimes called "Mollā Sadrā *redivivus*," has

---

23   See A. de GOBINEAU, *Oeuvres, vol. II: Les Religions et les philosophies dans l'Asie centrale . . .*, Paris, Gallimard (Bibliothèque de la Pléiade), 1983, pp. 448–83.

24   Three volumes published in the Bibliothèque iranienne of the French Research Institute in Iran, Paris and Tehran, 1971, 1975, 1976. The text of the analytical introductions in French was taken up in CORBIN, *La Philosophie iranienne islamique.*

produced many works to make known the thinking of the teacher of the Safavid era and his numerous Shi'ite heirs. He has saved several of their works from oblivion by publishing their manuscripts, unfortunately without much consideration for the rules of critical editing.

Two contemporary trends keep alive the flame of philosophical reflection in Iran. The more profound, but less fruitful, is a Heideggerian movement represented principally by an original thinker who has written virtually nothing, Ahmad Fardid. Born about 1920, Fardid received an Islamic and "modern" education; he first became a follower of Bergson then, after a brief stay in France, turned towards Germany and became Heideggerian, developing, in the course of his teaching at the University of Tehran and in many private and public talks, a new reflection on Islamic identity faced with desacralization: in his eyes, the West has been, since the Greek philosophers, to blame for reducing the divine to the dimensions of discursive rationality, which, in his opinion, can lead only to nihilism.

Daryush Shayegan, who has lived in France since 1980, was much influenced by Fardid although he denies it today. In his book *Qu'est-ce qu'une révolution religieuse?* he describes the evolution of western philosophy toward nihilism, and the parallel impasse in which oriental traditions (notably in India and Islamic countries) become bogged down when they are debased into "ideologies."

The second contemporary trend is Islamic esotericism, and its most illustrious representative is Sayyed Hossein Nasr. Born in 1933, Nasr was an outstanding student in the history of science in the United States before returning to Tehran to pursue a career midway between politics and university. Thanks to western thinkers as widely divergent (although both esotericists) as Fritzhof Schuon and Henry Corbin, he became aware of the richness of Islamic tradition. His excellent education and knowledge laid the very sources of Shi'ite and Sufi esotericism open to him, but his western connections, which brought him international celebrity, prevented him from finding a wide audience in Iran itself. Although very friendly with the Pahlavi regime, Nasr also kept company with *ulema* such as 'Allāma Tabātabā'i, Āshtiyāni and Motahhari; despite the traditional reluctance of Shi'ite theologians, he overtly professed Sufism and justified it, as we have seen, by doctrinal arguments. In 1975, together with Corbin and under the aegis of the Empress Farah, he founded the Iranian Imperial Academy of Philosophy, with a full research program and publications in Persian, Arabic, French, and English. Despite the reservations of the *ulema*, this institution gave a healthy impetus to Iranian philosophical studies and continued (minus Nasr!) after the Revolution.

Today, some fifteen years after the Revolution, a political barrier prevents freedom of expression on the principles of the organization of society or religion, but philosophy still holds a place of honor in Iran: the more the public is put off by legalistic religion, dominated by clerical morality, the more it is attracted to Islamic and mystic philosophy; bookshops sell much more Sufi or theosophical literature in Persian (Arabic texts are less easy for the public at large to obtain) than ideological or Islamist literature, and certain magazines, like the very earnest *Ma'āref*, edited by Nasrollāh Purjavādi (the author of erudite works on Sufism and neo-Platonism) have specialized in this field. The Academy of Philosophy, which is no longer Imperial but "Islamic," continues its programme, with lectures that are open to the public. Western philosophy is by no means forgotten, either at the University where it is still taught, or in the booksellers' windows, where among others there are published translations of Kant and Hegel. The great ideological debates of the Islamic Republic, notably between Rezā Dāvari, a Heideggerian doctor of philosophy and disciple of Fardid, and 'Abdo'l-Karim Sorush, a doctor of pharmacy, brilliant lecturer, and supporter of a pragmatic and liberal philosophical eclecticism (a partisan of Karl Popper), revolve around matters that would not be out of place on any European campus.[25]

In short, a century and a half after Gobineau, a foreigner passing through Iran could come to the same conclusions about the speculative curiosity and intellectual tolerance of the Iranian elite. Shi'ism and classical Persian culture are certainly not unimportant to it.

THE SCHISMS OF MODERN SHI'ISM

Up till now I have spoken of Twelver Shi'ism as if it were a monolithic doctrine about which everyone is in agreement. In reality, the slight deviations described in connection with Sufism and philosophy have their place only because the official doctrine itself is penetrated by contrary tendencies. The clerics who are currently in power in Iran represent only a dominant tendency. In a further chapter I will examine the differences bearing on the right to govern human society, but here I will recall the division between the traditionalists (*akhbāri*) and the rationalists (*osuli*). To simplify matters, it could be said that the argument resembles the one

---

25 See Y. RICHARD, "Clercs et intellectuels de la République islamique d'Iran," in G. Kepel and Y. Richard, eds, *Intellectuels et militants de l'islam contemporain*, Paris, Le Seuil, 1990, pp. 29–70.

which sets Protestantism against Catholicism; on the one hand, recourse to a personal, austere religiousness, based on foundational scriptures (a kind of fundamentalism); on the other, insistence on instituted religion, on tradition passed on by accredited intermediaries, the clergy (a kind of integrism, a term often applied to Roman Catholic traditionalism).

The definition of akhbārism is linked with the Occultation of the Imam.[26] In fact, in the absence of a spiritual leader to whom believers can address themselves for guidance in ethical, religious, and legal matters, the Shi'ite could choose between two solutions: to refer to the corpus of traditions (*akhbār*) recorded by the Imams and keep strictly to the directives vouched for by the latter. That is the solution adopted by the *akhbāri*. For them, anything that has not been explicitly authorized by the Imams is considered doubtful, and it is preferable to abstain from it. Neither the consensus of the community nor the exercise of analogical reasoning has any legitimacy: the *akhbāri*, who accept only the opinions expressly given out by the Imams, see no difference at all on this point between the period before and the period after the Occultation of the Twelfth Imam. They consider that all believers are "imitators" of the Imams and therefore place doctors of the Law (*mojtaheds*) and the simple faithful on the same level: it is the duty of them all to learn the doctrine of the Imams, if necessary learning Arabic, and to put it into practice.

In complete contrast, the "rationalists" (*osuli*) think that one should not "imitate a dead man" (*taqlid al-mayyet*): each generation needs a *mojtahed*, a theologian empowered to interpret and apply the Law according to circumstances. For the rationalists, it is obvious that the situation created by the Occultation is radically new and that, while awaiting the Return of the Imam, transitory solutions must be put into effect. In particular the use of analogical reasoning (*qiyās*) is essential in order to find solutions for new problems. Great importance is given to high-ranking *ulema* who may be chosen as *mojtaheds*. These, to some extent, take the place of the Imam: they are empowered to collect ritual taxes, to pass legal verdicts, to conduct the Friday prayers – things that the *akhbāri* reject.

The immediate political implications of religious choice can be seen here. The rationalists defend the hegemony of the clerical body as the only

26   See W. MADELUNG, "Akhbariyya," *Encyclopaedia of Islam*, 2nd edn (Supplement); E. KOHLBERG, "Akbariya", *Encyclopaedia Iranica*; A. J. NEWMAN, "The Development and Political Significance of the Rationalist (*usuli*) and Traditionalist (*akhbari*) School in Imami Shi'i History from the Third/Ninth to the Tenth/Sixteenth Century A.D.," unpublished PhD dissertation, UCLA, Los Angeles, 1986, 2 vols (see *Abstracta Iranica*, 10, no. 674).

acceptable intermediary between God and man. They have dominated the Shi'ite community since the Safavid era, as if to counterbalance the civil authority. In the eighteenth century, when the Safavid Empire foundered, when political instability became the rule and Shi'ism was in danger of losing its supremacy, the *ulema*, chiefly those who had settled at Najaf, withdrew from the public scene and the majority of them became *akhbāri*. One cannot claim overwhelming political circumstances to explain this *akhbāri* dominance. At all events a fierce campaign led by Mohammad-Bāqer Behbahāni (d. 1793) denounced the *akhbāri* as infidels and resulted in their persecution. They did not recover from it, as they were unable to convert the Qājār ruler Fath-'Ali Shah to their cause. Today Akhbārism is almost non-existent, apart from a few survivors in the south-west of Iran, near Abadan, and elsewhere in the Gulf.

Another division was to burst forth in the bosom of Shi'ism at the very moment when Akhbārism was beginning to disappear, Sheikhism. This school was founded by an Arab theologian born in Bahrain, Sheikh Ahmad Ahsā'i (d. 1826). Sheikh Ahmad had, since his youth, been predisposed to visionary states, and he came to settle in Iran, encouraged by the favor of Fath-'Ali Shah. His originality lies in having developed certain of Mollā Sadrā's theosophical arguments concerning the intermediate world between the spiritual and material world (*barzakh*), and having denied the resurrection of the material body and the material nature of the Ascension of the Prophet and the Occultation of the Twelfth Imam: these events take place in the between-world of *Hurqalyā*, described by the mystics, where bodies are spiritualized and escape from physical laws.[27]

Like the Akhbāris, the Sheikhis reject the division of believers into imitators and *mojtaheds*, for each Shi'ite is called to understand his faith if he is morally, spiritually, and intellectually capable: the notion of an elite that can claim authority is an aberration, the only authority that all must acknowledge being that of the hidden Imam. However, the Sheikhis have formulated a theory which has won them the mistrust and hostility of the "rationalists" who are in the majority. They say that in every era there is one *imam*, and one alone, who speaks in the name of God or the Prophet; this theory has been coined by them as "the uniqueness of the one who has the word," (*vahdat-e nāteq*). The Sheikhis have applied this term to those they call the "perfect" Shi'ites: since the time of the Great

27 See H. CORBIN, *Corps spirituel et Terre céleste*, Paris, Buchet-Chastel, 2nd edn, 1979, chiefly pp. 211–45: texts translated from Sheikh Ahmad Ahsa'i.

Occultation, in every era, they are the "representatives" (*nāʾeb*) or the "gate" or "portal" (*bāb*) of the Twelfth Imam, and it is absolutely ruled out that they should be known publicly. The Sheikhis do not claim to be vested with this esoteric dignity, for by publicly representing the hidden Imam, they would violate his secret and break the eschatological expectation. But they place themselves in the traditional Shiʾite line which insists that in any era God provides men with a sure Guide to lead them in the path of Truth.

In practice, these doctrines incurred anathema and the Sheikhis owed their survival only to the protection of the Qājār rulers, who prevented the *mojtaheds* from having them exterminated. Their worst troubles were caused chiefly by the affiliation claimed by the Bābis and Bahāʾis with Sheikhi doctrine. But their general attitude regarding the 'rationalists' led them to draw closer to the government as long as Iran was ruled by a regime mistrustful of the *ulema*, which offered a better guarantee to minority rights. This situation placed them in a delicate position after the Revolution. Some months after the beginning of the Islamic Republic, in September 1979, I met at Kermān the spiritual leader of the Sheikhis, "Sarkār Aqā" ʾAbdorrezā Khān Ebrāhimi, who in spite of his mulla's garb took pleasure in telling me that he was first and foremost an agronomist before being a theologian. He insisted on refusing to levy on his flock the Islamic tax (*khoms*) that the Shiʾite rationalists give to the *mojtaheds*: the Sheikhi clergy earn their own livelihood (*kasb*: trade, agriculture, industry, or teaching).

Today there are Sheikhis scattered in Iran and Iraq, but their chief centre was Kermān, from the time of Sheikh Mohammad Karim Khān Kermāni (d. 1870), the son of the Qājār prince Ebrāhim Khān who was governor of this town. There, at the beginning of the nineteenth century, the Madrasa Ebrāhimiya was founded, and until quite recently remained the most important place for the study and teaching of Sheikhism; there also numerous Arabic and Persian texts were edited and printed setting out the Sheikhi doctrine. Unfortunately, post-revolutionary tensions proved too strong. Sarkār Āqā was murdered during the autumn of 1979 and his successor, Sayyed ʾAli Musavi Basri, preferred to assemble the activities of the community at Basra, in Iraq. The Iran–Iraq war (1980–8) and the consequences of the Kuwait war (1990–1) hit this community hard, like all the Shiʾites in the region. The Sheikhis again have an Iranian leadership in Kermān, in the person of Zeyn al-ʾĀbedin Ebrāhimi, the son of ʾAbdorrezā Khān.

TWO NEW RELIGIONS, BĀBISM AND BAHĀ'ISM

The Sheikhis do not look upon themselves as schismatics, despite the violent attacks on them by Shi'ite rationalist clergy, who reproach them for their excessive worship of the Imams, which in their eyes is close to idolatry.[28] It is difficult to say as much for the Bābis and Bahā'is, who historically emerged from Shi'ism and were very quickly defined as a new religion.[29]

The founder of Bābism, Sayyed 'Ali-Mohammad, surnamed the *Bāb* ("the Gate" or "Portal" to the Imam), was born at Shiraz in 1819 or 1820. He was attracted to mysticism and followed Sheikhism after meeting Sayyed Kāzem Rashti. In 1844, 1,000 lunar years after the Occultation of the Imam, one of Sayyed Kāzem's emissaries recognized in 'Ali-Mohammad the resurrective Imam awaited by the Shi'ites: not only did he give brilliant answers to the most subtle theological questions, but he also edited in Arabic a commentary on the Joseph chapter in the Koran. Henceforward he wished to be known as the Gate, which in his idea seemed to imply more than a simple intermediary: he presented himself to his disciples as an Epiphany (or "manifestation") of God. The Bāb met an unexpected response from very varied social strata and caused many violent riots in several Iranian provinces. In the end he was arrested and executed in 1850, while about 5,000 of his supporters had perished in the disturbances he had provoked between 1848 and 1850.

The doctrine of the Bāb, chiefly laid out in the Persian *Bayān* ("exposition") and the Arabic *Bayān*, is an abrogation of the religious law of Islam and of all other religions, which must be replaced by a new, more universal law; it is not quite clear whether the Bāb himself was to be its Prophet, or if the world had to await the coming of a new prophet, who is called "He whom God will make manifest" (*man yozheroho'l-Lāh*). The commandments and legal punishments of the new religion seem milder than those of Islam: women would no longer be obliged to wear the veil; there would no longer be a death sentence, but only the imposition of sexual abstinence, etc. In contrast, in order to impose Bābism throughout the whole world, all the means of holy war (*jehād*) were admissible, which explains the violence

---

28   See for instance A. Kh. LIQAVANI, *In-ast sheykhigari*, [Tehran], Ketābkhāna-ye Vali-'Asr, 1354/1975.
29   See Ch. CANNUYER, *Les Bahā'is: Peuple de la Triple Unité*, Maredsous, Brepols, 1987.

of the disturbances occasioned by the Bābi rebellion.[30] The Bāb had doubt-less hoped in the beginning to have the backing of the Qājār ruler, Mohammad Shah, and massive adherence on the part of the Shi'ites. His downfall probably caused the later disciples to reflect, and they became partisans of Bahā'ollāh, being known as the Bahā'is.

Bahā'ollāh, or to give him his real name, Mirzā Hoseyn-'Ali Nuri, was born into a noble family in Tehran in 1817, and was one of the first disciples of the Bāb, whom he never met. Imprisoned, then exiled to Iraq, in 1863 in a garden near Baghdad he revealed that he was "He whom God will make manifest." The majority of the Bāb's disciples rallied to him, provoking violent reactions and murders on the part of the "hard-line" supporters of Bābism, who recognized the authority of his half-brother Mirzā Yahyā Nuri (d. 1912), to whom the Bāb had given the name Sobh-e Azal ("Morning of eternity"), whence their name *azali*. Bahā'ollāh died in 1892 under house arrest, near Acre in Palestine (modern Israel).

The Bahā'is, whose doctrine was widely disseminated and defined by 'Abd ol-Bahā, the son of Bahā'ollāh, seek to organize society in order to unite humankind and to build a world government. Their pacifism is not at all in accord with the bellicose methods recommended by the Bāb, and they even had to conceal certain of the founder's words which did not match their irenical spirit. Obedience to the constituted authorities is ob-ligatory for them, and, as pacifists, they avoid military service if they can. The Bahā'is forbid political and even trade unionist militancy. Since the end of the nineteenth century they have been solidly entrenched in the United States and Europe. Their world centre is to be found today at Haifa in Israel but, although they have a presence almost everywhere in the world, they are still most numerous in Iran (between 300,000 and 500,000 believers according to estimates in 1979), not without creating serious problems of toleration on the part of Muslims.

The Bahā'i problem is frequently mentioned in the media in order to condemn Iranian fanaticism: there is a desire to defend a persecuted minor-ity to whom even the most elementary human rights are not guaranteed. A few lines of explanation are called for here: in Islam, even more than in other religions, belonging to the faith has a collective value and if the believer is asked to utter his profession of faith (*shahāda*) "There is no god but God and Mohammad is His Prophet," it is only to confirm a sense

---

30 See D. MACEOIN, "The Babi Concept of Holy War," *Religion*, 12 (1982), pp. 93–129. A lively account is given by GOBINEAU, *Les Religions et les philosophies*, pp. 504–662.

of belonging to a Community that was acquired at birth. Anyone who
denies that he belongs is taking sides against the Community and is henceforward regarded as a traitor. Apostasy is punishable by death when it
involves a Muslim born of Muslim parents. This rule is valid no matter
which religion the Muslim turns to, or even if he subsequently retracts.
The casuistry and caution of jurists are such that, in reality, this penalty is
rarely put into effect: the death sentence is pronounced only if the apostasy
is public and imperils the Community.

In the case we are considering, dissidence began with the Bābis. They
were fiercely opposed to the mullas, whom they accused of every kind of
turpitude, and they contributed to feeding the Iranian reformist secular
trend which triumphed with the constitutionalist movement in 1906. In this
sense the Bahā'is were also the successors of the Bābis, and found themselves among the reformists and supporters of the West, chiefly when the
latter held power, to which on principle the Bahā'is had to submit. If one
adds to pro-western acculturation the fact that the Bahā'i world sanctuary
is in Haifa, first under British mandate then in the state of Israel, it may be
seen that things would hardly go well for the Bahā'is should they need to
seek the sympathy of Iranian nationalists. Bahā'i internationalism has little
chance of being understood in a nation which all too often believes itself
the victim of conspiracies and manipulation orchestrated from London or
Washington.

The Bahā'is, like other religious minorities, were very pleased about the
secular turn taken by political development under the Pahlavi dynasty, and
saw in the strong Pahlavi government a protection against Shi'ite abuses.
In reality, whereas Zoroastrians, Jews, Christians and Sunnis (and even to
a certain extent the Sabeans in Khuzistan) have enjoyed reasonably comfortable civic and political rights since the constitutional Revolution in
1906, the Bahā'is, despite their considerable number, have always been
treated as non-existent; figuring in the census as Muslims, their marriages
and inheritances have always run the risk of not being recognized, or of
being annulled. Even though they felt less vulnerable under the monarchy,
they were nonetheless liable to be exposed to public condemnation at any
moment. Under Rezā Shah in 1933, the Bahā'i schools were the first to be
subjected to state control, while Bahā'i places of worship were seques-
trated; in 1955 and 1956 Mohammad-Rezā Shah needed to find an easy
way of appeasing the clergy in order to reaffirm his authority inside Iran
and to gain a little elbow room in international negotiations that were not
proving very popular: he allowed a campaign of anti-Bahā'i persecution,
including profanation of cemeteries, destruction of the temple in Tehran

and various acts of oppression. The Iranian Bahā'is were able to resurface in the 1960s and 1970s. One of them, Amir-'Abbās Hoveydā, even became Prime Minister for more than twelve years (1965–77), while others, such as Hojabr Yazdāni, had been able to amass vast fortunes, or, like Parviz Sābeti, to become one of the heads of the political police. But they were never citizens like the rest.[31]

Under the Islamic Republic, the situation of the Bahā'is has worsened. Regarded as apostates, they are punishable by death (*makhdur od-damm*), and killing them is not a crime. Local authorities – and sometimes private firms – have been purged of all employees recognized or denounced as Bahā'is. The community's goods have been confiscated (notably the great temple in Tehran, the Mesaqiya hospital, etc.) and the Bāb's house in Shiraz, a great center for pilgrimage, was razed on the pretext that a road was to be put through. Starting in the summer of 1980, the president of the revolutionary tribunals, Sheikh Sādeq Khalkhāli, engaged in a campaign of persecution which chiefly affected all the members of the National Spiritual Assembly (the community's internal structure in each country) and numerous Bahā'i personalities, all executed on various charges (such as "conspirator," "Zionist agent," etc.: rarely do the sentences make mention of the victims' religion). A large number of Bahā'is have chosen exile, sometimes in very uncertain conditions. Those who remain (the executions generally affect only the principal leaders of the community) have to face a very precarious situation, on occasion defying all the dictates of prudence, as if they had absorbed the Shi'ite fondness for martyrdom.

These persecutions and injustices certainly have nothing to do directly with Shi'ism, and could equally well happen in a Sunni environment. On the other hand, violence is mentioned because it is happening now, and international opinion is more easily swayed when it is a matter of condemning a regime reputed to be "unpleasant." Apostasy is not accepted in any region of the Muslim world and is no more dangerous for converts to Bahā'ism than for converts to Christianity. Anyway, numerous counter-examples can be cited of the tolerance of Iranians, and of marks of friendship shown to the persecuted, to whom shelter or comfort is offered.

But another conclusion may be drawn from the Bābi-Bahā'i phenomenon: the eruption of this new religion little over a century ago demonstrates the dynamism of the religious factor in the Shi'ite community. Such daring would have been scarcely thinkable in Sunnism, but it happened

---

31 Actually, as he had entered politics, Hoveydā had been excluded from the Bahā'i community. He did not quash the discriminatory measures against it.

quite naturally within Shi'ism, a religion that began in an eschatological expectation and whose relations with political power are ambiguous. In other words, its clergy enjoy a greater autonomy and do not have an answer for everything. The eruption of Khomeynism could equally be interpreted as a new trend within the bosom of Shi'ism: better adapted to the present needs of the Iranian nation and less innovatory than Bābism, this trend is no less keenly striving for power – by violent means, if necessary – and world hegemony. There the comparison stops: Khomeyni was not accepted by every doctor of Shi'ism, but unlike the Bāb, he never tried to break with the Law of Islam.

4

A Destiny Linked with Iran

Shi'ism's ties with Iran are so strong today that in thinking of the one it is automatic to think of the other. How can they be dissociated? A non-Shi'ite Iranian would have difficulty in imagining his national identity: he would seek another homeland, an imaginary Kurdistan, the Armenian nation or an ideal Christendom in a vanished kingdom, Israel, the secular West, the Union of Soviet Socialist Republics, etc. And can a Lebanese or Iraqi Shi'ite forget that Iran is the only country where his religion is truly dominant? Conversely, would not an Egyptian or Saudi Sunni tend to view Shi'ism as a Persian heresy, Islam mingled with whiffs of Zoroastrianism? But these vague associations have as much to do with reverie as with history.

Firstly, Shi'ism is not an Iranian version of Islam. There is nothing in this religion to give the slightest encouragement to any Iranian tendency. Apart from the brief and regrettable episode of Imam Rezā, the Imams, who were Arabs, lived and died in Arab lands. All the prayers and theological texts of the Shi'ites are in Arabic, and their religious center, the chief place for pilgrimage and study for Shi'ite Iranians, up until 1920, was Najaf, in Iraq. So Shi'ism would tend rather to strengthen Iranians' awareness of belonging to a cultural community dominated by Arabs. At the start, as we have seen, Shi'ism was a legitimist party defending the political rights of 'Ali and the descendants of the Prophet's daughter, the Imams, who were of Arab blood. This line of descent is held in high esteem by the Shi'ites: those who today claim to be its heirs accord themselves the honour of the title *sayyed* – indicating their Arab ancestry – preceding their name and passed on from father to son. This title is so prized, moreover, that more than half the Iranian *sayyeds* pride themselves on a title they have wrongfully assumed, or so it is said.

It is true that Iran's "conversion" to Shi'ism at the beginning of the sixteenth century created a political and cultural split between that country and the rest of the Muslim world, which at that time was for the most part dominated by Sunni Ottoman Turks. Iran has followed a separate course of evolution and has left its mark on Shi'ite culture to the point of arousing the confusion just mentioned. I propose here to describe the Iranization of Shi'ism as twofold: the first is political, with the formation of a clergy and the radicalization of religious discourse; the second is cultural, with the development of powerfully emotive rites to celebrate the martyrdom of the Imams.

THE PLACE OF THE CLERGY

To talk of "clergy" requires some preliminary clarification. In Islam there is no sacrament or sacrificial form of worship needing duly ordained ministers, and the ideas of priesthood, monasticism, or consecrated celibacy make no sense in the religion of the Koran. The sole liturgy of Muslims is that of daily prayer, which every believer must fulfill, alone or in a group. At the very most, if the prayer is celebrated collectively, there may be recourse to a guide, "imam" (*emām* in Arabic, "he who is in front," or in Persian *pish-namāz*, "he who is in front for prayer"). The only criterion for singling out this guide among all the faithful is respectability, and in the ordinary way an older man would be chosen, better educated in religion, and one who had proved himself morally. His role is modest: to carry out the ritual prostrations in front of everyone so that all, copying him, may prostrate themselves simultaneously. He is not raised up like the priest at the altar in a Catholic church, but lowered, his face turned toward Mecca . . .

The professionals in the field of religious knowledge, the *ulema* (Arabic *'ulamā*, the plural of *'ālim*, "educated," "learned"), carry out the two eminently clerical functions of Islam, teaching and dispensing justice. In giving a place of honor to "savants," Muslims have found the chief criterion of distinction in the religious order. If there is a reluctance to speak of "clergy" in Sunnism, it is probably because for the Sunnis the *ulema* do not constitute a definitive authority of the kind Roman Catholic bishops share with the pope: they are financially dependent on the political order, from which they also receive their legitimacy. The political order is generally considered by Sunnis to represent the caliphal order, that is to say, the social order desired by God; the *ulema* are the agents of the authority instituted by the divine will. "O ye who believe! Obey God! Obey the Prophet and those among you who hold authority," says the Koran (IV, 59).

In Shiʾism, on the other hand, the clergy hold an important position, notably because of their institutional and financial autonomy in relation to the state.[1] A Persian word describes the body of *ulema* as if to emphasize its specific nature and distinguish it from the ordinary run of mortals: *ruhāniyat*, formed from the root *ruh* ("the spirit") in the same way as *spirituality* from *spirit*. The similarity with the notion of clergy in Christianity has been pointed out as a blemish by Shiʾite reformers since the beginning of the twentieth century, in an era when Iranian Shiʾite clerics, losing their role as teachers (henceforward in competition with secularized education) and judges or notaries (replaced by jurists responsible to a Ministry of Justice), had to redefine their social role on the basis of their expertise in the theology and sciences of Islam. From then on the term *ruhāniyat* has been used to designate the *ulema* collectively.[2] A "cleric" (*ruhāni*) is therefore by definition no longer someone who is "educated" in the sciences of Islam (ʾ*ālem*), but someone who attends to spiritual life, leaving worldly affairs to those more competent than himself . . . Neither Arabic nor any other Islamic language contains a comparable term. By becoming a cleric one is socially marginalized, one leaves ordinary status behind.

One of the unexpected consequences of the emergence of the clergy as a distinct social body is that it constitutes the ideal framework for a counter-society. In the Iran of 1977–8, when the movement of revolutionary mobilization was advancing, political parties had difficulty in asserting themselves as credible groups to effect a change in society. The "national movement" led by Dr Mosaddeq against the British seizure of Iranian oil and for the reestablishment of the democratic control of institutions, the last attempt to destabilize the authoritarian monarchy, had ended in 1953 in a *coup d'état* orchestrated by the CIA and the establishment of a virtually dictatorial monarchy. Repression then crushed any form of organized political challenge, and the imperial regime politically or socially brought into line – whether through venality, discouragement, or a desire at all costs to do something for the nation – renegades coming from all sides, including communists, nationalists, and liberals. The clergy, on the other hand, kept its distance from imperial society. It had a direct hold over the people, a flexible organization and a greater ideological independence *vis-à-vis* modern institutions. In 1977–8 it was therefore no trouble to replace the faltering state organisms at a moment's notice: the clerics used the mosque

---

1   See N. R. KEDDIE, "The Roots of the Ulama's Power in Modern Iran," in N. R. Keddie, ed., *Scholars, Saints and Sufis*, Berkeley, Los Angeles, and London, University of California Press, 1972, pp. 211–29.

2   A. MAMAQĀNI, *Din va shoʾun*, 2nd edn, Tehran, 1335/1956, pp. 73–5.

as headquarters for the revolutionary committees, distribution centre for essential goods, which had become scarce because of the general strike, and a center for popular mobilization. After the Revolution, the mosque retained those roles to a certain extent.

Why did secularization in Iran succeed in setting the clergy apart, distanced from the state and civil society, and in preserving it from decline, contrary to what happened in other Muslim countries despite the similarity in development due to modernization? Is the emergence of the clergy as an autonomous social category attributable to Shi'ism or to the particular history of Shi'ism in Iran? If one accepts the idea that the clergy will stay for some time at the head of the Iranian state, the answer to these questions may allow us to picture the evolution of the clerical system in the Islamic Republic.

Shi'ism has certainly placed a very special value on spiritual knowledge and its concomitant function of transmitting religious traditions. Because after 'Ali they occupied no political office, the Imams spiritualized their power. They would not be consulted over decisions concerning government, but for teaching.[3] Their authority was thus made use of in order to pass on knowledge. Can it be imagined that this function was forgotten after the Occultation?

If one accepts the dominant discourse of present-day Shi'ism, and notably of the Khomeynist tendency, the clerical function is an intimate part of Islam and to abandon it would be to place the Community in danger. Here Khomeyni, like one of his eminent predecessors of the Safavid era, Sheikh Karaki (d. 1534), refers to a tradition known under the name of its transmitter, Ibn Hanzala: the latter asked the Sixth Imam what he thought of two Shi'ites who went to a (Sunni) secular authority for arbitration on a court case concerning an inheritance.[4] Ja'far al-Sādeq replied: "Whoever has chosen such arbitration, whether he is right or wrong, has sought the judgement of a false god (*Tāqut*) and anything awarded to him by that judge will come into his possession illegally."[5] "What should they do,

---

3   E. KOHLBERG, "Imam and Community in the Pre-Ghayba Period," in S. A. Arjomand, ed., *Authority and Political Culture in Shi'ism*, Albany, SUNY Press, 1988, pp. 25–53.

4   M. MOMEN, *An Introduction to Shi'i Islam*, New Haven and London, Yale University Press, 1985, pp. 197ff; R. KHOMEINI, *Islam and Revolution*, trans. H. Algar, Berkeley, Mizan Press, 1981, pp. 87ff.

5   Reference to the Koran, IV, 60: "Knowest thou not of those who pretend that they believe in that which has been sent down to thee and that which has been sent down before thee, and yet they desire to seek judgement from the rebellious ones though they had been commanded not to obey them? Satan desires to lead them astray grievously."

then?" asks Ibn Hanzala. "They ought," retorts the Imam, "to seek one amongst them who is knowledgeable about our traditions, who has examined what we allow and what is forbidden, who has studied our laws . . . They should agree to let that person decide for them, for I have made that person a judge [*hākem*] amongst you."

The term *hākem* is taken in the sense of "judge", at least in the traditional interpretation.[6] The great theorist of Shi'ite jurisprudence in the nineteenth century, Sheikh Mortaza Ansāri (d. 1864), defined his role as doctor of the Law (*faqih*) in terms of three functions, as follows: the power to promulgate "religious decrees" (*fatvā*) on minor problems submitted by the faithful; the power to judge and arbitrate on personal conflicts (*hokuma*, which does not have here the modern sense of "political power"); and lastly administrative power over possessions and people (*velāya*).

The third function, as may be suspected, is subject to the greatest variations in interpretation: for Ansāri, only the Prophet, and after him the Imams, had full authority in both temporal and spiritual domains. During the Occultation of the Imam, the power to punish and to respond to new situations not provided for by jurisprudence is delegated to doctors of the Law. This authority with which the *faqih* is indirectly vested is therefore only a "residual" *velāyat*, to use Hamid Enayat's expression; in the interpretation given to it by Ansāri, it can be exercised only in a very restrictive sense, for certain types of power alone (not to exercise government) and solely with regard to Muslims who, for various reasons, would be incapable of managing their own affairs (minors, the mentally ill, etc.).

THE GUIDE OF THE COMMUNITY

The argument over the authority of the *faqih* (in Persian *velāyat-e faqih*) took on a much sharper edge in 1979 when the Iranians, after the libertarian enthusiasm of the Revolution, were recalled to order by the adjective *Islamic* with which Revolution had been bracketed. Those who had paraded calling for the return of Khomeyni then discovered the only available work in Persian of Iran's new guide. It had been disseminated during the months of insurrection but nobody had yet read it . . . Moreover, it had different titles according to the edition: "Islamic Government," or "the

---

6 Here I am taking up H. ENAYAT's presentation, "Iran: Khumayni's Concept of the 'Guardianship of the Jurisconsult,'" in J. P. Piscatori, ed., *Islam in the Political Process*, Cambridge, London, New York, etc., Cambridge University Press, 1983, pp. 160–80.

Authority of the *Faqih*," or "The Book of Imam Musavi, Who Reveals Hidden Things" (Musavi was one of Khomeyni's names).[7]

This book was not written by Khomeyni, but transcribed about 1971 from his lessons on Islamic political law at Najaf by theology students (notably Jalāloddin Fārsi and Hamid Ruhāni), and is the fruit of a radicalization of Khomeyni's political thinking since his exile from Iran in 1964. In fact, the repressed rising of which he had been the hero in June 1963, and the awakening of a politicized religious feeling as an antidote to the frenetic westernization of the Pahlavi regime had given rise to the idea that Islam could form a collective response to the modern challenge and that the clergy was the body best protected from any compromise with the impious state to direct the nation.

In the 1960s, in the light of the same events, a brilliant essayist named Āl-e Ahmad – a mulla's son who became a communist and then a third-worldist, and died in 1969 – became aware of the national, anti-imperialist nature of the clerical discourse and reinterpreted the history of modern Iran in a sense that was hostile to westernized secularism.[8] So when, at the end of the 1960s in a learned five-volume work in Arabic, Khomeyni rejected the principles of democratic government (*al-jomhuriya*) and constitutional monarchy (*al-mashruta*) – i.e. the regime in Iran since 1906 – he doubtless had only a few mullas for readers, but he was going in the same direction as part of the progressive Iranian intelligentsia.[9] His lessons in Persian on "Islamic Government," even though they had a slightly wider readership and though intellectuals continued to be unaware of them until 1979, only systematized the principle of theocratic clerical government. This principle, the *velāyat-e faqih*, would become the basis of the Islamic Republic's Constitution in 1979; it would be further strengthened in a decree of January 1988 before losing its substance on the death of the Imam in 1989.

What does Khomeyni say? Against the rule of human law dictated by non-Muslim foreigners, subject to opinion and thus to arbitrariness, injustice,

7　KHOMEINI, *Islam and Revolution*, pp. 25–166.
8　See for instance J. AL-E AHMAD, *Plagued by the West (Gharbzadegi)*, trans. from the Persian by P. Sprachman, New York, Caravan Books, 1962. Another trans.: *Weststruckness*, by J. Green and A. Alizadeh, Lexington, Mazda, 1982. Another posthumous, more explicit work in Persian, "Concerning the Betrayal and Servility of the Intellectuals," was secretly printed before the Islamic Revolution and circulated by politicized clerics, notably Ahmad Khomeyni, the Imam's son.
9　See Y. RICHARD, "Le Rôle du clergé: tendances contradictoires du chi'isme iranien contemporain," *Archives de sciences sociales des religions*, 55, 1 (1983), p. 18.

and disorder, he sets the divine Law of Islam, based on reason and revelation, as the guarantee of stability, justice, and order. That Law was
entrusted to the Prophet in his lifetime, then to his heirs, the Imams. It is
not reasonable to suppose, continues Khomeyni, that God abandoned men
to their own devices after the Occultation of the Twelfth Imam.[10] There is
no more difference between the just *faqih* and the Imam than there is
between the Imam and the Prophet. The nation may be compared to a
child needing to be "guided" by a guardian. For Khomeyni it is therefore
clear that doctors of religious Law (*foqahā*, plural of *faqih*) must establish
an Islamic government, placing at its head either one among them or a
"college" of several *foqahā*. This government will have to see to the application of the Law, the levying of religious taxes and the defence of Islamic
territory.

That the *ulema* are the Prophet's successors is confirmed, according to
the head of the Islamic Revolution, by a Shi'ite tradition:

> The Commander of the believers ['Ali] records that the Prophet exclaimed
> three times: "Oh God! Have pity on those who will succeed me." He was
> asked: "Oh, Messenger of God! Who are they who will succeed you?" He
> replied: "Those who will come after me, pass on my traditions and put them
> into practice [i.e. the Imams] and teach the people after me."

Khomeyni further quotes these words of the Sixth Imam: "The *ulema*
are the heirs of the Prophets. The Prophets left not a halfpenny to their
heirs, but [religious] knowledge." With the support of these sacred references, the Guide of the Islamic Revolution really seeks to systematize and
enlarge the competence of the *mojtahed*. In traditional Shi'ism, in fact,
religious matters are managed in an informal way by a clerical hierarchy; in
Iran, since the Safavids (1501–1722), this hierarchy has served as a relief
and counterweight to political power, sometimes going as far as opposing
the rulers: following Said Amir Arjomand, it may be described as a veritable *hierocracy*.[11]

The *mojtaheds* are the clerics who, after a complete course of theological
studies, receive written authorization from their teacher (and generally
several teachers) to teach in their turn and to interpret Islamic Law. They
are given the honorary title *hojjat ol-eslām* (literally "proof of Islam").

10 KHOMEINI, *Islam and Revolution*, pp. 61ff.
11 See S. A. ARJOMAND, *The Shadow of God and the Hidden Imam*, Chicago and
London, University of Chicago Press, 1984.

Among the *mojtaheds*, of whom there are several hundreds if not thousands, an internal consensus selects high-ranking theologians of a respectable age who will be known as *āyatollāh* (literally "miraculous sign of God"). There is no fixed criterion to determine qualification for this title, awarded to some extent by co-optation: when Khomeyni gave 'Ali Khamena'i, then President of the Republic and his successor after 1989, the title "*hojjat ol-eslām*," others continued to call him *āyatollāh*, no doubt through a touch of natural sycophancy which became the rule when Khamena'i was designated for the office of Guide.

The *āyatollāhs* can gather round them "study circles" (*howza*), "classes" attended by young mullas, the nuclei of the great Muslim "schools" of theology (*madrasa*, "medresseh") which survive at Najaf, Qom and Mashhad. A new form of selection, less informal than previously, operates among the *āyatollāhs*: by co-optation of those who have already attained this stage, those *āyatollāhs* who have written their "Practical Treatise" (also called "Explanation of Problems," *Towzih ol-masā'el*) are henceforward acknowledged as suitable to become "models to be imitated" (*marja' al-taqlid*) for the simple believers, and bear the title "great ayatollah" (*āyatollāh ol-'ozmā*).

When the original French version of this book was written in 1990 there were five "great ayatollahs." Sayyed Mohammad-Rezā Golpāyegāni, born in the Isfahan region in 1889, died in 1993 at Qom; Abo'l-Qāsem Kho'i, born at Kho'y (Azerbaijan) in 1899, who lived at Najaf, died in 1992; Sayyed 'Abdollāh Musavi Shirāzi, born at Shirāz in 1901, died in 1991; Sayyed Hasan Tabātabā'i Qommi, born at Najaf in 1911, lives at Mashhad; Hoseyn-'Ali Montazeri, born in 1922 at Najafābād near Isfahan, was Khomeyni's designated successor between 1985 and February 1989, but was set aside by Khomeyni himself, who reproached him for defending opponents of the Islamic Republic and criticizing the death sentence on Salman Rushdie. He still lives at Qom, where he teaches: he is the hope of "liberal" Muslims. (Sayyed Shehāboddin Mar'ashi Najafi, born at Najaf in 1900, died in 1990.)

This gallery of aged men altered on the death of Kho'i and Golpāyegāni, two theologians who had resisted the revolutionary wave and had maintained a profound following among the people. Faced with the efforts of the Iraqi Ba'athist government to have a resident of Najaf appointed, over whom it would have some control, the leaders of the Iranian Islamic Republic put pressure on teachers in the Islamic schools in Qom to appoint ayatollah Sheikh Mohammad-'Ali Arāki, who lives there. Born in 1894 at Soltānābād (or Arāk), he is the doyen of them all, which gives him indisputable primacy. In 1973 a biographer described him as "a model of learning, wisdom and virtue" . . . This choice appears to have been widely accepted in Iran and by Shi'ites in India and Pakistan. In January 1994, those in charge of Islamic teaching in Qom met to designate a successor to Arāki in the event of his death. They were in agreement in choosing one of their own men, ayatollah Hājj Sayyed Musā Shobeyri Zanjāni, aged about 70. Theologians at Najaf proposed ayatollah Sayyed 'Ali-Hoseyn Sistāni, who had been a student of ayatollah Kho'i: his following is spread in Iraq, Kuwait, Lebanon, and even, to a certain extent, in Iran. Finally, besides the previously nominated ayatollah Montazeri, who is the guide of Shi'ites in the Isfahan region and also in Afghanistan, among the great *mojtaheds* of Qom some claim to favour ayatollah Sayyed Mohammad Ruhāni, born in 1917, whose following covers part of Iran, and also Kuwait and Saudi Arabia (Qatif and Ahsā); others, chiefly among the Shi'ites of Azerbaijan, have chosen ayatollah Sayyed Mohammad Shirāzi.[12]

A Shi'ite who is not a specialist in theological science must choose from among the ayatollahs the one who will be his guide in the application of secondary points of law, his "model to imitate." He agrees to follow the religious dictates laid down in the "Practical Treatise" by this ayatollah and to pay the ritual religious taxes to one of his authorized representatives. Obviously, therefore, not all Shi'ites have the same religious guide: though Khomeyni had gathered a large number of Iranians at the start of the Revolution, it is estimated that by 1988 the majority of Iranians preferred Kho'i, a conservative theologian who was strongly in favour of not mixing religion with politics. The consequences of the believers' choice are immense for the resources of the principal ayatollahs who collect the Islamic taxes voluntarily paid by their "imitators;" this money is used to fund the studies of young mullas, charitable foundations (hospitals, aid for the needy) and pious works.

Thus a relative amount of freedom is granted to the believer in choosing his "model to imitate:" the criterion is the general respectability of the candidate and his "greater knowledge." If the believer does not feel capable of deciding between two ayatollahs, he refers to a trustworthy mulla who will direct his choice. The 1979 constitution of the Islamic Republic of Iran tried to systematize this principle by having the *Faqih* elected in a two-stage ballot: the whole population (including non-Muslim minorities . . .)

12 A Shi'ite theologian (who wishes to remain anonymous) staying in a western university has kindly supplied me with this information. See also Sharif RĀZI, *Ganjina-ye dāneshmandān*, Tehran 1352/1973, vols I and II.

elect a Council of 70 "experts," all *mojtaheds* (*Shurā-ye khebragān*), who choose the *Faqih* from among the *ulema* most suitable to exercise the function of Guide (*rahbar*).

There will doubtless be surprise that the Guide elected in June 1989 was not one of the "models to imitate" listed earlier. This anomaly, which arose from the fact that the constitution had actually been drawn up for Khomeyni in person and that he was irreplaceable, did not escape the legislators' notice, as the constitution was revised by referendum on July 28, 1989. By lowering the theological rank required to be Guide, a clear line of demarcation was drawn between political institutions and the religious institution, and the veiled hostility to the excessive politicization of religion on the part of large numbers of the high-ranking clergy was formally recorded.

Khomeyni did not content himself with re-assuming the most strongly clerical traditions and justifying by all possible means *ulema* control of public affairs. After some years of power, finding that the institutions of the Islamic Republic were blocked by the many barriers to absolute power that had been set up in the 1979 constitution, he decided to add further to the weight of the *Faqih* and, on January 7, 1988, issued the following decree: "The government, which is a branch of the absolute authority of God's Prophet, stems from one of the fundamental institutions of Islam and takes precedence over all other institutions, which may be regarded as secondary, even prayer, fasting and pilgrimage."[13]

There is no need to stress the gravity of that declaration, or its unrealistic nature, to be revealed some months later when the sole candidate recognized as suitable to succeed Khomeyni was found to be a simple *mojtahed*. Let us briefly restate its boldness and the general direction it indicated. In the face of institutional difficulties, it is tempting to reinforce the indisputable nature, above the laws and common precepts of religion, of the Guide of the Community, who acts as guardian toward the young children who are entrusted to him.

SHI'ISM "MINUS THE CLERICS"?

Contrary to this clerical tendency, certain Muslim ideologists have realized the danger of clericalization and are trying to liberate religion from the hold

13   J. REISSNER, " Der Imam unde die Verfassung: Zur politischen und staatsrechtlichen Bedeutung der Direktive Imam Khomeinis vom 7 Januar 1988," *Orient*, 29, 2 (June 1988), pp. 213–36.

of the *ulema*. Since the middle of the nineteenth century, in the era of the Bābi movement, anticlericalism and para-Masonic or rationalist secularism have given food for thought to those who remain attached to the Islamic faith but are aware of the inability of Muslim nations to resist European powers.[14] Certain *ulema* famous for their progressive and anticolonial political positions, such as Sayyed Jamāloddin al-Afghāni (d. 1896) or Sayyed Mohammad Tabātabāʾi (d. 1918), were even closely involved with Masonic lodges.

In the years of heavy secularization of Rezā Shah's reign (1925–41), mullas and sometimes renowned theologians within the Iranian clerical circle took the side of modernity against the reactionary defenders of clerical prerogatives: for instance, Shariʾat Sangalaji (d. 1946), a religious reformer who had great influence on young intellectuals and who was anathematized by the *mojtaheds* of Qom for wanting to rid the doctrine of parasitical beliefs; or Hakamizāda, a young mulla who published at Qom a magazine inspired by the desire for social and religious reforms.[15] It was in reply to a virulent little work by Hakamizāda which came out in 1943, "Thousand-Year-Old Secrets" (i.e. the "secrets of clerical imposture"), that Khomeyni published his first major book intended for the public at large, a systematic and no less polemical retort entitled "Unveiling the 'Secrets.'"

Following in the footsteps of interwar modernist precursors – although he certainly never knew them and had probably never read their works – ʾAli Shariʾati, the son of a cleric unfrocked by the secularization of Rezā Shah's era, also inherited some of the liberal nationalist and anticolonialist ideology of Mosaddeq. After "modern" university studies, he lived for five years in France, at the end of the Algerian War, and became aware of the mobilizing force of Islam in struggles for independence. In Paris he used to visit and attend the lectures of the anticolonialist scholars of Islam, Louis Massignon and Jacques Berque, and also wrote a (mediocre) doctorate in Iranian philology. Returning to Iran in 1964, ʾAli Shariʾati became a popular lecturer, and was then imprisoned in 1973 because of a hardening of the Shah's regime and the enmity he had incurred from the clergy. Freed two years later, he succeeded in leaving Iran but died of a heart attack in London in 1977, at the age of forty-four.

14 Bābism, at the origin of Bahāʾism, was founded by Mohammad-ʾAli, known as the *Bāb* ("the Gate") executed in 1850. See above, ch. 3.
15 See Y. RICHARD, "Shariʾat Sangalaji: A Reformist Theologian of the Ridā Shāh Period," in S. A. Arjomand, ed., *Authority and Political Culture in Shiʾism*, Albany, SUNY Press, 1988, pp. 159–77.

His attack on the clergy begins by postulating its defects in the very genesis of the Shi'ite hierocracy in Iran, in the Safavid era. Shari'ati reassesses the values of combat and humanist militancy in the Koran and the holy history of the Imams, and bluntly criticizes the compromises arranged over the centuries between the clergy and the iniquitous monarchy. In a book which unleashed the fury of Qom's *mojtaheds*, Shari'ati made a distinction between the early Shi'ism "of 'Ali" and "Safavid" Shi'ism.[16] The first is movement, dynamism, progressive minority in opposition to the already institutionalized majority (Sunnism), a religion of awareness, social commitment, justice, and fighting for the liberation of the underprivileged. On the other hand, the Shi'ism that came to power in Iran in the sixteenth century, that of the Safavids, is a fixed social order, sidetracked from its mission by compromise with government; it alienates the people whom it seeks to beguile amid tears for the holy martyrs and the dream of a recompense at the end of the world. Losing its universal value, the Islam of the Safavids has become a sectarian Shi'ism, bound up with the Iranian nation (inventing a legitimate patriotism for itself through the legendary tale of Imam Hoseyn's marriage to the daughter of the last Sassanid emperor). Instead of being a way of perceiving and interpreting the Koranic message, Shi'ism then becomes a political instrument with which to oppose the Sunni Muslims dominated by the Ottomans. The agents of this deviation of Shi'ism, according to Shari'ati, are the clergy: he gives several caricatural examples of theologians of the Safavid era, prototypes of the parasitic mullas of the twentieth century, who are more concerned with making the faithful weep over the Imams' martyrdom and drawing their attention toward minor scruples than with regenerating their faith by following the Imams' examples.

In Shari'ati's view, the rigid conservatism of the clergy has turned Islam into a literalist, soulless religion, unfit to deal with contemporary problems. Such critical observations stirred those young Iranians who blamed the traditional *ulema* for their passive complicity in the injustices they witnessed. These young intellectuals realized that people could read the Koran with a fresh eye and live in the Islamic faith without being prisoners of the outmoded forms of clerical tradition. Shari'ati used the expression "Islam minus the clerics," adapting Mosaddeq's slogan when he nationalized the Anglo-Iranian Oil Company in 1951 and recommended an "economy minus oil." In 1972 Shari'ati wrote to his father:

---

16 'A. SHARI'ATI, *Tashayyo'-e 'alavi va tashayyo'-e safavi* (Collected Works, vol. IX), Tehran, Tashayyo', 1359/1980.

Thanks to this argument [Islam without clerics] Islam is in turn freed from its medieval shackles and imprisonment in the "priests' churches," freed from that petrified and decadent philosophy, from that deformed, superstitious vision of the world that stultifies and encourages passive imitation, turns people into a bleating flock of sheep and transforms intellectuals into enemies of religion, terrified and fleeing before Islam . . .[17]

In another work, devoted to Imam Hoseyn, which he himself modified in order to soften its overviolent nature in subsequent editions, Shari'ati stigmatizes the ignorance of the clerics who see nothing in God's Book

> but superstitions and wild flights of imagination, their desires and their own interests. They change God's words, turn them round, place obstacles in the path to God, steal the good of mankind. They carry God's Book about with them, but understand nothing of it and do not obey it: they are like asses, beasts of burden carrying books [an allusion to the Koran LXII, 5, against the Jews "bearing the Torah who, afterwards, no longer accepting it, are like a donkey laden with books"]. They are like dogs that bark and bite.[18]

Elsewhere Shari'ati makes a clear distinction between "two religions:" clerical Islam, which justifies wickedness in order to preserve institutionalized forms, and living Islam which, taking its example from the Prophets, overturns rigid traditions in order to substitute a spirituality committed to the service of the oppressed. He also attacks the so-called theological "specialization" on which clerics depend to establish their dominance.

To replace this unsuitable clergy with a new generation of Muslims educated in their religion, Shari'ati had found an appropriate training ground in the Hoseyniya Ershād, an Islamic institute founded at the end of the 1960s in the residential suburbs of Tehran. There, to a certain extent but on a larger scale, he continued the work that his father had begun in the 1940s at Mashhad with the Center for the Propagation of Islamic Truth (*Kānun-e nashr-e haqāyeq-e eslāmi*). Although the Hoseyniya Ershad was the work of several Muslim reformers, including certain eminent members of the clergy (such as ayatollah Motahhari) it was Shari'ati who soon became its major star. The clientele was composed mainly of university

---

17 'A. SHARI'ATI, *Bā makhāteb-hā-ye āshenā* (With Familiar Penfriends) (publication of this volume was banned in Iran after the Revolution) (Collected Works, vol. I), Tehran, Hoseyniya Ershad, 1356/1978, p. 8.

18 In the definitive edition of this text, *ruhāniun* ("clerics") was altered to *ahbār* ("erudite"), a less pronounced term: 'A SHARI'ATI, *Hoseyn vāres-e Ādam* (Hoseyn, Adam's Heir) (Collected Works, vol. XIX), Tehran, Qalam, 1360/1981, p. 24.

students and young secularly inclined laymen of the middle and lower
middle classes.

In this framework the man they called "the Doctor" outlined a program
of Islamic studies which, had it been realized, could have rivalled the
madrasa of Qom. There were several sections: research, teaching, propaganda, organization. Here are some of the areas set out by Shari'ati:

1   Research: Islamology, consisting of studying the idea of God and His revelation;
    the knowledge one can gain of the Prophet (including through the works of
    orientalists), the Islamic ideal, the Islamic state; the history of Islam, and Is-
    lamic culture and sciences; the sociology of Islamic countries; art and literature.
2   Teaching: Islamology (definition of the ideal society and the ideal man), know-
    ledge of the Koran (understanding the text, hermeneutics, and exegesis), rheto-
    ric (grammar, classical and modern literature, Arabic and European languages,
    beliefs, and ideologies).
3   Propaganda: the various means of diffusing thinking, sermons, mass media,
    pilgrimages, lectures, and seminars, etc.
4   Organization: an information and documentation center, modern library (in-
    cluding cassettes, films, etc.); varied range of publications of original texts and
    translations.[19]

If Shari'ati worked out such a program it was because, in keeping with
Shi'ite tradition, he believed in the role that the elite must play in guiding
a society not prepared to take itself in hand. In a work written in 1969, he
analyzed the role of the Imam in society and discussed the decadence of
western democracies whose political system is based on the law of the
majority: revolution and progress are not the product of the will of the
majority, but of those who are more clear-sighted. Was not the election of
Caliph Abu Bakr – denounced by the Shi'ites as a bid for power – achieved
by a majority?[20] A people anaesthetized by an ossified culture and the long
experience of dictatorship cannot awake by itself, but needs leaders. And the
people, says Shari'ati, are like children who cannot choose their tutor: they
will choose the one who most fulfills their desires. (Here is something that
strongly calls to mind Khomeyni's paternalist view of the people.) "If 'command' and 'progress' [*rahbari va pish-raft*], i.e. the revolutionary alteration
of men, are taken for political principles, then it is not possible for individuals in this society to choose this command."

19   'A. SHARI'ATI, *Che bāyad kard?* (What is to be Done?) (Collected Works, vol. XX),
Tehran, n. p. 1360/1982, pp. 333–472.
20   'A. SHARI'ATI, "Ommat va emāmat" (The Community and the Imam) in *'Ali* (Collected Works, vol. XXVI), Tehran, Nilufar, 1361/1982, pp. 600ff.

No hope can ever lie in the western democracies, says Shari'ati, partly because of the fundamental weaknesses of the majority principle, and partly because western societies continue to pillage and exploit the wealth of the third world even when they show concern for their underprivileged classes. In place of tainted liberal democracy our ideologist proposes the institution of a "guided" or "committed democracy," which he defines as follows:

> It is the government of a group which, on the basis of a progressive revolutionary program, wants to change and guide in the best possible way individuals, people's language and culture, social relations, and the standard of living . . . If there are some who do not believe in this [revolutionary] path, and whose behavior and opinion entail the underdevelopment and corruption of society, and if there are some who abuse their power, their money, and this liberty, and if there are social habits that hinder man from flourishing, these traditions must be suppressed, these ways of thinking must be condemned, and society must be liberated by all available means from its fossilized yoke.[21]

One can see the danger of such a justification for the seizure of power by an enlightened minority. Here Shari'ati, with his intention to liberate and save, is fitting in with a genuine Shi'ite tradition, both deeply elitist and pessimistic, about the ability of men to steer their own course. However, that interventionist aspect caught the attention of the young Iranian intellectuals in the Islamic Revolution far less than the "progressive" aspect of his thinking and his religious inspiration stripped of its rags of clerical tradition. This appeal was strongly felt when the Iranian old regime's censorship, pressed by President Carter's more liberal administration, freely allowed publication of Shari'ati's work: Shari'ati died precisely then, in 1977, when his thinking was exploding the old schemas. A portrait of "the Doctor" was borne aloft in the great demonstrations of the Revolution and his books were read by everybody. The infatuation even reached the young theologians of Qom.

THE CLERGY AND THE NATION

Between these two conceptions of the clergy, minimal agreement was reached in giving supreme importance to the role that Shari'ati – like Khomeyni, although in a different way – wished to see played by a ruling elite. In

21   Ibid., p. 618.

practice, whether enlightened or obscurantist, this role is held today by the clergy. Since the nineteenth century, Iranian clerics have constantly intervened in political affairs. There is not, however, complete agreement as to whether the mullas have always gone to the defence of the people against the government or whether they have quite simply tried to preserve their social position.

Let us take an example: in 1890 Nāseroddin Shah sold a monopoly on the growing, marketing, and exporting of Iranian tobacco to one Major Talbot, a British citizen. Some months later, a strong mobilization of the people against this concession brought about the failure of the monopoly bid and the great *mojtahed* of Najaf, Mirzā Hasan Shirāzi, confirmed a *fatvā* (religious decree) forbidding any Muslim to sell or use tobacco. This boycotting of tobacco was so strictly obeyed that the Shah was obliged to repurchase the concession at the cost of an unprecedented humiliation and a loan from the British Imperial Bank. What was the clergy's attitude in this Tobacco Affair?[22] Apparently, it was the *ulema* who steered the popular revolt and, through the boycott order, gave it its determining force (here, the clergy presented itself as defending the oppressed nation, challenging absolutism and undermining the authority of colonial powers . . .). But an Iranian historian, Fereydun Ādamiyat, has argued that the strength and spontaneity of the popular revolt frightened the *ulema*, who did all they could to calm and channel it for fear of a revolutionary movement: if they joined the demonstrators it was in order not to lose their influence and in the hope of getting them to accept a compromise with the monarchy as quickly as possible.

The same ambivalence hangs over the role of the *ulema* in the Iranian constitutional revolution of 1906–9. Incontestably they played a central part in the mobilization of the people, both to bring them together and to form a block opposition to royal absolutism; for instance, in 1906 the principal *ulema* of Tehran – who were at the same time the magistrates and notaries – left the capital to withdraw to Qom, 120 km to the south, as a mark of protest, and returned only when Mozaffaroddin Shah (1896–1907) agreed to convoke a parliament. Of the three eminent members of the clergy who automatically took their place in the First Assembly one was a pure opportunist, Sayyed 'Abdollāh Behbahāni, one a democrat who sympathized with the Masonic movement, Sayyed Mohammad Tabātabā'i, and

---

22   Excellent presentation of the dominant point of view by N. R. KEDDIE, *Religion and Rebellion in Iran: The Iranian Tobacco Protest of 1891–1892*, London, Frank Cass, 1966; anticlerical revision, F. ADAMIYAT, *Shuresh bar emtiyāz-nāma-ye Rehzi*, Tehran, Payām, 1360/1981.

the third an "integrist" who turned against the Revolution, accusing it of wanting to destroy Islam, Sheikh Fazlollāh Nuri. By his stubbornness, Nuri managed to gather a large number of mullas who were worried about the secular turn taken by the movement. He allied himself with the absolutist reaction of Mohammad-'Ali Shah, suppressed the Constitution in 1908. Nuri was executed the following year in the public square in Tehran by constitutionalists who had swept triumphantly back to power.[23]

Nuri's case is especially interesting for the impassioned way in which Iranians appraise him: secular historians pour scorn on this reactionary cleric who chose retrograde Islam rather than the popular will; on the other hand, the clerics – including Khomeyni – praise him to the skies as defender of the faith. Since the 1960s certain intellectuals, feeling let down by secular ideologies and seeking a militant identity, following the essayist Āl-e Ahmad (d. 1969), have found in this figure of the stubborn cleric a model for refusing to submit to the leveling influence of the West. In short, according to them, Nuri rejected the ascendancy of colonial societies over the Iranian Muslim, and by doing so to some extent anticipated the Islamic Revolution.

Among the great clerical figures in twentieth-century Iran, one of the most controversial is ayatollah Abo'l-Qāsem Kāshāni: after being involved in the 1920 Shi'ite revolt against the British Protectorate in Iraq, Kāshāni champed at the bit in Iran during Rezā Shah's reign (1925–41), like many another cleric and nationalist. Making his comeback in the anti-British disturbances in 1941, Kāshāni was imprisoned by the Russo-British occupation forces. After the war he became a hero and threw himself deeply into political action. In turn the ally of nationalist liberals and the most violent Islamic militants (the *Fedā'iyān-e eslām*), together with Mosaddeq, until 1952, he was a leader of the campaign for the nationalization of the Anglo-Iranian Oil Company and became president of the Iranian parliament. But personal and ideological rivalries with Mosaddeq brought about a split between the two men, which facilitated the organization of a *coup d'état*, supported by the CIA, and Mohammad-Rezā Shah's return to the throne in August 1953. Kāshāni died forgotten in 1962, despised by the nationalists. He was rehabilitated only after the victory of the clerical supporters in the Islamic Revolution, in 1980. In order to blacken the liberal nationalist leaders, Mehdi Bāzargān and Abo'l-Hasan Bani-Sadr,

---

23   See A. HAIRI, *Shī'ism and Constitutionalism in Iran*, Leiden, Brill, 1977; V. MARTIN, *Islam and Modernism: The Iranian Revolution of 1906*, London, I. B. Tauris, 1989; Y. RICHARD, "Le Radicalisme islamique du Sheykh Fazlollah Nuri et son impact dans l'histoire de l'Iran contemporain," *Laïcité*, n. s. 29, 2 (*Les Intégrismes*) Brussels, 1986.

who were claiming to be Mosaddeq's heirs, importance was henceforward to be given to the part played by the former nationalist leader in the weakening of the national movement. If the support of the religious wing of the National Front had not been repulsed by the liberals, or rendered impossible by their refusal to share power, so it was said, the Shah would never have regained his throne. Despite Kāshāni's exceptional openness of mind and his gift for making use of the media, his political opportunism had in reality caused his downfall, and later reinstatement cannot conceal the inconsistencies of his ideas.[24]

One last dramatic phase, liable to varying interpretations of the role of the clergy, was to prepare more distinctly, fifteen years ahead of time, for the coming of the Islamic Revolution: in 1963, in order to protest against various measures of social reform imposed by the Shah in the framework of the "White Revolution," theology students at Qom began to demonstrate, with a 60-year-old *sayyed* at their head, Hājj Āqā Ruhollāh, otherwise known as ayatollah Khomeyni. Little known until then, this mulla headed the movement, openly challenged the Shah's political police and became the public star of the popular opposition. His arrest during the mourning celebration of Moharram in 1963 (5 June, "15 Khordād" in the Iranian calendar) was the occasion for a general uprising that was brutally crushed.

It is undeniable that at the moment when the classic political opposition was foundering and the White Revolution's program (notably agrarian reform, so long desired) seemed to be outstripping all its opponents, Khomeyni went much farther than the rest. After over a year of disputes (or compromises?) with the police, he denounced as a return to the "Capitulations" (the legal and commercial advantages which European colonial powers had succeeded in obtaining in the Ottoman Empire and in Persia and which were abolished only after the First World War) the granting by the Iranian Parliament in October 1964 of legal extraterritoriality to American military personnel in Iran. The ayatollah paid the price for this denunciation by being sent into exile in Turkey. The failure of his movement was transformed in the long term into an extraordinary success, since he made everyone – notably the intellectuals – aware of the clergy's importance in political mobilization.

---

24   See Y. RICHARD, "Ayatollah Kashani: Precursor of the Islamic Republic?" in N. R. Keddie, ed., *Religion and Politics in Iran*, New Haven and London, Yale University Press, 1983, pp. 101–24; *idem*, "L'Organisation des Fedā'iyān-e eslām, mouvement intégriste musulman en Iran (1945–1956)," in O. Carré and P. Dumont, eds, *Radicalismes islamiques*, vol. I, Paris, L'Harmattan, 1985, pp. 23–82.

But unless one wants to fall into hagiography, the limits of Khomeyni's action must also be pointed out: first, his intransigence was far from being as complete as it is sometimes said to be, as is indicated by the very deferential tone of the telegrams which he was sending at the time to the Shah, corroborating the thesis according to which Khomeyni several times reached an "understanding" with the political police (the SAVAK).[25] The substance of the revolt is even more ambiguous. For the clergy two things seemed of prime importance. The first, that the Shah was paying no heed to Islam's traditions, for instance with regard to women (who were granted, horror of horrors! the right to vote, and shortly afterwards the right to seek divorce).[26] Secondly, Islam was treated on a par with other religions: in the new law on the election of regional and local councils the oath was no longer to be sworn on the Koran, but on the "holy book" – which might therefore just as well be the Avesta, the Gospel or one of the Bāb's writings!

A motive less pure than the defense of the faith could also have determined the intervention of the Iranian *ulema*: they were (and still are to a large extent) linked with the large landowners with whom they have a shared interest because, through the intermediary of mortmain foundations (*vaqf*) of which they are generally the institutional managers, the *ulema* are the biggest property-owners in Iran. They knew full well that, after the redistribution of the great private domains, it would be the turn of the pious foundations. The removal of those revenues would not only be in the nature of a violation of the sacred right of the donors, but would above all render precarious the material situation of the clergy, the theological schools, and charitable organizations, a large part of whose resources came from the *vaqf*.

The biggest Iranian pious foundation is the Āstān-e Qods-e Razavi ("Sacred Threshold of the Imam Reza") at Mashhad.[27] This *vaqf* owns 58 percent (7,000 ha) of the land of this regional capital with 1,000,000 inhabitants. In the province of Khorasan alone, about 400,000 ha divided into

25   See M. ZONIS, *The Political Elite of Iran*, Princeton, Princeton University Press, 1971, p. 45. On the 1963 revolt, clerical version, DEHNAVI, *Qiyām-e Khunin-e 15 Khordād 42 be-revāyat-e asnād*, Tehran, Resā, 1360/1981: anticlerical version in W. M. FLOOR, "The Revolutionary Character of the Ulama: Wishful Thinking or Reality," in N. R. Keddie, ed., *Religion and Politics in Iran*, pp. 73–97.

26   It was to be confirmed for them in the Islamic Republic, as was eligibility for Parliament.

27   B. HOURCADE, "Vaqf et modernité en Iran: Les Agro-business de l'Āstān-e Qods de Mashhad," in Y. Richard, ed., *Entre l'Iran et l'Occident*, Paris, Maison des sciences de l'homme, 1989, pp. 117–41.

438 properties, belong to the sanctuary, the largest domain exceeding 60,000 ha. The Shah's agrarian reform included these immense stretches of land bequeathed to the Imam's Foundation, but everyone agrees that the Foundation was very little affected by the measures. In order to be legally in the clear, it granted the 99-year lease allowed by the proposals only to those peasants who farmed in traditional fashion the land surrounding the villages. A precise assessment of these transfers of the use of the land – which were hardly ever legalized – was not carried out systematically. This legal lacuna poses grave political and social problems, for the Islamic Revolution allowed the Āstān-e Qods to challenge the religious legitimacy of "selling" *vaqf* lands to the peasants in the 1960s. A religious legacy to a mortmain foundation cannot in fact be modified, except in the case of a "change to better status" (*tabdil be-ahsan*). The sanctuary's administration undertook to recover its property inheritance in its entirety after the Revolution . . .

In spite of their great wealth, and unlike the westernized intellectuals, the mullas remained apart from "civil society" until 1979. The government mistrusted them, and they themselves retained their reserve in the face of a secular government that was unacceptable because it was the enemy of Islam's exclusive dominance over public life.

Iran's recent history and the ease with which the clergy has passed from a situation of counter-society to one of a central institution of the state, provide a good illustration of this social body's originality, and one would look in vain to find its equivalent in other Muslim countries. Theoretical discourse on the role of the clergy thus came up with more than one gratuitous speculation. Without the clergy there would be no religious tradition independent of the state, no ready-made alternative to secular administration, no Islamic Republic.

This kind of interpretation of Islamist movements in the large countries of the Muslim world shows in fact that everything is in readiness for an explosion similar to the one which took place in Iran: a galloping demography, the culture shock of modernity, the feeling of frustration of locally trained elites which can find no honourable outlet after their studies . . . and even a revolutionary ideology based on a return to Islamic Law. All that is missing is a clergy. One cannot help thinking, for example, that the failure of radical Islamist movements in Egypt and Syria is due only to the absence of an elite of responsible executives, capable of taking over from the state should it fall short of its primordial task of guaranteeing people the hope that their efforts are not in vain, and that their identity is protected. (In Algeria the Islamic Salvation Front has tried to vest local administrations with the ability to set up centres of Islamic society: such assumption of control over existing state institutions will not of course compensate for the absence of an organically structured body of *ulema*, but will perhaps allow the gaining of power by stages.)

MOURNING AND DANCING FOR THE MARTYRS

Mourning is the most moving aspect of Iranian Shi'ism. It is not an absolutely exclusive peculiarity of this religion. Christianity also celebrates Christ's Passion and glorifies its martyrs. In Sunni Islam people are not unaware of the meaning that human suffering can impart; the Sunnis even recognize Imam Hoseyn, killed at Karbalā with his companions by the Omayyad army, as a genuine martyr who was unjustly sacrificed. But the Shi'ites more particularly know the harrowing epic of the Prophet's twelve successors, each reputedly dying a martyr's death, and their religious literature bears witness that, since the earliest times, they have known how to weep in order to share in their Imams' fight, as tradition invites them to do: "Whosoever weeps or causes others to weep for Hoseyn will enter Paradise."[28] In Iran, however, the ceremonies commemorating the tragedy of Karbalā are quite another matter . . .

Like all Iranian townships, in August 1988, Arak, a small town in the centre of Iran where Khomeyni began his theological studies at the age of 18, celebrated the days of Tāsu'ā and Āshurā, on the 9th and 10th of the lunar month of Moharram, the days when Imam Hoseyn was subjected to torture. The celebrations were on a vast scale, with processions of flagellants, lamentations, music (drums, cymbals, fifes, and fine male voices), following behind banners, huge and magnificent insignia or emblems ('alam), occasionally the symbolic coffin of Zeynab, the Imam's sister. The whole town was in a ferment! Groups of weeping people came from every alley and paraded to the town centre, thence to return to their starting-point where a meal was provided by benefactors.

It is difficult to describe the impact of this spectacle: grave-faced men and women clad in black, the men rhythmically beating their breast, or

28 See M. AYOUB, *Redemptive Suffering in Islām: A Study of the Devotional Aspects of 'Āshurā in Twelver Shī'īsm*, The Hague, Mouton, 1978, written by a Lebanese Shi'ite; Ch. BROMBERGER, "Martyre, deuil et remords: Horizons mythiques et rituels des religions méditerranéennes" (regarding the "passions" of Christ and Imām Hoseyn: an essay in comparative analysis), in *Études corses*, 12–13 (1979), pp. 129–53. On the celebration of Moharram among Shi'ites in India, see D. PINAULT, *The Shi'ites*, London, I. B. Tauris, 1992.

flagellating themselves, sometimes very hard, with a little whip of small chains, apparently without feeling the slightest pain. Several men walk barefoot, perhaps fulfilling a vow. Certain participants show great heroism, notably those who take it in turns to carry the heavy emblems mounted on a metal frame that may reach a span of four metres, adorned with silver figurines (doves, camels) and long flexible strips bending in time with the bearers' steps, and decorated with oil lamps and precious cloths. From time to time, before resuming their pall-bearers' pace, those carrying the emblems halt opposite a group of women sitting in the shade of a mosque and begin an astonishing and disturbing demonstration of their courage, spinning round with their burden as if in defiance of its weight and dancing the most unreal and dangerous ballet imaginable: two men stay close alongside in case anything unforeseen occurs, but if the carrier were to stumble, his massive burden could well injure or kill innocent spectators.

The procession comprises only men, unshaven (I am the only man to have shaved this morning), and boys, some of whom wear a sort of shroud to signify their acceptance of martyrdom. On the day of 'Āshurā (10th day of Moharram), many men have smeared mud on the top of their head and on their shoulders, a sign that they are prepared to be buried with Hoseyn. Elsewhere, people have witnessed numerous processions of men who deliberately wound their scalp with a knife to let the blood flow freely down their face. Slowly walking in the sunshine and repeating, when invited to do so, a slogan or refrain, they follow the directions of the cantor who, into a microphone linked up to a mobile amplifier, makes himself hoarse chanting his text, which he deciphers from some ancient book, or improvises when inspiration permits. If there were but one procession, one might imagine it to be a carefully organized and executed folk phenomenon. But there are hundreds of them in this small town. It is collective hysteria, a taste for *thanatos* that has swept away the bounds of all human respect. Wherever one goes, there is mourning. Radio, television, public service buildings, everything is punctuated by this throbbing, this color; everything is mobilized to demonstrate death.

Iranians, ordinarily so sober in their collective demonstrations, so little given to "performance," so little inclined to empty spectacle, gather together in the *hoseyniya*, the *takiya* (theaters, meeting halls), in mosques, to listen to preachers tell them for the hundredth, the thousandth, time about the death of Hoseyn at Karbalā, massacred with his 72 companions by the army of the impious Omayyads. And they weep. They come in order to weep and they are told what is necessary to make the tears flow. They really do shed tears, together, in public and with sincerity. They get rid of the pent-up emotion that they contain at other times, when they are prudish and timid. No sooner does the voice of the preacher begin to quaver than there is an explosion of sobbing and beating of breasts.

Elsewhere, in towns but above all in villages, the *ta'ziya* (tazieh) is held. This religious theater is so extrordinary, so popular and so spontaneous. It is both a mystery and a celebration, a game and a tragedy, where the public gathers all around a scene improvised in the open air (or in the *hoseyniya*). The spectators and actors are interchangeable: everyone knows Yazid, 'Ali Akbar, Zeynab, and Hazrat 'Abbās . . . they are the ones in the village who can read and have decked themselves out for the occasion in the costumes of the drama. They have their script in their hands and the director asks them to read their part, handing each the microphone in his turn. There is magic, with horses stampeded through the midst of it all, firecrackers that explode during the battle, the hand of 'Abbās that flies through the air before managing to get water from the Euphrates (symbolized by a bath-tub) to assuage the thirst of Hoseyn's companions. There is blood, the clashing of sabers whirled round over heads, the beating of drums and the sound of death cries.

A friend recalling the *ta'ziya* of his childhood, in which he himself had acted, is surprised that the people of the village where we are attending the drama do not weep. Is it the introduction of microphones, saturation by the filmed pictures seen on television, or the – typical – upset caused by a procession of flagellants who insist on going through the middle of the *ta'ziya*, breaking the rhythm of the action?

This exuberant display of mourning and demonstration of a morbid kind of heroism is accompanied by a surrealistic festival atmosphere. Everywhere refreshing syrups are being handed out, to make up for the miseries of Hoseyn in the arid plain of Karbalā. Everywhere copious repasts are being given, very often to correspond with prayers that have been answered. People stay on the streets till late in the evening: shattered with fatigue after walking around on the eve of Āshurā, from my bed I can still hear, past midnight, the cantors and the preachers, the cymbals and the bass drums; everywhere illuminations pierce the night, putting the mourning out of mind. Women and children, men and boys become intoxicated with the throbbing of the processions and the fumes of *esfand* burnt to ward off bad luck.

Amid the confusion and tiredness of the evening, amid the repasts, in the mosques, contact between boys and girls becomes less hazardous, less noticed. All my informants confirm that 'Ashura is a day for fondling, furtive caresses and flirtations. All at once the sexual nature of this festival of death hits me. The pole of the majestic emblem supported on the belly and raised skywards to be exhibited to the women's view. The masochistic display of virility to attract compassion and admiration. The sweetness of the syrups, the tenderness of stolen glances, of love for Hoseyn and his companions. The bewitching rhythm of the processions, usually in four-time – three flagellations and one pause, or three lightly swung flagellations and one step forward – is more like a dance than a funeral march. And the whip with the little chains that the men twirl round to lash their shoulders suddenly resembles the multi-coloured scarves that the tribal women wave over their heads while dancing lightly in their finest dress at weddings . . . The *ta'ziya* reminds us that Qāsem, the son of Imam Hasan, was killed at Karbalā on his wedding day, a myth that was used on many occasions during the Iranian Revolution to make death more moving: the alliance of eroticism with martyrdom, the victims killed before they could consummate their amorous union, their death doubtless being that union itself.[29]

The potent collective celebration which I had just attended seemed to me to prove the great strength of the Iranian nation. After eight years of war, with about 300,000 dead (out of a population of about 50 million), all those men in the streets, orderly, sticking together, demonstrating their love for the Imams, displaying their virility . . . Shi'ism's power to mobilize has not waned, quite the reverse. The objection will be raised that, because of their excessive Shi'ite sentimentality, because of their Iranian roots so deeply entrenched in the land, in urban bodies, in villages, these mourning celebrations make the Iranian Revolution absolutely unexportable. Yet politics seemed to have no part in these processions. There was no allusion to the Islamic Republic, except for portraits of the martyrs (war victims) from each area, sometimes attached to banners, or more often exhibited amid flowers in front of the *hoseyniya*. There were also portraits of Khomeyni and Iranian flags in the processions, but without any particular ideological slogans.

The coherence, the gravity, and the grandeur of those 'Āshurā demonstrations almost scared me. Who would halt an army whose marching pace is a dance, and whose leader is Hoseyn who died 1,300 years ago in Mesopotamia?

In this collective "happening," in this profound and joyous sorrow of Shi'ite mourning, it is not a matter of an amorphous mass obeying some

---

29 See S. HUMAYUNI, "An Analysis of a Ta'ziyeh of Qasem," in P. Chelkowski, ed., *Ta'ziyeh: Ritual and Drama in Iran*, New York, New York University Press, and Tehran, Soroush, 1979, pp. 12–23.

agitator or other, but of little local processions, of parochial, communal Islamic groups, in a street or a guild in the bazaar, of religious associations who proudly inscribe their name on their procession's banner. Of course, they encounter one another in the main street, but each group keeps its own "soundtrack," its own rhythm and "togetherness," and eventually returns to its own *hoseyniya* where kebabs, rice, and sweet drinks are waiting. In the main street, rivalries between local quarters, groups, and associations may give rise to aggressive attitudes and manifestations of pride that are not in keeping with the fusion and self-forgetfulness one would expect from a unitarian demonstration. The depth of feeling is in no way diminished by being divided. A Sunni Muslim attending these ceremonies would probably be disgusted by the orgy of Imamolatry in which Iranians indulge here. I am not trying to reassure those who would be alarmed by the collective merging of religion and nation but, even if its breakdown into parishes shatters any leanings towards political exploitation, the phenomenon goes deeper and is more complex than a simple ideological mobilization.

In the whole town of Arak, amid the scores or hundreds of processions converging in the direction of the town centre, afterwards to disperse to the localities from which they had come, I noticed only one solitary mulla in his religious habit, a *sayyed*. Was he conscious that he was an exception? It is public knowledge that the *ulema* have never been in favour of the ostentatious displays of mourning in the form of flagellation, or of the *ta'ziya* which are its more elaborate expression: they recommend only meetings where the clerics themselves are the leading actors, as preachers, to recount the martyrdom of the holy Imams. It is a matter, therefore, of a spontaneous ritual, against which neither police nor clergy would dare to attempt the slightest movement, but which organizes itself *by* itself, in the name of a solid and unshakable tradition.

RELIGIOUS FEELING: FROM THE RITUAL TO THE MYTH

The popularity in Iran of the celebrations of Hoseyn's death is an ancient phenomenon. Some authors have unhesitatingly drawn a parallel with a pre-Islamic cult borne out by literature – notably in the *Book of the Kings* by Ferdowsi, a tenth-century Persian epic narrating the foundational events in the mythical history of Iran – and certain vestiges of this cult are still attested in the provinces of Iran. It is about the celebration of a hero, Siyāvosh, the incarnation of perfection, purity, and bravery. Unjustly accused by his father's wife, whose amorous advances he has repulsed, Siyāvosh emerges triumphant from an ordeal by fire and then, following a brilliant military expedition, he makes an alliance, for the sake of peace, with the vanquished enemies of the king, his father. Repudiated by his own people, Siyāvosh will perish, the innocent victim of men's hatred, decapitated by Afrāsyāb, a relation of the king who has given him refuge.[30] "The population of Bukhara," an ancient chronicle tells us, "make much lamentation over the murder of Siyāvosh, which is known throughout the provinces, and the minstrels have composed songs about it that the singers call the 'Laments of the Magi.' "

In the *Book of the Kings*, Siyāvosh has a presentiment about his death and uses it as an example:

> Open your ears to what I have to say;
> Not many days shall pass before I shall,
> Though innocent, be murdered wretchedly
> By our shrewd-hearted king; another will
> Adorn this crown and throne; through my bad Fortune
> And through the calumny of one who hates me
> My guiltless head will meet an evil fate.
> This murder will make life intolerable,
> Iran and Turan will rise against
> Each other and from end to end the earth
> Will fill with pain; then vengeful swords will swarm
> Through both our countries; in Iran and in Turan . . .
> What lamentations will rise up then
> From Iran and from Turan! My spilt blood will
> Convulse the world. Almighty God Who rules
> The Earth has written in the heavens thus –
> And by his order what is sown is reaped.

Siyāvosh has a dream that he describes to his wife:

> But Siyavosh replied, "My dream's come true;
> My glory's darkened now and life for me
> Draws to its end; sorrow and pain and grief
> Are mine, as is the turning heaven's way
> Which shows now joy, now wretchedness; and if

---

30   See Sh. MESKUB, *Sug-e Siyāvash* (The Mourning of Siyavash), Tehran, Kharezmi, 4th edn, 1354/1975; E. YARSHATER, "Ta'ziyeh and Pre-Islamic Mourning Rites in Iran," in Chelkowski, *Ta'ziyeh*, pp. 88–94.

My palace dome should touch the sphere of Saturn,
The poison of this world must still be tasted.
If for a thousand and two hundred years
We live, the black dust is our home at last –
And in this night no wise man hopes to find
The brightness of the day . . .
Thus turns
The whirling circle of the heavens, and men
Will never see this ancient dwelling change.
And now, through Afrasyab's commands, my dark
Luck sinks to sleep. They'll hack my guiltless head off
And in my body's blood they'll soak my crown;
I'll find no coffin, grave or shroud, and of
The company who's there not one will weep;
My final resting place will be Turan.
This ancient world is like a lion's maw:
Such is the fate the heavens will bring to me,
No happiness is promised me, or kindness,
But from the shining sum to darkest earth
No being can escape the will of God."[31]

No Iranian, reading this thousand-year-old passage, could fail to make the comparison with the hero of the cause of faith martyred at Karbalā. One must admire, in passing, the genius of nations for reinterpreting and retranslating into a new symbolic language those intense emotions on which they feed in order to face up to the ordeals inflicted by fate.

Although literary works celebrating the death of Hoseyn abounded in the early centuries, and emanated as much from Sunni circles (turning a critical gaze on the Omayyads) as from Shi'ites, it was only with the advent of the Safavids and Iran's conversion to Shi'ism, starting from the sixteenth century, that public celebrations of mourning for Hoseyn were organized in Iran.[32] Here, "public celebrations" does not mean "religious theater" (*ta'ziya*) as we know it today, this spectacular form being truly vouched for only since the end of the eighteenth century.

31 Abol' Qasem FERDOWSI, *The Book of the Kings*, trans. and presentation by Dick Davis, *The Legend of Seyāvash*, London, Penguin Books, 1992, pp. 85–6, and 111–12.
32 See J. CALMARD, "L'Iran sous Nāseroddin Chāh et les derniers Qadjar: Esquisse pour une histoire politique culturelle et socio-religieuse," *Le Monde iranien et l'islam*, 4 (1976–7), pp. 165–94; *idem*, "Le Culte de l'Imam Husayn: Étude sur la commémoration du drame de Karbalā dans l'Iran pré-safavide" (unpublished dissertation), Paris, EPHE, VIth section, March 1975.

Between the procession of flagellants and the *ta'ziya*, there exists a whole range of commemorations which doubtless explain the recent development. For example, there is the recitation of elegies for the dead (*marsiya*); commemoration meetings where a cleric who specializes in dramatic effect preaches in almost theatrical fashion to invoke tears for the martyrdom of the Imams (*rowza-khāni*); gestural demonstrations, both declamatory and pictorial, performed in public squares by popular orators using simple pictures (*parda*) representing the battle of Karbalā; historical processions, in some Iranian provinces, with characters from the tragedy of Karbalā, Hoseyn, Yazid, Shemr, etc., in which the costumed players, mounted on horses or camels, are the inhabitants of the village; ritual funeral processions, in the towns, when an imitation ceremonial catafalque (*nakhl*) is carried symbolically . . . As the misfortunes as well as the martyrdom of Hoseyn and his family are known to all, it is easy to improvise a commemoration: tears will fall naturally at any reminder of Karbalā.

The importance assumed by the *ta'ziya* in the nineteenth century is a subject for disputes among historians. For the public, besides the attraction of the spectacle, what matters most is the telling of the story. It is clear that royal patronage played a decisive part in the spread of these representations, which brought together all social classes. The example of Tehran, where an immense *takiya* had been built near the royal palace, prompted the provincial elites in their turn to finance troupes of performers and the construction of *takiya* or *hoseyniya*. In the villages, troupes could get together spontaneously. The reluctance of the clergy in respect of these demonstrations is doubtless not unconnected with the success of the *ta'ziya*, a way of demonstrating without the mullas one's attachment to religion at the time when clerical power was beginning to take the form of opposition to political power. Under the Pahlavi dynasty (1925–79), *ta'ziya* performances were officially banned, but continued in two forms: spontaneous, as a sign of cultural resistance, in villages where the central government could less easily make itself heard; and artificial, to revive as pure spectacle a popular theater that fascinated westerners. It was in that second form that the *ta'ziya* was introduced into an artistic festival striving to be both Iranian and avant-garde, at Shiraz in 1967, and at the time of an international symposium organized in 1976 on the lines of the same festival.[33]

This link between the royal sponsorship of the *ta'ziya* performances and the belated revival, for aesthetic reasons far removed from religious feeling, made popular religious theater very suspect in the eyes of certain

33 The works were later published in Chelkowski, *Ta'ziyeh*.

revolutionary Islamists in the 1970s. Shari'ati particularly attacked those theatrical demonstrations in which he saw manipulation of religious feeling.[34] He sought their origins in imitation of the West: the Shi'ite dynasties of Iran, hostile to the Ottoman Empire, found natural allies among those European peoples who lived in fear of Turkish conquests. That is why, said Shari'ati, very early on they established diplomatic relations and brought Christians to their capital (the Armenians from Jolfa, an Armenian town near Azerbaijan, deported to Isfahan by Shah 'Abbās in the seventeenth century). In the religious field, they imitated the medieval "mysteries" commemorating Christ's Passion on church forecourts, and like the Christians, set up a clerical hierarchy.

The idea pursued by Shari'ati in this book rests on the feeling that religion has been manipulated by the government to the point of being in flagrant contradiction with Koranic revelation. But the details of his argument run up against historical and philological unlikelihoods: thus, in the time of Shah 'Abbās, the "mysteries" were no longer current in Europe; the presence of a character called the Frank (or the "westerner," *farangi*) in certain *ta'ziya* is a recent phenomenon (nineteenth century) and the Frank becomes a sympathetic character in the end only because, like the Christian monk in the old stories, he is convinced of Hoseyn's holiness and converts to Islam (here the Frank is merely the counterpart of the Magi adoring the baby Jesus: the dimension of universality conferred, by an external recognition, on an event quite anodyne in itself); there is only a distant and accidental resemblance between the standard (*'alam*, or in Khorasan Persian, *jaride*, which Shari'ati says derives from the Latin *crux*!) carried in the processions of flagellants and the cross of Christian processions.

Even if Shari'ati's prejudices have more to do with fantasy than reason, they reveal the primordial importance of the mourning rituals in the Iranian collective consciousness. The history of modern Iran is closely bound up with the symbolism of Karbalā and the strong emotive charge created by the memory of Hoseyn's martyrdom.[35] Indeed it is not by chance that certain very serious events have taken place on the day of 'Āshurā, such as the violently crushed demonstrations of June 5, 1963 that marked Khomeyni's entry into history, or the spectacular procession of December 10, 1978 during which, for the first time, the slogan "Death to the Shah" (*marg bar Shah*) was used on a large scale and with much enthusiasm in

34 SHARI'ATI, *Tashayyo'-e 'alavi va tashayyo'-e safavi*, pp. 148ff.
35 J. HJARPE, "The Ta'ziya Ecstasy as Political Expression," in N. G. Holm, ed., *Religious Ecstasy*, Stockholm, Almquist & Wiksell, 1982, pp. 167–77.

place of the ritual funeral litanies. The mourning celebration turned from a sad lamentation to the jubilation of an imminent victory over the tyrant. The Shah, in fact, had been likened to Yazid, the wicked caliph.

"Everyone must know that obeying the order to fire on the people and kill constitutionalists is like obeying Yazid, the son of Mo'āviya, and is incompatible with Islam." So wrote the *ulema* who were in favour of the constitution, after the 1908 *coup d'état* which reestablished absolutism. Mirzā Mohammad-Hoseyn Nā'ini, who in 1909 provided a theological justification for the rallying of Muslims to parliamentary democracy, gave an even more precise description of the *ulema* who collaborated with the absolutist ruler Mohammad-'Ali Shah: he compared them to Hoseyn's murderers at Karbalā. And as the victims of Karbalā around the Imam numbered 72, the number of victims of the spectacular bomb attack which destroyed the Islamic Republic Party's headquarters on 28 June 1981 is still put at 72: the 72 martyrs of Islam around ayatollah Beheshti, who thus becomes the Imam Hoseyn's faithful imitator. Here, the *ta'ziya* is a performance that dramatically resembles the original . . .

Since the wicked caliph Yazid is the paradigmatic figure of the dictator, it comes as no surprise that the nation's savior should be the "Imam of the End of Time," a title pertaining to the Twelfth Imam as eschatological Saviour. In Iran, the title of *Imam* given to Khomeyni is not commonly attributed to a living person: it is reserved for the twelve successors of the Prophet Mohammad. For Arab Sunnis, an *imam* is the prayer leader in charge of a mosque. The Lebanese were therefore stretching the point when they conferred this sacred title on Musā Sadr, an Iranian cleric who, at the beginning of the 1960s, had very ably adapted himself to becoming Lebanese; *Imam* Musā Sadr bore this wrongfully assumed title until he paid the ultimate price for it since, in the summer of 1978 during a journey in Libya, he physically disappeared, "occulted" like the Twelfth Imam.[36]

Musā Sadr's precedent certainly worked for Khomeyni, but in reverse: Khomeyni lived for 15 years in "occultation" in Najaf, and Iranians had heard little of him before the first large demonstrations in 1978. During that occultation he nonetheless continued to communicate with the Iranians with the aid of a few messengers who carried his declarations to the religious militants. Actually being a descendant of the Imams (since he was a *sayyed*), Khomeyni was comparable with Hoseyn, for he had fought wickedness by leading the revolt that took place during the month of

36 F. AJAMI, *The Vanished Imam: Musa al Sadr and the Shia of Lebanon*, London, Tauris/Cornell University Press, 1986, pp. 24, 119ff.

Moharram in 1963. During the winter of 1978–9, from Paris, Khomeyni could more easily send his intransigent messages to Iran. The myth then took on its eschatological dimension: the "return of the Imam" had been envisaged by the majority of the revolutionaries as that of a saviour of the country, and no one really dared to believe in it. This much-awaited return became the event that eclipsed all opposition, even if the uprising of February 11, 1979 actually occurred outside the explicit directives of the Imam. The myth imposed itself in its all-encompassing and almost dictatorial reality, gaining for Imam Khomeyni's advantage all the subsequent development of the Revolution, even when its logic seemed to go astray.

Contrary to his own earlier declarations, ayatollah Khomeyni ran everything, but without appearing to govern directly. Whether at Qom or Tehran, he was the authority no one dared to cross and to whom the new leaders referred at the slightest difficulty. Despite the early democratically inspired plans that Khomeyni himself had approved, the 1979 constitution was developed to suit the charismatic leader he personified. In reality, the Imam enjoyed more power than the Shah had ever had. At the same time, the sacred role of "Guide of the Revolution and Founder of the Islamic Republic" (according to the official titles) was in no way diminished: having emerged from his "occultation," he was accessible only to a few personalities in the new regime. Any ordinary people who were privileged enough to approach him – his speeches were recorded and later broadcast like prophecies in all the media – came into his presence only in carefully shepherded bunches. These emotional and tearfully trembling pilgrims were coming to consult a soothsayer, to whom they brought prayers and sacred ovations, beseeching him to be kind enough to touch their children in order to ward off the evil eye. There was a real communication between him and them, but a profound ambiguity between the theologico-political sense of his words, and the genuine religion of the believer performing an almost magical deed.

In popular consciousness the vague likening of Khomeyni to an Imam brought in its wake some surprising attitudes, both peculiar to Shi'ism and also deeply marked by Iranian cultural customs. Even before Khomeyni boarded the aircraft that was to take him from Najaf to Paris, it was rumoured in Iran that his face could be seen in the moon: at night, when the curfew was mocked by cries of "God is great" (*Allāh akbar*), people vied with one another in perceiving the Imam in the luminous orb. Some months later, when he emerged from his occultation and finally arrived in Tehran (February 1, 1979), some peasants who had been in the town for a few days to go to meet him on the road between the airport and the cemetery, called at my home to come and perform their ritual ablutions so that they could be in a state of purity to meet *him*. The pilgrims from Jamārān (at the foot of the mountain, north of Tehran) similarly made their ablutions before entering the modest chapel where the Imam appeared to them. Several of the regime's dignitaries came to visit Khomeyni, during his first months at Qom, to ask him insistently for an immediate reply to the question: was he or was he not the Imam of Time? It is said that Khomeyni did not answer, thus leaving his questioners baffled . . .

The question of Khomeyni's imamate, or his closeness to the Imam, also divided the ruling circles in the Islamic Republic: the majority tendency had spread throughout the nation a slogan which everyone repeated at the Friday solemn prayers: "O! my God, while we await the Revolution of the Saviour Imam [by this was understood the return of the Hidden Imam], preserve Khomeyni for us!" In a manner perfectly in keeping with tradition, they meant by that to present Khomeyni as the one who – by virtue of his charisma – would let them await the longed-for eschatological salvation. Others, however, notably the members of a radical Islamic association founded in the 1950s to fight Bahā'ism, the Hojjatiya association, took a poor view of direct intervention in politics by the *ulema* and the secularization of religion: with everyone else they repeated the phrase asking God to preserve Khomeyni until the End of the World, but immediately added another slogan to put an end to that wait and neutralize the apparent desire for Khomeynist power to go on for ever: "Saviour Imam, come quickly, Saviour Imam, come quickly!" (*Mahdi biyā, Mahdi biyā!*).

Khomeyni was not immortal. He died on June 3, 1989. This event of course gave the lie to the illusions of some devoted believers. In itself, however, it represented a fine victory: for the first time since 1907 an Iranian head of state had died peacefully in his own country, surrounded by his nearest and dearest and his helpers. It is easy to draw up the list: Mohammad-'Ali Shah Qājār deposed by the constitutionalist Revolution in 1909, died in Savona in Italy in 1925; Ahmad Shah Qājār, shaken by a *coup d'état* in 1921, deposed by a Constituent Assembly in 1925, died in Paris in 1930; Rezā Shah Pahlavi, deposed by the British in 1941, died in 1944 in Johannesburg; and lastly Mohammad-Rezā Shah, deposed by the Islamic Revolution in 1979, died the following year in Egypt.

With the death of Khomeyni, would the central pillar of the Islamic Republic disappear, and the relief of some and despair of others leave room only for chaos? It seems that the spontaneous fervour which broke out around the remains of the vanished leader, and the vast throngs who attended his funeral, surprised even the authorities, for the burial had to be postponed several times and the body, jostled by the crowds trying to obtain mementoes, fell to the ground. The mausoleum erected over his burial-place in record time completes the consecration of the eminently Shi'ite nature of the cult devoted to Khomeyni.

LEARNED OR POPULAR SHI'ISM?

Khomeyni is the finest example of a clerical career supported by popular religiosity, the meeting of two types of religion one would have believed permanently ill-matched.

On the one hand, the cleric from the depths of the country, the son of a provincial mulla, speaking the most provincial language filled with those unmistakable peasant intonations; on the other, a long-standing hierocratic tradition. It was the career of mulla that served in this instance as a springboard for social ascent. Khomeyni's brother-in-law tells how, when the village mulla that Āqā Ruhollāh was in the 1920s asked his teacher, ayatollah Saqafi, a rich and renowned theologian originally from Tehran, for his daughter's hand in mariage, Mrs Saqafi was at first very much against it. But the professor had detected qualities in the young mulla, and gave his consent. Ruhollāh Khomeyni had not chosen the path of an *arriviste*: his penchant for mysticism and philosophy did not lead him into public preaching or the career of a great jurist to be "imitated" by the faithful. His contact with the crowds happened only belatedly, in 1963, and was interrupted by a long exile. It was his hardline determination, in a period of crisis, that won Khomeyni the devotion of his former students in Qom and the prestige he later enjoyed among the Iranians. The bloody tragedy of the Revolution, with the spontaneous need to find a figure diametrically opposed to the Shah to hound him out and take his place, afforded Khomeyni his success.

The social wretchedness of the old regime, its inability to respond to the expectations aroused by the 1973 oil boom, its betrayals with regard to the Islamic ideal, could all confer on the revolutionary struggle the aspect of an immense *ta'ziya* in which the Iranian nation itself was at war, together with its Imam, against wickedness, corruption, etc. But the *ta'ziya* spectators are content just to weep and the master of ceremonies is not the Imam; when it is all over, everyone returns to his or her place in society. The rules had been overturned and no one knew any longer who was the wicked caliph.

5

The Shi'ites outside Iran

Originally, nothing but the pure Arab lineage of the Prophet seemed to link Shi'ism with any nation, but today Iran has so transformed and acclimatized it that Persian culture and the cult of the Imams can no longer be dissociated. Persia's prestige since ancient times, the large number and high rank of Iranian Shi'ite *ulema* and the spread of their influence through all Imamite communities are the fundamentals of Shi'ite identity on which political habits have been built. This paradox then arises: whereas certain secular and "modern" nationalist Iranians try to define Islam – notably in its Twelver Shi'ite version – as a foreign, Arab religion, the majority of Muslims worldwide, Shi'ite or not, involuntarily and unconsciously establish a correlation between Imamism and Persia. The Iranian Revolution has further accentuated this association.

IRAQ

There have been Shi'ites in Mesopotamia since the time of the first Imams. The Shi'ite Community was enlarged by Bedouin tribes, who came from the Arabian peninsula up until the eighteenth century, and by conversions. For those Arabs who glorified virility, feats of arms, and a spirit of fierce independence, converting to Shi'ism was a way of escaping the control of Ottoman authority. Shi'ite proselytism was made easier "by the similarity, in the eyes of the tribesmen, between Sunnism, power, and repression; the traditional spirit of tribal independence could thus find religious expression."[1]

1 See P. MARTIN, "Les Chi'ites d'Irak: Une majorité dominée à la recherche de son destin," *L'Irak, le pétrole et la guerre, Peuples méditerranéens*, 40, Paris (July–September 1987), pp. 127–69 (here p. 129); and, further, P.-J. LUIZARD, *La Formation de l'Irak contemporain*, Paris, CNRS, 1991.

Through Shi'ism certain tribes demonstrated opposition to their own sheikhs who had remained Sunni. The absence of religiously justified allegiance to the government in power allowed them to stand back in relation to the dominant political community. This attitude was rendered easier by the scarcity of clerical leaders among the Bedouins, a fact which engendered a certain laxity in the exercise of fasting and prayer. Tribal customs mattered more to them than the law of Islam, of whatever persuasion.[2]

Present-day Iraq, carved by the 1916 Sykes–Picot agreement out of the still-smoking tatters of the Ottoman Empire, shelters a majority of Shi'ites who are today still socially disadvantaged. The Shi'ites were the ones who most violently challenged the creation of the state of Iraq, which never represented a clear national entity, by rebelling against the British in 1920. From the sixteenth century, the mausoleums of the Imams, at Najaf, Karbalā, Kāzemeyn and Samarra, were the stake in bloody conflicts between the Iranian Shi'ite empire of the Safavids and the Sunni Ottoman Turks, and remain the symbol of the Shi'ite Community's failure to win its dignity. In the eighteenth century, when the frontier of the two empires was stabilized – broadly along the present line, the Shatt ol-'Arab, a navigable river but not strategically important prior to the twentieth century – Najaf and Karbalā became great centres of Imamite theological studies.

The decline of Isfahan and Qom, subsequent to the collapse of the Safavid state (1722), was moreover accompanied by a debate on religious authority from which the Najaf clergy emerged strengthened: the *osuliyun* or rationalists recognized a kind of clerical hierarchy headed, until 1920, by one or more of the great theologians residing in Najaf.[3] These religious leaders were almost all Iranians, who had left for Iraq in order to pursue their clerical career, rather like a Catholic priest going to the Vatican. The fact that they were living outside Iranian political frontiers gave the religious dignitaries greater independence, which they used in periods of crisis to defy Tehran's political authority.

The Shi'ite social explosion in 1920 against the British Protectorate was also directed against the Sunni establishment which was taking over from Ottoman domination. The insurrection lasted a few months: it was limited to Shi'ite tribes and orchestrated by certain great *ulema*. The repression that followed a clerical ban on British-sponsored elections forced

---

2   H. BATATU, "Shi'i Organizations in Iraq: al-Da'wah al-Islamiyah and al-Mujahidin," in J. I. Cole and N. R. Keddie, eds, *Shi'ism and Social Protest*, New Haven and London, Yale University Press, 1986, pp. 186ff. On the Shi'ite tribes of South Iraq, see W. THESIGER, *The Marsh Arabs*, London, Longman & Green, 1964.
3   See above, ch. 3.

the religious leaders to go into exile shortly afterwards at Qom, in Iran; they returned to Iraq only to accept a compromise with King Faisal (1921– 33). British domination had not really been weakened, nor had Sunnite supremacy been called into question, and in a politically stabilized Iran the theological centre of Qom would henceforward take over from Najaf, accentuating the isolation of the Iraqi Shi'ites.

Under the monarchy their situation improved. Starting from 1930 some great Imami merchants broke away from the poverty of their community. A larger number of Shi'ite children received secondary education, thus gaining access to modern careers. In 1947, for the first time, a Shi'ite was appointed Prime Minister, and four out of the eight heads of government who followed until 1958 were Shi'ite; this denominational rebalancing of political life gave rise to vehement protests from the Sunnis.[4] But the Shi'ites stayed poor, and their poverty, which fueled permanent social unrest, was often used by politicians to obtain personal advantage and maintain relations with their supporters.

Social demands then overtook the demand for religious recognition, despite the transitory backing of a few *ulema*, such as ayatollah Mohammad-Hoseyn Kāshef ol-Qetā in the 1930s (he gave up political action well before his death in 1954) or later Mohammad al-Sadr, who was Prime Minister in 1948. From the 1950s communism tempted many young people, and Shi'ites joined the party *en masse*, especially in rural areas:

> Numerous points were common to Shi'ite dogma and communist ideology: defence of the oppressed, fighting injustice, opposition to the government, hatred of foreign domination, and also a certain taste for martyrs. Even the word *shoyū'i* (communist), which some people link with *shī'i* (Shi'ite). It is undeniable that these similarities favoured communist penetration into Shi'ite circles and that certain militants played on this ambiguity of words and rousing subjects, notably among peasants who were illiterate and influenced by religion.[5]

Communist leaders were well aware of what they could derive from this situation. For their propaganda they used symbols embodying Shi'ite

---

4   Ch. MALLAT, "Iraq," in S. Hunter, ed., *The Politics of Islamic Revivalism: Diversity and Unity*, Bloomington, Indiana University Press, 1988, pp. 71–87; H. BATATU, *The Old Social Classes and the Revolutionary Movements of Iraq*, Princeton, Princeton University Press, 1978; W. ENDE, "Erfolg und Scheitern eines schiitischen Modernisten: Muhammad ibn Mahdī al-Hālesī," in U. Tworuschka, ed., *Gottes ist der Orient – Gottes ist der Okzident: Festschrift für Abdoldjavad Falaturi*, Cologne and Vienna, Böhlau, 1991, pp. 120–30.
5   MARTIN, "Les Chi'ites d'Irak," p. 146. On the Iraqi Communist Party, ibid., pp. 143– 56; BATATU, *The Old Social Classes*, p. 422.

piety, such as the mourning ceremonies for Hoseyn during the month of Moharram, in which they spotted revolutionary potential. The first Ba'athist *coup d'état* in 1963 was a catastrophe for Iraqi communists, as for the Shi'ites who supported General 'Abdolkarim Qāsem (Kassim). "As the Shi'ite areas were the poorest, they were naturally the bastions of resistance to an anti-communist *coup d'état* which carried a strong whiff of social revenge . . . Everywhere in the country it was the revenge of Arab nationalists and the wealthy, in particular the Sunni bourgeoisie."[6] The subsequent repression and decline of the Communist Party drew the Shi'ites into a mobilization that was much more centred on religion.

When the Ba'athists seized control of the state in 1968, Shi'ite participation in running the Ba'ath Party, which had been equitable before 1963, fell to 6 percent. The Shi'ites were excluded, marginalized, and from then on the Iraqi government ruling party turned Sunni. From 1968 to 1977, among the fifteen members of the Revolutionary Command Council, not one was Shi'ite, and only 5 percent of the leaders of the Ba'ath Party were Shi'ites. Starting from that date, those close to Saddam Hussein, mostly Sunnis from the village of Takrit, took over key posts for themselves. The militarization of the regime still further disadvantaged the Shi'ites, who have never attained higher ranks in careers as officers.

This unfavorable political climate and the social distress must be borne in mind if we are to understand the politicization of religious feeling detectable among Iraqi Shi'ites since the 1950s. The high-ranking clerics, dominated by a "quietist" trend, took no part – a fact that further distanced them from the mass of the people – although they were already concentrated in the religious towns, mainly Najaf, and burning problems such as the proclamation of the state of Israel, social questions and problems of independence in relation to colonial powers (Mosaddeq, Nasser) were stirring up the masses. However, in 1959 at Najaf, the spectre of communism caused the creation of the Association of *Ulema* (*Jamā'at 'olamā' al-din*) and the publication of a cultural magazine, *al-Adhwa' al-eslāmiya* (The Enlightenment of Islam), to which a certain Mohammad-Bāqer al-Sadr (nephew of the former Prime Minister Mohammad al-Sadr) contributed. The aim was to fight the influence of communism which was penetrating clerical circles in Najaf itself. When the Iraqi ayatollah Mohsen al-Hakim Tabātabā'i became supreme chief of the Shi'ite Community, he encouraged a resocialization of youth through Islam in order to regain control of a Community dreaming more of Moscow than Najaf. In the crucial period from 1961 to his death in 1970, Hakim was recognized as a "Guide to

6 MARTIN, "Les Chi'ites d'Irak," p. 153.

imitate" (*marja' al-taqlid*) by the majority of Shi'ites, including – with a certain amount of pressure on the part of the Shah, who was seeking to de-Iranize Shi'ism the better to de-Shi'itize Iran – Iranians. Khomeyni, in exile at Najaf at that time, had learned a lesson from the failure of the 1963 uprising and was fighting against the apolitical tendency of part of the Shi'ite clergy.[7]

The first movement to see the light of day was the *Da'wat al-eslāmiya* ("Call of Islam") Party, commonly known as Da'wa. It was born from a background of Shi'ite disaffection from their religious institutions, with a disturbing slide in the number of theology students. In 1957 only 20 percent of the students at Najaf were Arab, 46 percent being Iranian, which shows the marginalization of clerical office and its lack of attraction for the young Shi'ites of Iraq.[8] According to some, the Da'wa party was the continuation of the Association of Fighting *Ulema*, so called after 1960. It seems, however, that in the 1970s this organization was clearly rid of its clerics and even earned the disapproval of the clergy because of its connections, real or supposed, with the Shah of Iran. Prior to 1975, he appears to have used this lever (by funding or internal manipulations) as he then made use of Kurdish autonomists in order to put pressure on Baghdad.[9] On the occasion of demonstrations of discontent in rural areas, notably during the Moharram mourning period, the Da'wa militants launched slogans hostile to the Ba'athist regime and Saddam Hussein. Although in theory the Shah ceased all pressure after the Agreement of Algiers (which on March 6, 1975 put an end to a long period of hostility between Iran and Iraq), the Shi'ites' discontent remained strong and rose in parallel with pre-revolutionary tension in Iran.

Loyal to its secular line, the Iraqi government tried at all costs to avoid a politicization of religion which would soon have escaped its control.[10] Saddam Hussein chose a stick-and-carrot policy. He had five members of the Da'wa executed in 1974, and another eight in 1977. He ruthlessly put down demonstrations in the wretched Shi'ite quarter of Baghdad, al-Thowra, and had no hesitation in sending in tanks to attack the procession celebrating the 40th day after 'Āshurā at Najaf in 1977. On several occasions he had thousands of Iranian citizens who had lived in Iraq for generations expelled

7   H. ALGAR, "The Oppositional Role of the Ulama in Twentieth-Century Iran," in N. R. Keddie, ed., *Scholars, Saints and Sufis*, Berkeley, Los Angeles, and London, University of California Press, 1972, pp. 231–55 (here, p. 244).
8   BATATU, "Shi'i Organizations in Iraq," p. 189.
9   Ibid., p. 194.
10   Ibid., p. 196.

from the country. Over 75,000 Shi'ites took refuge in Iran in the 1970s, victims as much of their ethnic origin (dangerous in the context of the latent war developing between Iran and Iraq) as of their Imamite persuasion: they were a difficult minority to assimilate in a state boasting of its Arab and secular qualities, and very marked by Sunni dominance. But at the same time, the Iraqi government made an effort to satisfy non-political *ulema* by allocating vast funds to the upkeep of mausoleums, mosques, *hoseyniya*, and other religious buildings. The Imam 'Ali's birthday was decreed a public holiday, and when the head of state visited the sacred places of Shi'ism he delivered speeches punctuated with references to the Imams to gain approval for his policies. If the occasion warranted, Saddam Hussein even declared himself to be a descendant of the Prophet and Imam Hoseyn . . .

In the face of this aggressive policy, the Iraqi clergy adopted contradictory attitudes. Those who were more realistic, headed by a nonagenarian Iranian who, despite his age, was one of the most influential of all the Shi'ite clerics, ayatollah Abo'l-Qāsem Kho'i (1899–1992), adopted the most rigorous "quietism:" in his view the Shi'ite *ulema* were not to intervene in the affairs of the state, and religion belonged to the domain of personal conscience, which must at all costs be preserved from government pressures. The advantage of this attitude was that Kho'i was never troubled by the political power except in 1991 when Saddam forced him to appear on television to condemn Shi'i uprisings after the Kuwait War.

The other line was political militancy, chiefly that of ayatollah Mohammad-Bāqer al-Sadr. Born in 1935 at Kāzemeyn, into a great Iraqi clerical family of Lebanese origin, he followed a religious career at Najaf, where he was notably the disciple of ayatollah Kho'i.[11] His first work, published in 1955, defends the Shi'ite point of view in an old polemic: the right of ownership over the estate of Fadak, which had belonged to the Prophet, demanded by his daughter Fatima, contrary to the opinion of the Sunni caliphs. Some years later, as we have seen, al-Sadr became the editorial writer of the Association of *Ulema* magazine, *al-Adhwa*, which brought him much renown. In his publications of that time, al-Sadr tackled the burning ideological problems, starting with communism, in the face of which he presented

11   P. MARTIN, "Une grande figure de l'islamisme en Irak (Muhammad Baqer al-Sadr)," *Cahiers de l'Orient*, 8–9 (1987–8), pp. 117–42; Ch. MALLAT, *The Renewal of Islamic Law: Muhammad Baqer as-Sadr, Najaf and the Shi'i International*, Cambridge, New York and Oakleigh, Cambridge University Press, 1993; *idem*, "Religious Militancy in Contemporary Iraq: Muhammad Baqer as-Sadr and the Sunni–Shia paradigm," in A. Gauhar, ed., *Third World Quarterly: Islam and Politics*, 10, 2 (April 1988), pp. 699–729.

Islam as the source of a philosophy superior to other currents of thinking, chiefly Marxism and materialism. He similarly attacked capitalism.

In *Eqtesādonā* (Our Economy), which remains his fundamental work, he endeavours to use only references that are acceptable to both Sunnis and Shi'ites, which signals a development compared with his first book. He recommends a system of limited private ownership, that has consideration for serving the Community and avoids usury and monopolizing. It is a market economy in which the state plays a regulatory role. In all his analyses, Islam has a central role and appears as "the one and only alternative for solving the problems of our times."[12] A prolific writer, Bāqer al-Sadr tackled the widest variety of topics and even drew up the plan of a constitution for the Islamic Republic of Iran in 1979: its echoes were noticeable in the constitution adopted by the constitutional experts in Tehran, but also in the writings and thinking of all his contemporaries, in Iraq as well as in Iran and the Lebanon, where his works were disseminated and translated. His militant activity took him to places where religious preaching had hitherto seemed impossible, on university campuses, at great ritual gatherings, and mass meetings.

The effervescence created among Iraqi Shi'ites at the time of the Iranian Revolution had its hero, Mohammad-Bāqer al-Sadr, who was already regarded as the theoretician behind that revolution because he had been the first to impart a constitutional dimension to the Khomeynist principle of the *velāyat-e faqih*. The Iraqi Shi'ites believed they had found in him someone who would help them to attempt, between the Tigris and the Euphrates, an experiment similar to that of Iran. Social unrest increased and terrorist attacks were perpetrated. Bāqer al-Sadr was first arrested then released in 1979. Having assigned him a forced residence in Najaf, the Ba'ath Party tried to extract concessions from him, notably that he should withdraw his *fatvā* anathematizing party members. Political pressure tightened on Shi'ite institutions. On April 1, 1980, Tareq 'Aziz, the deputy Prime Minister, escaped a murderous attack by the Da'wa. Four days later Mohammad-Bāqer al-Sadr and his sister, Bent al-Hodā, were executed.

The conflict between the Shi'ites and the Iraqi state seems rooted less in ideological opposition than in past history and the social situation. Less rich and fertile than in Iran, Iraq's Shi'ism enjoyed a strategic position because of the holy places that for over two centuries were the principal theological centre for all Shi'ites. But it was the Iranians who most frequently played the leading role there. Only a few exceptional figures, such

12   For a detailed analysis of *Eqtesādonā*, see MALLAT, *The Renewal*, pp. 109ff.

as Mohammad-Bāqer al-Sadr, stood out from this provincial and disadvantaged Community whose chief rival was the Communist Party. In this young country, made wealthy too quickly by oil, the autocratic political culture did not allow the game of challenging the establishment to assume sophisticated forms, and brutal executions were the only remedy that the Ba'athist government could find to neutralize opposition. The Iraqi Shi'ites tended to turn to Iran as to their brothers, without realizing that Tehran's intentions were not wholly pure, and in return used this Community – in the majority but treated like a minority by the state – as a Trojan horse which the Baghdad government always mistrusted.

Such was, indeed, the great unknown factor in 1979, when ayatollahs who were suddenly far more interested than the Shah in their Arab neighbours were establishing themselves in Iran. As they had lived in Iraq, Khomeyni and some of his close associates thought that the Shi'ite Community in that country would offer easy access to their propaganda. It would be difficult to imagine a stronger ideological antagonism than that between the young Islamic Republic of Iran and the secular nationalism of the Ba'ath party. The strategic *rapprochement* between Baghdad and Tehran in 1975 had been effected at the expense of the Kurds and had also resulted in the tightening of the surveillance measures restricting ayatollah Khomeyni's contacts in Najaf. Shortly after the head of the Iranian Revolution had gone to France, the Iranian empress made a pilgrimage to Najaf as a last attempt on the part of the monarchy to manipulate to its own advantage the connection between Iranians and the principal Shi'ite places in Iraq . . .

The war did not produce, on the population of either country, the effects expected by the rulers of the enemy nation. The Khuzistan Arabs, whose territory became the principal battlefield after September 1980, chose for the most part to withdraw into the interior of Iran; as for the Iraqi Shi'ites, heavily surrounded and intimidated by the police, they did not budge in favour of Iran. It is possible that Iraqi propaganda managed to arouse patriotic reactions among the Shi'ite population, an Arab solidarity against the "aggression" of the Persians. Saddam Hussein was careful to handle Shi'ite sensitivity tactfully in his speeches, presenting Khomeyni as a miscreant innovator, and himself redoubling his gestures of piety, visiting holy places, showing particular deference in regard to the apolitical Iranian ayatollah Kho'i, making references to his own lineage which he traced back as far as the Prophet, etc. The Iraqi president blew hot and cold on the Shi'ites: on the one hand, he carried out massive expulsions to Iran of Shi'ites having family links (distant ancestry or union by marriage) with

Iran, alarming all the many people who could also be liable to this fate; on the other, he granted funds to those *ulema* who had remained kindly disposed to the regime, and distributed enormous sums for the renovation of the sanctuaries of Najaf ($220 million) and Karbalā ($60 million), with all the beneficial repercussions for the local economy of these places of pilgrimage.[13]

In March 1991, after the Kuwait War and the Iraqi defeat, a huge uprising of Shi'ites in the south of Iraq rudely reminded the world of their large number in that country. One of the leaders of the religious movement in opposition to the Ba'ath Party, ayatollah Bāqer al-Hakim (son of ayatollah Mohsen al-Hakim), prepared himself for a national future. Exiled to Tehran since the beginning of the Iran–Iraq war (1980), his determination to fight the Baghdad Ba'athist regime could only be reinforced in 1983 by the execution at Najaf of seven of his close relatives and the arrest of about 100 others. He led the Iraq Higher Council of Islamic Revolution, a body which was unsuccessful in rallying opponents to the Ba'athist regime (either Kurds, or certain other parties, such as the Da'wa, which supported an alliance with non-religious tendencies). Another organization, *'Amal al-eslāmi* (Islamic Action), was founded in 1982 at Damascus by the *hojjat ol-eslām* Mohammad-Taqi Modarresi, and managed a few successful attacks on Iraqi soil.

Even in isolation, Bāqer al-Hakim demonstrated a certain ability in mobilizing volunteers to help Iran in the war between 1980 and 1988; after the Kuwait War, he lacked Iran's political and military backing to confirm his ability to dominate the Shi'ite revolt in southern Iraq: it was doubtless proof that reasons of state were beginning to win the day in Tehran, where the dismantling of Iraq stirred up a series of concomitant problems, such as the demand for Kurdish autonomy and the Syrian and Turkish anxiety over regional stability. Iran also had to strike a balance with those states in the region which had participated in the anti-Iraqi coalition in 1990–1. Iran's regaining of a leading regional position was by way of this concession.

The failure of the Shi'ite revolt and Iran's caution did not settle the Iraqi problem. Following the Kuwait War the international embargo most affected the Shi'ite populations in the south, whose international isolation is greater than the others'. The death of ayatollah Abo'l-Qāsem Kho'i in 1992 gave even further help to the state's attempts to control this minority. Iran

13   P. ROBINS, "Iraq: Revolutionary Threats and Regime Responses," in J. L. Esposito, ed., *The Iranian Revolution: Its Global Impact*, Miami, Florida International University Press, 1990, pp. 83–99.

would like the future *marja' al-taqlid* recognized by all Shi'ites to be an Iranian, and one in favour of the Khomeynist spirit of politicizing religion. In the absence of a candidate obtaining an unanimous vote, things seem on course for a division of the Community, the Iraqis having managed to gain recognition for the authority of a cleric from Najaf who is more receptive to the pressures of the Iraqi government than those of Tehran. In Iran itself, the supporters of ayatollah Montazeri, who was turned down by Khomeyni before he died, are confronted by both a strong apolitical current and the radical heirs of the Revolution.

THE ARABIAN PENINSULA

Whatever their proportion in each of their countries, in the minority in Saudi Arabia, or in the majority in Bahrain, the Arab Shi'ites of the Persian Gulf have for a very long time been subjected to a regime of discrimination on the part of the Sunnis.[14] Even with the more effective protection they have enjoyed for half a century, they are everywhere under-represented at the political level (parliaments and governments). Only the economic prosperity resulting from oil production (notably in Saudi Arabia where enormous stocks lie in a region peopled by Shi'ites) has allowed certain members of these communities to acquire wealth and alleviate social tensions.

One of the weakening factors of these Shi'ites is the diversity of their origins. Some come from old local stock, others from former Iranian colonies (the Baharna of Bahrain), and others have arrived recently from poor Iraqi tribes. The economic and human influence of Iran, to which it is so natural to turn if difficulties arise, does not put matters right here any more than in Iraq. But what makes coexistence between Sunnis and Shi'ites particularly difficult is the domination over the Arab kingdom by the most puritan and fundamentalist sect of Islam, the Wahhābis (they call themselves the monotheists, *movahhedun*) who abhor Shi'ism. To give but one example, the Wahhābis have no minaret on their mosques, and raise no tomb or mausoleum for their dead, whatever their rank may have been. Kings and beggars alike are buried in the bare earth, and not a single stone lies above the level of the ground. In their eyes, the cult of the Imams is a form of polytheism, and the devotions of pilgrims at the saints' tombs – even if it were that of the Prophet himself – is sheer paganism.

14 J. KOSTINER, "Kuwait and Bahrain," in Hunter, *The Politics of Islamic Revivalism*, pp. 116–29, notably p. 118.

The Shi'ite pilgrims going to Medina weep (and hide their tears because of the Wahhābis) as they pass a spot where, according to the ancients, Fatima's tomb lies, no longer marked by any distinguishing sign, close to the tomb of the Prophet. As for Fatima's Orchard, situated in the courtyard of the same mosque, it has quite simply vanished in the course of extension work carried out under the Saudi dynasty. The Baqi' cemetery, at Medina, which contains the mausoleums of several Imams and which Shi'ites visit without fail during the Pilgrimage (*Hajj*), was first destroyed by the Wahhābis in 1804, and a second time in 1926: 'Abdol'aziz Al Sa'ud gave the order to destroy the cupolas built over the tombs, which aroused great indignation in all the Shi'ite regions, notably in Iran and India. A European traveller who had come to Medina in 1926

> found that al-Baqi' looked like a razed town. It was strewn with a rubble of earth, timber, iron bars, bricks, cement, etc., through which paths had been cleared. It was said that 10,000 of the Companions of the Prophet had been buried there, but all graves, from those of the Prophet's family, of 'Uthmān ('Osmān), Mālik b. Anas and other well known Muslims, to the palmfrond graves of the poor, were systematically destroyed.[15]

The degree of oppression suffered by the Shi'ites in this country will be better understood when we learn that those who were given the task of destroying the Baqi' tombs were themselves Shi'ites from Medina, the Nakhāvila. These pariahs, who had only the most menial work, numbered about 10,000. They lived in an area kept for them alone (today destroyed by the Saudis), for they were not permitted to live within the town's walls, or to pray at the Prophet's mosque. They claimed to be descended from the *Ansār*, who were associated with the Prophet after he settled in Medina, but others think they are descended from African slaves.

Although the Iranian Islamic Revolution caused great anxiety to the monarchies of the peninsula, who suddenly discovered, when comparing their situation with that of the Shah, that their prosperity based on oil revenues was no protection against profound crises, there was no direct threat in these societies, which were relatively little politicized in the modern sense, and dominated by Sunnis.

The seizure of the great mosque in Mecca on November 20, 1979 by a visionary, Juheyman b. Mohammad b. Seyf al-'Oteybi, whom it required

15 B. WINDER, "Al-Madina," *Encyclopedia of Islam*, 2nd edn, vol. V (1986) s.v.; recent description: S. ZEGHIDOUR, *La Vie quotidienne à la Mecque de Mahomet à nos jours*, Paris, Hachette, 1989, pp. 335–46.

over a fortnight to dislodge with heavy arms and the help of French gendarmes, had nothing to do directly with Iran. Juheyman was a Saudi, a former member of the national guard, and the one he wanted to proclaim Mahdi ("saviour") was his brother-in-law, Mohammad b. ʾAbdollāh al-Qahtāni, a young man of 27 who had been a theological student in Medina. Both were even more fundamentalist than the Saudi monarchy, that is to say, there was nothing Shiʾite about them, except perhaps their desire to impart a profound millenarian sense to the advent of the fifteenth century of Islam (in the lunar calendar, that very day marked the entry into the year 1400 of the Hegira). Among the insurgents, 63 of whom were beheaded in public, there were Saudis, Egyptians, Kuwaitis, Pakistanis, and American members of the Black Muslims.[16]

LEBANON

In this small country created by the French after the First World War with the aim of establishing a territorial unit where the Christians of the Levant would be in the majority, the Shiʾites exist only as a relic of the long-distant past, gone to ground in the mountains of Jabal ʾĀmel where they took refuge in the Middle Ages to escape the intolerance of triumphant Sunnism. They were dominated by feudal *bey* who cared little about religion or social reform.[17] It was at the end of the eighteenth century, so it would seem, that this Shiʾite Community suffered most, under the attacks of the fierce Ottoman governor Ahmad Pāshā al-Jazzār, "the Butcher," who ruined and annihilated a region which until then had had the reputation of being prosperous and trouble-free for the Imamis. Those who survived practiced dissimulation (*taqiya*): they were crushed and forced into subjection. Stifled by enterprising Maronites and despised by the Sunnis, the Shiʾites of this region never had the means of making themselves heard by the Ottoman administration, if they had a voice, that is, or wanted to be heard. Moreover, they were not known as "Shiʾites" or "Imamis," which would have been tantamount to acknowledging that they had an identity, linking them with a Community and a belief, but as *metwāli* (*motavāli*), a term obscure in origin, associated with derogatory

16 ZEGHIDOUR, *La Vie quotidienne à la Mecque*, pp. 397ff.; W. OCHSENWALD "Saudi Arabia," in Hunter, *The Politics of Islamic Revivalism*, pp. 103–15, notably 108ff.
17 F. AJAMI, *The Vanished Imam: Musa al Sadr and the Shia of Lebanon*, London, I. B. Tauris and Cornell University Press, 1986, pp. 52–84.

gibes, humiliation, and persecution.[18] In reality this humiliated Community was making ready to enter the world's history: it was more complex and varied than the Iraqi Shi'ite Community, at all events much more so than it appeared.

Did the Shi'ites emerge from their torpor at the advent of a modern state and citizenship? As early as 1925, at the time of the Druze rebellion, French administrators had put their cringing submissiveness to the test: they made no move. Promises of road-building projects, irrigation works, the founding of schools and hospitals remained in the archives of official speeches and electoral campaigns. Nobody worried. Neither Lebanese identity, taken over by the Maronites, nor Arab nationalism, monopolized by the Sunnis, could have motivated political movement on the part of such an impoverished community, estimated on the eve of independence (1943) at about 200,000 inhabitants, that is, well below the Maronite or Sunni communities.

After the Second World War, many young Lebanese Shi'ites who had struggled to make their way to Beirut and college, were led on to the path of communism or the secular socialism of the Ba'ath by the ineffectuality and egoism of the feudal lords. There was certainly very little likelihood of their turning towards the *ulema*, whose socio-economic status was disastrous and who had made it a rule not to intervene in political matters. The low level of education and social consciousness of the Lebanese Shi'ite clergy in the 1960s is harshly described by one of Imam Musā Sadr's companions:

> The man of religion in our midst covered himself with his *abaya*, put his head on his hand, and went to sleep. He woke up only to tell others to sleep. He lives a stagnant life; don't be fooled by any motion he makes for it is usually backward. The man of religion does two kinds of harm: once when he falls behind, and once when he pulls others with him . . . He, the man of religion, has stuffed his mind with the most impossible fantasies and miracles and myths.[19]

Against this sombre horizon, the first breath of change was the inescapable opening up of the rural areas. Despite the lack of roads, poverty drove the Shi'ites to join their bolder cousins who had preceded them in the rural

18 AJAMI, *The Vanished Imam*, p. 155. According to Dozy, *Supplément aux dictionnaires arabes*, vol. II, p. 852, they are called this because they are "close (*tavallu'*) to 'Ali and his family."

19 Najib Jamal al-Din, quoted by AJAMI, *The Vanished Imam*, pp. 74ff.

exodus, to huddle in the shanty towns of Beirut. Harsh contact with what sociologists call "world economy" was also made through exile in Black Africa where powerful networks of Lebanese Shi'ite traders allowed links to be maintained with the home country. Other factors played their part, such as the Palestinian problem which destabilized the artifical equilibrium of the Lebanon, beginning with the south, where operations against Israel and reprisals generally resulted in harming innocent populations who suffered the attacks without being able to defend themselves.

Even before the arrival of Musā Sadr, Lebanese *ulema* who had done their theological studies in Najaf were worried about the weakness of their community. They were revitalizing a certain intellectual life that had been kept up since 1908 by the magazine *al-'Erfān*.[20]

One of the *ulema* who made his mark on the development of Lebanese Shi'ism, Mohammad-Javād Maqniya (or Moghniya, 1904–79), is relatively well known outside Lebanon, and some of his works have even been translated and published in Iran.[21] Born into a family of *ulema* of southern Lebanon, orphaned at the age of 12, he was acquainted with poverty. In 1925 he managed to join clandestinely (for want of a passport) his elder brother in Najaf, in Iraq, and became a pupil of the Iranian ayatollah Abo'l-Qāsem Kho'i. With British domination over Iraq he discovered politics and, in the course of eleven years, formed solid friendships among the *ulema* in all Shi'ite regions, in Iran, Iraq, and Lebanon. Coming back to Lebanon, he took on the ministry of his deceased brother in a village near Tyre. He soon realized that the theology he had learnt in Najaf was no help in improving his contacts with the peasants or solving their problems. His refusal to cooperate with the rich landowners brought him threats from the feudal lords. After acquiring the reputation of an upright and active cleric, having mosques built and defending the poor, in 1948 he obtained a post as judge on a *ja'farite* (Shi'ite) legal tribunal in Beirut. But he was put under a great deal of pressure to stop taking progressive stands or to quit his office as magistrate. "Each of my works," he wrote, "is like a lightning bolt striking communists, atheists, capitalists, imperialists, and their treacherous maneuvers." Maqniya committed himself in favor of Nasser and was fired with enthusiasm for Algerian independence.

Apparently little inclined to let his cause lie idle in order to accept

20 Ch. MALLAT, *Shi'i Thought from the South of Lebanon*, Oxford, Centre for Lebanese Studies, 1988, pp. 9ff.
21 K.-H. GÖBEL, *Moderne schiitische Politik und Staatsidee*, Opladen, Leske and Budrich, 1984, pp. 65–139.

honors, Maqniya had strained relations with Musā Sadr, whose success must have put him in the shade.[22] He seems to have reproached him for pushing ahead too far in denominationalism and a "politicking" type of politics, which worked in favour of the common enemy, Israel. On several occasions, notably on a journey to Cairo in 1963 during which he met Sheikh Shaltut and spoke with him about the ecumenical *rapprochement* between Sunni and Shi'ite Muslims, and during his pilgrimage to Mecca in 1964, Maqniya evinced his interest in interdenominational dialogue. He saw its limitations when visiting the ruins of the Baqi' cemetery at Medina and noted the hardening of the Wahhābis' doctrinal positions *vis-à-vis* the Shi'ites.

But what particularly distinguished Maqniya was his definition of political power, a subject of great controversy among Imamite Shi'ites. Maqniya expressed himself on this topic in 1961 in a first book on "*Shi'ism and Rulers*", then in 1970 in a study on "*The Imamate of 'Ali between Reason and the Koran*"; and lastly "*Khomeyni and the Islamic Government*," published in 1979 shortly before his death, criticizes Khomeynist positions on the *velāyat-e faqih* (supervision by the theologian-jurist). A progressive Lebanese cleric, trying to elevate the political discourse of his community to rival the westernized discourse of the Maronites or the Nasserian socialist and nationalist discourse of the Sunnis, could do nothing other than minimize the true inclination of Shi'ism to favour a dictatorial power or at least an inspired (if not enlightened) despotism. Maqniya was moreover acquainted with other different types of Shi'ite Community besides that of the Lebanon: in 1966 he had been invited to Bahrain, where he noted the ossified nature of the clergy and their tendency to Akhbārism (a doctrine giving primacy to tradition over interpretation and, in his opinion, leading to the numbing of thought); in 1976, also, he was invited by ayatollah Shari'at-madāri to teach at Qom; there he formed fruitful contacts with a classic Shi'ism, very lively and restless, but well established and unrivalled in the country.

For Maqniya the tradition of the Shi'ite Imams justified rebellion against any despotic power. Revolution against corruption and tyranny must be preached wherever submission would lead to a denial of Islam. The best type of government would be a form of democracy, a way of expressing, for our own times, the Imamate or caliphate. Maqniya kept his expressions of opinion moderate as long as possible, so that a too clearly Shi'ite position should not estrange the Sunnis. But at Qom, before a public that was

22   Ibid., pp. 88ff.

Shi'ite and relatively restricted, Maqniya stated more clearly his great fear of the western influence that works through the cultural research done by Islamologists and the fascination felt by Muslims for their methods of research; he directly approached the problem of the claim of Islamic legitimacy to govern, moving slightly away from his previous "progressive" stance.[23] According to him, the Sunnis have no *democratic* superiority compared with the *aristocratic* doctrine of Shi'ism which recognizes that no one other than descendants of the Prophet has a legitimate right to manage the government. In fact, says Maqniya, unanimity of opinions is rarely achieved, and a majority is not of necessity rational; it may even let itself be led astray by base argument and go as far as imposing its will on minorities by dictatorial means. There is therefore nothing to equal a doctrine that is independent of men's capriciousness. As regards the economy, there is no absolute formula, and any system that respects the rights of the weak is compatible with Islam.

In these moderate Shi'ite positions one can recognize the sphere of influence of the great ayatollah Shari'at-madāri who, at the beginning of the Islamic Republic, was Khomeyni's conservative rival. And if, only a few weeks after the Islamic Revolution's victory in Tehran, Maqniya published his last book, criticizing the new regime's over-radical principles, it was because he was in profound disagreement with Imam Khomeyni over the interpretation of the *velāyat-e faqih*: the "supervision by the religious jurist" defined by nineteenth-century Shi'ite theologians is confined, according to our Lebanese cleric, to the juridical and private sphere.[24] There is danger in entrusting too great powers to professionals in religious law (*mojtaheds*), who at the very most are empowered to verify that laws conform to Islam. No one man or group, Maqniya continues, is entitled to monopolize political power, over which men should have ample control through elections (a guarantee granted in theory in the Iranian Islamic constitution of 1979).

With Maqniya, two trends of Lebanese Shi'ism appear clearly: the recent and painful awakening of that community to political problems, and its fascination with Iran, the mother-community from which it cannot avoid seeking support, even while wanting to dissociate itself. It was traditionally the concern of the Iranian state, even well before the 1979 revolution, to

---

23   Ibid., pp. 128ff.
24   Ibid., pp. 131ff.; H. ENAYAT, "Iran: Khumayni's Concept of the 'Guardianship of the Jurisconsult,'" in J. P. Piscatori, ed., *Islam in the Political Process*, Cambridge, Cambridge University Press, 1983, pp. 160–80.

present itself as the Shi'ite realm, the only country in the world where power was exercised in the name of the absent Imam. The photograph of the Shah of Iran was pinned up in the homes of poor Lebanese Shi'ites in the nineteenth century, a sign of the spread of influence already extended by Iran.[25]

From Submission to Revolt

Moreover, it was an Iranian, distantly connected with Lebanese soil but speaking Arabic with a Persian accent, who would crystallize the Lebanese Shi'ite Community's immense potential for violence into a veritable political movement. This man, of superior physical and intellectual stature, Musā Sadr, one day came up with the formula that sums up the later development of Lebanese Shi'ism: on 18 February 1974, about a year before the start of the civil war and four years before the unleashing of the Iranian Islamic Revolution, he declared before a large audience:

> Our name is not *metwāli* [a name for the Lebanese Shi'a with derogatory connotations, see above]; our name is "men of refusal" [*rāfidun*], "men of vengeance," "men who revolt against all tyranny" [*kharijun*], even though this costs us our blood and our lives. Hoseyn faced the enemy with seventy men; the enemy was very numerous. Today we are more than seventy, and our enemy is not the quarter of the whole world.
>
> We do not want sentiments, but action. We are tired of words, feelings, speeches . . . I have made more speeches than anyone else. And I am the one who most often called for calm . . . I have made enough appeals for calm. From today on I will not keep silent. If you keep quiet, I will not . . .[26]

By rejecting the degrading name of *Metwāli*, Musā Sadr restored hope and dignity to the Lebanese Shi'ites. The name *rāfezi* was also, historically, the one the Sunnis called them, but it had a connotation of militancy, of struggle freely engaged in. From then on, the despised and resourceless masses had an identity jealous of its honour. Lebanese Shi'ism was born.

Who was Musā Sadr? Born in 1928 at Qom, in Iran, the son of a *sayyed*

---

25 T. JABER, "Le Discours shi'ite sur le pouvoir," *Liban, remises en cause, Peuples méditerranéens*, 20 (July–September 1982), p. 91, no. 26.

26 AJAMI, *The Vanished Imam*, p. 155; A. R. NORTON, "The Origins and Resurgence of Amal," in M. Kramer, ed., *Shi'ism, Resistance and Revolution*, Boulder, Colo., Westview Press, and London, Mansell, 1987, p. 205.

who had spent the greater part of his life in Najaf, Sadr had distant paternal ancestors, the Sadroddins, who had left the Lebanese mountains for Mesopotamia in the eighteenth century, driven out by the persecutions and attracted by the holy places and theological studies.[27] Through his mother, he was descended from an Iranian clerical family. Coming to Najaf in the 1950s in order to perfect his Arabic and do his apprenticeship in religious studies, the young Sayyed Musā Sadr had placed himself under the protection of the great ayatollah Mohsen al-Hakim, who later became the spiritual leader of all the Shi'ites (1961–70). In Najaf, among the Lebanese clerics, he met a certain Sayyed 'Abd ol-Hoseyn, whose "see" was Tyre in southern Lebanon, where he had acquired a reputation for a fiercely independent spirit, chiefly in regard to the French. The supranational dimension of Shi'ism here came into full play: by writing into his will an invitation to this young and brilliant Iranian mulla to succeed him, Sayyed 'Abd ol-Hoseyn doubtless had the presentiment that he would be injecting new blood into a community that had grown too parochial and humdrum. By accepting this ministry, Sayyed Musā Sadr renounced the outstanding religious career to which he had been destined at Qom. He left to venture into a small country where the Shi'ites were a minority group, dominated and wretched. He abandoned a country where distances were measured in hundreds of kilometres for a territory where kilometres were counted almost one at a time.

From his height of over 6 ft, this man, who was always elegant, immaculate, with a well-trimmed beard and polished shoes, inspired spontaneous respect. He had the aura of an Imam. Shi'ites are very sensitive to the physical attractiveness of those they honor: a one-eyed or lame Imam is unimaginable (in Iran, Khomeyni's successor, 'Ali Khamena'i, thus had to overcome the paralysis of his right arm, due to a terrorist attack, which theoretically rendered him unsuitable for supreme office).

> By his charisma (wrote Ghassan Tueni) he obliged his enemies and friends alike to venerate him, to respect his insight. His credibility was never questioned, in spite of the rumors concerning his origins . . . [He was] tall, very tall: to the point of seeming to soar above the often frenzied crowds that his presence drew together: black turban tilted with a slight negligence. His enemies seemed charmed by his enigmatic and benevolent smile, whereas his friends found that his bearded face constantly reflected profound melancholy . . . One often had the impression, watching him, that his immense head was

27 AJAMI, *The Vanished Imam*, pp. 42–51.

constantly trying to rise even higher. And his hands gave the impression of gathering up his floating robe, the *abaya* in which he wrapped himself, as if he were preparing to step out of some antique miniature.

Even while he harangued the masses, his words were calm and sibylline, an oracle of love and hope, punctuated with the mysterious accents of some mystic vision that appealed as much to reason as to the heart.

His personal contacts were a ritual of seduction. When he would humbly open the door and invite you to enter a modest office or an ordinary salon of some home which sheltered him, one would wonder why this man was there, by what mystery, and how such a mythic persona could seem so familiar.[28]

Replying to the objections of the best-intentioned Lebanese *ulema*, like those of Javād Maqniya quoted earlier, Sayyed Musā Sadr addressed the clerics as follows:

> There are those who cannot deal with dedication and commitment. They have linked my initiatives to political movements – local, Arab, and foreign – without shame, without any evidence. There is no reason for suspicion. The only reason is that I took the man of religion [*rajul al-din*] into the social realm, that I removed from him the dust of ages.[29]

A man of action, Musā Sadr had the good fortune to arrive in Lebanon in 1959 (after a preliminary trip in 1957), in the era when Shi'ite rural enclaves were being opened up, when the car, the radio, and soon television were bringing villages out of their isolation. At the same time, the upsurge in African nationalisms and the coming of independence drove many Lebanese merchants in Africa to return to their homeland and reinvest their wealth in a way that developed their communities' economy. This was also the period, after a short civil war, when the Lebanese state was taken in hand by an efficient military man, Fu'ād Shehāb (1958–64). Musā Sadr – and he was blamed for this – chose to collaborate with the new president. He had the temerity to join with Christians in development schemes. On various occasions he preached in churches, which created a scandal – and photographs of him in front of the cross were shown in order to discredit him. In Tyre, where the Shi'ite majority systematically boycotted small Christian businesses, after a meeting he drew journalists towards the stall of a Maronite icecream seller: "What flavor will you give me today?" he asked him, knowing full well that with this simple sentence he was saving

28 Gh. TUENI, *Une guerre pour les autres*, Paris, Jean-Claude Lattès, 1985, pp. 97–8.
29 AJAMI, *The Vanished Imam*, p. 85.

the poor man from bankruptcy. He traveled openly in Europe to meet the scattered Shi'ite communities. In 1968, at Strasbourg University, he took part with orientalists (including Henry Corbin) in an international symposium on Imamite Shi'ism.

His style, it may be seen, was resolutely "modern", with no "hang-ups." For Musā Sadr no subject was taboo: he accepted the idea that – in certain circumstances – abortion was permissible, that a Christian could marry a Muslim woman without recanting, and he doubted that polygamy was really in keeping with religious law.[30] This man, whose high level of education was acknowledged by all and who showed himself so much at ease, inspired confidence and was able to gather funds to finance his undertakings: was he not the man who enabled the Shi'ites to hold up their heads again? People were certain of his complete personal impartiality.

As a cleric, Musā Sadr had a natural distaste for a "politicking" type of politics: he thought only in terms of community of faith and adherence to a doctrine. His first achievement was the founding of the Lebanese Shi'ite Islamic Higher Council (*Majles al-shi'i al-a'lā*), where he encountered clerical rivalry. In 1969 he was appointed president of this official institution which allowed the Shi'ites, following the example of other religious communities in the Lebanon, to be given official representation. The Council took away from the Sunnite Grand Mufti the claim to represent the Imamis, whom in any case it regarded with condescension as schismatics. On election day, the president of the parliament, a Shi'ite feudal lord from the Biqa', symbolically kissed Musā Sadr's hand in public, thereby overturning the former social order in which clerics were subservient to the traditional chiefs.[31]

Musā Sadr's next step was to create the Movement of the Deprived (*Harakat al-mahrumin*) in 1974. This time, it was a matter of liberating the Shi'ite Community from its feudal bonds and forcing the Lebanese state, if it was to survive, to give Shi'ites full recognition. In the very first months the movement won success with the masses and, during a legislative election, the candidate backed by Imam Musā Sadr obtained 20,000 votes against 7,000 for the feudal candidate and 5,000 for the two left-wing candidates.[32]

30 Ibid., p. 94.
31 Ibid., p. 117.
32 S. NASR, "Mobilisation communautaire et symbolique religieuse: L'Imam Sadr et les chi'ites du Liban (1970–1975)," in O. Carré and P. Dumont, eds, *Radicalismes islamiques*, I: *Iran, Liban, Turquie*, Paris, L'Harmattan, 1985, p. 140.

Today we have chosen Fatima, the Prophet's daughter [said Sadr in May 1974]. O Prophet, O God, we have passed the stage of puberty and have reached maturity, we no longer need guardians, we are no longer afraid, we have freed ourselves in spite of all the means they have used to prevent people from learning, we have united to affirm the end of supervision for we are following in the footsteps of Fatima and shall have a martyr's end.[33]

Going further still beyond the simple internal defence of his community's rights, Musā Sadr established close links with the Palestinian resistance. He thus set aside his reservations on the subject of the relations between the Lebanese state and the armed organizations operating against Israel out of southern Lebanon. His alliance with them allowed the Iranian cleric to benefit from military backing in order to rival the Jabal 'Āmel's traditional leaders and later, in 1975, to profit from material support (supply of arms and training) when the Amal Shi'ite militia was officially established.

By overtly recognizing the existence of this militia, Musā Sadr clarified which interpretation of Shi'ism he favoured: not the soothing compromise of Imam Hasan, but the sword-in-hand revolt of Imam Hoseyn. He was no Shi'ite Gandhi, but actually a prefiguration of Khomeyni. *Amal*, in Arabic, means "hope," a word formed from the initials of *Afvāj al-moqāvamat al-lobnāniya*, the "battalions of Lebanese resistance." The Amal militia was conceived in principle to assist the Lebanese army against Israeli incursions. It was also a way of regaining some control of the anti-Zionist cause, and not leaving it exclusively in the hands of the Palestinians who had been held responsible for too many of the south's misfortunes. After the unleashing of the Lebanese civil war, Musā Sadr would noticeably change his attitude toward Palestinian organizations, and some harsh words of his have been recorded. "The Palestinian resistance is not a revolution," he declared, shortly before his disappearance, to a Maronite politician close to the Phalange Party. "It does not seek martrydom. It is a military machine that terrorizes the Arab world. With weapons, Arafat gets money; with money he feeds the press; and thanks to the press he can get a hearing before world public opinion." And he then added, "The PLO is an element of disorder in the south. The Shia have finally gotten over their inferiority complex vis-à-vis the Palestinian Organization."[34]

In 1978 when Musā Sadr took off for Libya, from where he had planned to go on to Italy, and vanished from our sight like the Twelfth Imam, the

33 JABER, "Le Discours shi'ite," p. 85.
34 AJAMI, *The Vanished Imam*, p. 178.

Islamic world was on the eve of an immense upheaval which had already begun in Iran in the autumn of 1977. In the space of a few months, after January 1978, various Iranian towns flared up: Qom, Tabriz, Isfahan, Tehran. On August 23, 1978, two days before the historic journey to Libya, *Le Monde* published in Paris an international forum entitled "The Call of the Prophets, by Imam Musā Sadr." It said:

> Unarmed though they [the people] may be, they endure bloodshed heroically and create a force that nothing can break. The Iranian revolutionaries are not representative of any particular social stratum. Students, workingmen, intellectuals, and men of religion are together taking part in the revolution . . . This movement is motivated by faith and its objectives are those of an open-minded humanism and a revolutionary ethic . . . The moral values of civilized man are under threat in Iran. They cannot be preserved, no matter how much world support the regime receives, as long as the latter sheds blood and suppresses liberties while claiming to defend "progress" and "democracy."

This final stance makes what followed even more dramatic, and for some uncritical believers the disappearance of the great Shi'ite leader assumed messianic proportions: he will return, he has already come!

The precise circumstances of the disappearance are controversial, since Libya has always claimed that Musā Sadr had taken a plane for Rome.[35] None of the official or unofficial inquiries by the Lebanese state, the Islamic Republic of Iran or journalists eager for a media "scoop" managed to discover what became of Musā Sadr after 31 August, the last day he was seen, in his hotel in Tripoli, when he was setting off for a meeting with Colonel Gaddafi . . .

Amal, Hezbollāh and Others

Until the disappearance of Musā Sadr, the position of Shi'ites in Lebanon seemed relatively clear, even if their attitude toward Israelis and Palestinians changed several times according to whether this or that camp showed itself more arrogant or less heedful of the Shi'ite frontier populations. The dynamism of Amal was revived in 1979 by the example of the Iranian Revolution and the arrival from Tehran of a brigade of 300 armed Iranian Revolutionary Guards (*Pāsdārān*). Henceforward commanded by Hoseyn Hoseyni (a lawyer from a Biqa' family of notables) and Nabih Berri (also a lawyer, but younger and Americanized, who had originated from a village

---

35 Ibid., p. 182.

of the Jabal 'Āmel but had been born in Freetown, Sierra Leone), the organization was allied *de facto* with Syria.[36] The latter made use of it to balance Iraq's influence over the Palestinian groups of the PLO. Damascus also wanted a Shi'ite militia to use in opposition, should the need arise, to Sunni Islamic militias who might challenge the 'Alavites' grip on the Syrian state (after the violent repression of the Muslim Brothers at Hama in 1982, which caused 12,000 deaths in three days). Amal was just as much in control of the southern outskirts of Beirut as the Biqa' or south Lebanon.

The decisive factor in the radicalization of the Shi'ite movement was Israel's invasion of Lebanon in 1982, followed by Nabih Berri's acceptance of participation in the Committee of National Safety created by President Sarkis with the commander of the Lebanese forces, Bachir Gemayel. A branch more clearly committed to the side of Iran, *Amal Eslāmi*, led by Hoseyn Musavi (or Moussawi, a teacher from the Biqa'), was excluded from the movement in that year. A third militant section, *Jehād al-Eslāmi* (Islamic Jehad), even more obviously pro-Iranian and benefiting in the Biqa' from direct military aid thanks to a permanent expeditionary corps of Revolutionary Guards who had come from Iran, went over to a terrorist offensive: they carried out a series of bloody attacks, notably on 23 October 1983 against American (241 dead) and French (57 dead) contingents charged with an international peacekeeping mission.

It is clear that the transport of the explosives necessary for these operations could not have taken place without the effective backing of Syria. But was the *Jehād al-Eslāmi* part of a concerted plan by Tehran to reestablish a hegemony, revolutionary if not Shi'ite, over the region? It is difficult to give a precise answer, since everything relating to terrorism has for a long time been lost in a cloud of very complex counter-information. It is certainly possible that Shi'ite militants, recruited and trained in Lebanon, could have carried out operations commanded from Iran. But who will ever prove that Iran controlled the the progress of the spate of hostage-taking carried out by commandos boasting of their Khomeynism? There were no doubt other motives for those isolated actions which, in a completely disorganized country, required only a limited set-up: the lure of gain (ransom), rivalries between militias trying to ensure their control of a sector, easy access to the international media . . .

---

36 See L. and A. CHABRY, *Politique et minorités au Proche-Orient: Les Raisons d'une explosion*, Paris, Maisonneuve æ Larose, 1987, pp. 137ff.; M. DEEB, "Shia Movements in Lebanon: Their Formation Ideology, Social Basis, and Links with Iran and Syria," *Third World Quarterly*, 10, 2 (1988), pp. 683–98 (here, p. 687).

As far as Lebanon was concerned, the withdrawal of the multinational force following the two attacks in October 1983 left the Lebanese army face to face with militias that provoked it constantly. In February 1984 Nabih Berri gave the order to all Shi'ite soldiers in the regular (i.e. government) army to desert with their weapons: the Amal militia, strengthened by these deserters, took control of west Beirut.[37] Henceforward the Lebanese state had no means of securing its survival without dealing via Damascus and by recognizing the Shi'ite militias as military forces: Berri, now a minister, demanded that south Lebanon be entrusted to him. Syria, hostile to Yaser 'Arafat, encouraged Nabih Berri to launch the Amal troops into an attack on the Palestinian camps of Sabra, Shatila, and Borj ol-Barajna in the spring of 1985: this military campaign, in which the Shi'ites did not win a victory, cost them additional shame. Doubtless it benefited the more radical, who were less sensitive about political alliances than ideological passions.

On March 5, 1986, Islamic Jehad announced the "execution of the specialist-researcher spy Michel Seurat." This French sociologist from the Centre national de la recherche scientifique (CNRS), who in actual fact was trying to understand and make known the Islamist movements of the Near East, had been taken hostage on May 22, 1985, and had died – it was later discovered – well before the publication of this sinister and wretched communiqué.[38] He had died from exhaustion and ill treatment. This dramatic episode illustrates the baseness of the group holding him: as they had not been able to make effective use of him alive to gain political or financial advantage, and unable morally to justify his death, they tried to turn it into a deed of heroism, a revolutionary execution. During this time in Tehran, where I was on a research mission, Iranian academics and officials I spoke to admitted their impotence in the face of Lebanese groups who were taking hostages and claiming to be associated with Iran. They were probably sincere, even though they knew that, quite close to them, similarly Iranian "sorcerer's apprentices," unleashing forces beyond their control, were regularly making the journey to Beirut via Damascus to manipulate these horrors, believing – no less sincerely – that they were reinforcing worldwide "Islamic Revolution." All the hostages freed since 1986 were

37 See G. CORM, *Le Proche-Orient éclaté*, 2nd edn, Paris, La Découverte, 1988, pp. 248ff.; H. COBBAN, "The Growth of Shi'i Power in Lebanon and its Implications for the Future," in Cole and Keddie, *Shi'ism and Social Protest*, pp. 151ff.
38 See chiefly O. CARRÉ and G. MICHAUD (alias M. SEURAT), *Les Frères musulmans*, Paris, Gallimard/Julliard, 1983; M. SEURAT, *L'État de barbarie*, Paris, Le Seuil, 1989.

liberated after an improvement in diplomatic relations between their country and Tehran. All have described the inhumane nature of their detention: they were chained up like animals, beaten, isolated from the world. Therein lies a violence that cannot be explained by any religious or ideological affiliation, still less, justified.

Another label often disconcerts westerners as much as it intrigues them – *Hezbollāh* (or *Hizbullah*), which appeared after the Israeli invasion of the Lebanon in 1982. Literally, it is "the Party of God" and not, as has frequently been heard or seen in the media, "God's Madmen." In actual fact, no more in Lebanon than in Iran is it a matter of a "party," complete with doctrine and duly listed members, even though there is no doubt of the existence of a Consultative Council of twelve members, turbaned clerics and military men. Among them there seems to be a majority of people from the Biqa' and certain *ulema* who had studied at Najaf or Qom, such as Ebrāhim al-Amin and Sobhi al-Tofeyli. (There is also a higher *shar'i* (dealing with religious law) Council serving as Hezbollāh's international coordinators, with its headquarters in Tehran: its president apparently an Iraqi opposition member, Sheikh Mohammad-Taqi Modarresi, and the Iranian official a young cleric, known since the Islamic Revolution for having led strong-arm groups with the job of beating up liberal intellectuals and left-wing militants, the *hojjat ol-eslām* Hādi Qaffāri.)

Is *Hezbollāh* no more than a mercenary militia, directly financed by Iran, or is it a fairly informal federation of militants seeking a revolutionary party? The program of the Lebanese Hezbollāh, published in an "open letter" in February 1985, makes reference to a a universal Islamic Community (*Omma*) obeying the orders of the jurisconsult Guide, as in the Khomeyni era. It lays stress on the struggle against "America, its allies of the Atlantic Pact and the Zionist entity that has usurped the holy land of Islamic Palestine." It attacks Amal, blaming it for its moderation, and denounces Nabih Berri's participation in Amin Gemayel's government, dominated by Maronite Christians.[39] For Hezbollāh, any compromise with Maronite rulers is illicit, because Muslims must live in a state governed by Muslims. Thus its aim is to create an Islamic state of Lebanon, the replica of the Iranian Islamic Republic, with the "supervision of the theologian-jurist" (*velāyat al-faqih*) as its cornerstone, a state where Christians can live

---

39 A.R. NORTON, "Shi'ism and Social Protest in Lebanon," in Cole and Keddie, *Shi'ism and Social Protest*, pp. 172ff; M. DEEB, "Shia Movements in Lebanon," p. 696; (anonymous) "Islam au Liban: Tendances et structures," *Cahiers de l'Orient*, 2 (1986), pp. 237–59.

in complete freedom, unlike the many restrictions which, according to the programme, Muslims suffer in a state dominated by Christians.

Behind Hezbollāh there is frequent mention of a turbaned cleric who enjoys a wide audience among Shi'ites and whom people have been quick to label a "fanatic" because of his entourage of violent militants: Sheikh Mohammad-Hoseyn Fazlallāh.[40] Born in Najaf in 1935, this Lebanese from a clerical family of Aynata, a village in south Lebanon, pursued his theological studies in Iraq. After the death of Mohsen al-Hakim, in 1970 he became a disciple of the apolitical Iranian ayatollah Abo'l-Qāsem Kho'i and his legal representative: he was empowered not only to transmit religious knowledge but also to manage the sums entrusted to him by way of religious taxes to finance Islamic schools, community clinics, etc. In Najaf he was equally very close to Mohammad Bāqer al-Sadr, a more politicized Iraqi theologian (see above, pp. 113–16) whom he sometimes consulted. At the age of 31 he returned to Lebanon and settled in the poor outskirts of Beirut. In 1986, on a visit to Iran, he was acknowledged by Khomeyni as a "model to imitate" (marja' al-taqlid), that is, competent to issue judgements on the application of religious Law without consulting any other ayatollah. Meanwhile Fazlallāh had found his audience among the young people and lowly poor and had exchanged his "quietist" ideas, received from ayatollah Kho'i, for an ideology of active defence of the oppressed. He had become the head of Hezbollāh and the most celebrated of Lebanese Shi'ite clerics. Did he supply funds, if not his blessing, to those responsible for the suicide-attacks on the French and American forces in October 1983? His ambiguous position does not permit a categorical reply. In a number of interviews he has expressed his feelings on recourse to violence, which he does not justify but can understand when the enemy is clearly identified. In this instance, the enemy is America because it is Israel's protector. "I believe that in all cases violence is like a surgical operation that the doctor should only resort to after he has exhausted all other methods. Every person needs to defend himself. If a man needs to use violent ways, he must use them."[41]

Among Sheikh Fazlallāh's works one may pick out exegetic studies on

40   As well as the anonymous article in Cahiers de l'Orient, 2 (1986), see M. KRAMER, "Kurzbiographie: Muhammad Husayn Fadlallah," Orient, 2 (1985), pp. 147–9; O. CARRÉ, "Quelques mots-clefs de Muhammad Husayn Fadlallāh," Revue française de science politique, 37, 4 (1987), pp. 478–501; idem, "La 'Révolution islamique' selon Muhammad Husayn Fadlallāh," Orient, 29, 1 (1988), pp. 68–84.

41   R. WRIGHT, "Lebanon," in Hunter, The Politics of Islamic Revivalism, pp. 57–67.

the Koran, on the social dimension of religious practice, the "missionary" role of women, collections of poems, and some more striking titles, such as "Islam and the Logic of Force" (1976) and "Following the Path of Islam" (1977). But he is principally known as a preacher widely listened to in Beirut's suburbs and the entire Arab-speaking world, where his cassettes are broadcast, as in western Europe. As a committed theologian, he approaches the political problems that are most vital to the Lebanese: the Palestinian problem, western ascendancy, Maronite domination over the Muslims, and inter-community violence. Obviously, all these matters go beyond Lebanese boundaries: can a believer in Allāh accept being governed by non-believers who are agents of American imperialism?

Sheikh Fazlallāh also replies to other burning questions. Can methods such as hostage-taking or suicide-attacks be justified in the name of the Revolution? When a complete change in individuals and society becomes essential, as at Islam's coming to Mecca in the time of the Prophet, he says, one must first of all seek peaceful and reformist solutions. Did not Mohammad wait 12 years between the first revelation and the Hegira? By preaching, one can breathe "an Islamic mentality" into every man; thus society will gradually change.[42] Kamikaze attacks pose a legal problem: is it permissible to wish certain death upon oneself? In martyrdom it is the enemy who desires the death of the Muslim fighter: is suicidal (*entehāri*) violence also martyrdom (*esteshhādi*)? Sheikh Fazlallāh, a fine casuist, gives his answer in three parts: first, it is possible to coexist peaceably with a bad ruling power without being compelled thereby to recognize the legitimacy of its government; next, any means that conflict with Islam must be avoided, even if it is in the service of Islam; lastly, one must not "miss taking decisive steps towards the Islamic goal."[43]

How can the Islamic Revolution be promoted? One way, according to our Sheikh, would be to draw Shi'ites and Sunnis closer together, as their differences are not fundamental – it is the "specialists" of the western countries who try to emphasize the divisions. For that, it is necessary to start from concrete realities, notably the offensive launched by Khomeyni against imperialism; the torpor induced by rigid traditions must be shaken off and a return made to basic principles. Control of power by the *ulema*, as set up in the 1979 Iranian constitution, is a good thing, but one must beware of the personal absolutism that could result from the principle of the *velāyat-e faqih* (governorship of the theologian-jurist). Standing slightly

42   CARRÉ, "La 'Révolution islamique,'" p. 72.
43   Ibid., p. 74; CARRÉ, "Quelques mots-clefs de Muhammad Husayn Fadlallāh," p. 484.

back from the Hezbollāh adherence to Khomeynist arguments, Mohammad-Hoseyn Fazlallāh is certainly in favour of strengthening clerical authority (*marja'iya*), but reluctant to reduce to one the number of ayatollahs who could be regarded as a "source of imitation" (*marja' al-taqlid*).

Did the Iranian Islamic Revolution have an impact on Lebanese Shi'ism? This question seems to overlook that for a long time, at least since the Safavids in the sixteenth century, Iran has been the territorial reference point for a Shi'ism that managed to win power. It was in Najaf that Shi'ite *ulema* from every region met together until Qom became the principal theological focal point. There, too, went the trends and alliances when Qom was temporarily unable to fulfill that role. Lebanon, lacking organization, bordering on Israel, a place of violence and social inequality, tempted Iranian mullas, who did not all equal Imam Musā Sadr's success there. Thus in April 1980, on a visit to Beirut, the *hojjat ol-eslām* Sādeq Khalkhāli, a Qom deputy and president of the expeditious revolutionary tribunals in Iran, declared that Musā Sadr "had been killed in Rome by Zionists," which unleashed the fury of Nabih Berri and Mohammad-Mahdi Shamsoddin.[44] For these Lebanese Shi'ites, Iran was trying in this way to reopen a dialogue with Libya to justify the excellent political relations maintained with Gaddafi . . . The best intermediaries between Amal and Iran, Mostafā Shamrān (Minister of Defence, who died at the beginning of the war in 1980 in circumstances that were never made clear) and Sādeq Qotbzāda (Ghotbzadeh, executed in 1982), seem to have been eliminated in order to make room for less committed men alongside the Palestinians.

The degree of alliance with Iran was the chief criterion distinguishing Lebanese Shi'ite militants.[45] The Iranian camp was clearly that of Hezbollāh. Nabih Berri went as far as to say that 'Ali-Akbar Mohtashami, who had been ambassador to Damascus before becoming Minister of the Interior in the Musavi government in Tehran, was directing Hezbollāh's operations. Even after losing his ministerial portfolio in the outcome of Hāshemi-Rafsanjāni's election to the Iranian presidency (July 1989), Mohtashami continued to make journeys to the Lebanon to meet Hezbollāh officials.[46] (His loss of political credibility in Iran, however, lessened the scope of these contacts.) Put simply, more pro-Iranian Hezbollāh supporters were

44 Sh. SHAPIRA, "The Origins of Hizbollah," *Jerusalem Quarterly*, 46 (Spring 1988), p. 120.
45 A. R. NORTON, "Lebanon: The Internal Conflict and the Iranian Connection," in Esposito, *The Iranian Revolution*, pp. 116–37.
46 Ibid., p. 127.

to be found in the environs of Beirut; in south Lebanon, where the need to compromise with other political affiliations (pro-Syrians, Sunnis) and hostility to the PLO were an unavoidable reality, the Amal movement's pragmatism gave it some advantages and allowed it occasionally to have talks with UNIFL (United Nations Intervention Force in the Lebanon), which was glad at last to have a relay point legitimately entrenched in this region (unlike the Lebanese forces linked with Israel). In the view of Tehran, whose opinion was subsequently taken up in Beirut, UNIFL became Israel's potential ally. The common enemy of the two Shi'ite groups was the Maronite force, which until the Kuwaiti–Iraqi crisis of 1990 was supported by Baghdad.

Iranian diplomacy had no reason to hide its interest in the Lebanese cause. It sometimes tried to be of assistance between the various factions on which it had some influence. In 1985 Iranian mediation prevented Syrian forces from crushing the Towhid movement, led by the Sunni Sheikh Sa'id Sha'bān in Tripoli, Iran's ally. In January 1989 'Ali-Akbar Velāyati, Iranian Minister of Foreign Affairs, announced the truce obtained in Damascus between Amal and Hezbollāh, which had been tearing each other to pieces. Even if hope increasingly faded that an Islamic Republic would see the light of day in the Lebanon, the Iranian Republic's influence was noticeable over hostage-takers and various Lebanese Islamist factions.[47]

Iranian money had been pouring into Lebanon by way of Ba'albek since 1982, finding its way just as much into military training for Hezbollāh militiamen as into social organizations, hospitals, schools, etc. It is certain that this manna aroused envy among Lebanese politico-denominational groups trying to cling on to their strongholds. This does not mean, however, that there was a real political dialogue between them in order to effect a very clear plan, even if the plan was Iranian. In October 1989, just when the Lebanese members of parliament were meeting at Ta'ef in Saudi Arabia with the Arabian, Moroccan, and Algerian Ministers of Foreign Affairs, under the aegis of the Arab League, and deciding on a limited political reform of the Lebanese state, Tehran was receiving other Lebanese, leaders of Amal, Hezbollāh, Sheikh Sha'bān from Tripoli, the Druze Walid Jumblatt and several radical Palestinians. Tehran's efforts to keep up the pressure against the Maronites in Lebanon were unavailing, brought to nought by Syria and the defection of Amal, which resumed its quarrel with Hezbollāh.

The fall of General Aoun, Baghdad's ally, and the fall of Baghdad itself before the American coalition, once again called into question the equilib-

47   Ibid., p. 118.

rium of this Lebanon where – without a doubt – the greed and meddle-someness of many countries, both near and far, leave little hope of finding a Lebanese solution.

AFGHANISTAN

This country came under growing influence from Moscow after a *coup d'état* abolished the monarchy in 1973. In December 1979 Soviet troops were sent in to support a communist regime opposed by various resistance movements using Islam as their ideology. The majority of anti-communist combatants were funded by Pakistan and Saudi Arabia, helped by the Americans; but others, for ethnic reasons or because they followed Shiʾism, were subject to Iran. After the fall of the communist regime, in 1994 a ferocious war set rival groups against one another in an attempt to dominate the capital, Kabul. Neither Iran nor Pakistan succeeded in imposing itself as an effective mediator.

The fascination exercised by Iran on Afghan Shiʾites is comparable with that found in Lebanon: religion gives an ethnic minority (the Hazāra) a powerful external protector to make up for their poverty and isolation in their national community. Before the Islamic Revolution, that protector was the Shah, whose photograph was replaced after 1979 by Khomeyni's in the inns of the Hazājarāt (the mountainous centre-west of Afghanistan).[48] This influence is more emblematic than real. Nevertheless, spiritual ties can be traced going back to teachers in the theological schools of Qom or Mashhad, Iranian clerical influence working on mullas who, returning to their own country, become the religious elite. This model serves equally well for written culture, when the Persian book printed in Iran circulating in Afghanistan is more highly prized because of Iran's greater progress in "modernity." Several institutions of Shiʾite teaching were created in the decade preceding the fall of the monarchy in 1973: they saw the development of young people who, copying the Iranian model, became strongly politicized. Among the nascent Islamist movements, mention must be made of groups in which Sunnis and Shiʾites were side by side, for example the student organization of Young Muslims (*Javānān-e mosalmān*), or the School of the Koran (*Madrasa-ye Qorʾān*), the latter run by a Sufi leader. Other forms of mobilization relied on criteria that were more ethnic than religious.

48   O. ROY, *L'Afghanistan: Islam et modernité politique*, Paris, Le Seuil, 1985, p. 70.

For the Hazāra, the fact of belonging to a minority (15 percent of the population) that was always bullied in the national community further accentuated their political radicalization. It was the more urbanized Qezelbāsh Shi'ites, longstanding servants of the monarchy, who traditionally provided Shi'ite religious elites, whereas the Hazāra, for the most part, had no mosques.[49] They retain a vivid memory of their persecutions: at the end of the nineteenth century, the Emir 'Abdorrahmān had a *fatvā* published by the theologians of Kabul decreeing that Shi'ites were infidels; it was therefore legitimate to pillage their belongings. There followed a spate of massacres and raids lasting two years (1891–3), which resulted in numerous conversions (at least in appearance) to Sunnism, mostly in the towns, and diminished the power of the *sayyeds*. Many Hazāra chose to go into exile in India and Khorasan, a north-eastern province of Iran adjacent to Afghanistan.

Other Afghan Shi'ites vainly tried to reverse the accursed fate of their community: thus in 1949 a Hazāra cleric from the Balkh region in the north of the country, Sayyed Esmā'il Balkhi, bungled a *coup d'état* and was imprisoned.[50] His fame spread beyond the Imami community and his example, which was compared with that of Imam Hoseyn's revolt, prefigured the strongly Islamized mobilization that took place after the communists seized control.

The social structure of the Hazāra, a Shi'ite and Persian-speaking minority of Mongol descent, remained very feudal, dominated by the *mir* and the *arbāb* (traditional local authorities) whom the later Afghan sovereigns had tried to involve in the political life of the state. In the Hazārajāt, the *sayyed* were held to be different because of their Arab origin, and enjoyed a special prestige. They often became mullas or sheikhs. Among the young who had benefited from a modern education many, ultra-politicized and conscious of the collective injustice of which their race was victim, turned toward Marxist or nationalist organizations, but no religious leader emerged from their ranks.

The recent development of Afghanistan presents strange chronological coincidences with that of Iran, as Olivier Roy has pointed out. In 1978: revolts against the Shah in Iran, and the communist regime in Afghanistan; 1979: triumph of the Iranian Islamic Revolution, Soviet invasion of

---

49   D. B. EDWARDS, "The Evolution of Shi'i Political Dissent in Afghanistan," in Cole and Keddie, *Shi'ism and Social Protest*, pp. 201–29 (here, p. 204).
50   EDWARDS, "The Evolution of Shi'i Political Dissent in Afghanistan," pp. 214ff.

Afghanistan; 1988, cease-fire between Iran and Iraq, Soviet withdrawal from Afghanistan.[51] But these external *rapproachements* had nothing to do with the development of the Islamist movement and the denominational division between resistance organizations according to whether they belonged to Sunnism or Shi'ism.

In fact, whereas the majority of Afghans, notably the Pashtuns, were affected by fundamentalist propaganda and Saudi influence, those who pledged allegiance to ayatollah Khomeyni and the Iranian Islamic Republic were recruited only from specifically Shi'ite circles and were isolated in the resistance. On the Iranian side, despite the arrival of over two million Afghan refugees, the government remained circumspect: the war with Iraq on the one hand and the crisis over hostages in the American embassy on the other caused Tehran to exercise extreme caution in its relations with the USSR. Unlike Pakistan, Iran is in direct contact, over about 1,800 km, with the erstwhile Soviet state. Moreover, the Afghan movement, often led by tribal or "feudal" chiefs, failed to inspire much sympathy in young Iranian revolutionaries dreaming of land reforms and social justice.

On the Afghan side, there was doubtless a certain degree of mistrust toward Iranian ideological interference in a movement for independence that already had no shortage of offers of aid from outside. The greatest present-day Afghan clerics, such as Sheikh Āsef Mohseni, who directs the *Harakat-e eslāmi* (Islamic Movement, first based in Iran, then at Islamabad, i.e., in Pakistan), Qorbān-Ali Mohaqqeq, or Sayyed 'Ali Beheshti who in 1979 founded the Islamic Council for the Union of Afghanistan (*Shurā-ye ettefāq-e eslāmi-e Afqānestān*, confined to the Hazārajāt), became radicalized before the Iranian Revolution and for the most part did not consult Khomeyni, but apolitical ayatollahs like Kho'i (Najaf) or Shari'atmadāri (Qom).[52]

The Iranians, who continued to recommend a hard line against the USSR while at the same time refraining from encouraging engagement with its army, lost much of their credit among the leaders of the Afghan resistance. Internal struggles in Iran, notably the pretension of the *hojjat ol-eslām* Mohtashami (Iran's Minister of the Interior until 1989) to manage relations with the Afghan Mojāhedin, contributed to weakening aid for the Resistance. In 1986, for the first time, Iran invited to Tehran the leader of

51   O. ROY, "The Mujahidin and the Future of Afghanistan," in Esposito, *The Iranian Revolution*, pp. 179–202.
52   Ibid., p. 187.

the Sunni organization *Jami'at-e eslāmi*, Borhānoddin Rabbāni. Leaders of Sunni organizations were invited to a conference on Afghanistan in Iran in January 1989: the chief Sunni leaders, such as Rabbāni, Mojaddedi, and Nabi attended, while radicals and royalists abstained. Henceforward Iran tried to recognize that Afghanistan had an Islamic identity, without further insistence on a Shi'ite avant-garde and its role in an improbable revolution.

THE INDIAN SUBCONTINENT

The first Shi'ites to be recorded in large numbers in India were Ismailis, whose presence is attested from the tenth century, even though the different conquests of the subcontinent by Sunni armies brought their expansion to a premature close. In Gujarat, north of Bombay, Mosta'li Ismailis of Hindu descent, established since 1067, are known as *Bohras* (merchants);[53] but part of the Bohras are Sunni Muslims. Ismailis from the other main branch, the Nizari (Nezāri) are called the Khojas (from the Persian Khāja, "Lord") or Aga-Khanis (from the nobiliary title *Āqā Khān*, "Lord," which their Imam Hasan-'Ali Shah received from the Qājār king Fath-'Ali Shah when he was appointed governor of the city of Qom at the beginning of the nineteenth century). In the modern era, chiefly because of the exodus of Iranian Ismailis persecuted in their homeland until the nineteenth century and beyond, the Nizari Ismaili community is very well represented in India. The Ismailis are extremely active today in this country where they particularly control banks and important commercial sectors. The third Āqā Khān, Soltān Mohammad Shāh (born in Karachi in 1877, died in 1957 in Switzerland), played an important role in the Muslims' anticolonial battles, in which he usually sided with the British, and the majority of his faithful opted for Pakistan at the time of partition in 1947. The first Governor-General of Pakistan, Mohammad-'Ali Jinnah, was a Khoja by origin although, extremely westernized, he never referred to his religious faith: he defended the Muslims as a cultural and political entity, not as a religious community. The Ismaili community emigrated in great numbers to East Africa. From there the Ismailis, who became prosperous, were forced into exile to western countries, mainly North America, owing to

---

53   See F. DAFTARY, *The Isma'īlīs: Their History and Doctrines*, Cambridge, Cambridge University Press, 1990, pp. 299ff.

racial intolerance in the aftermath of independence. Over 10,000 Ismailis live today in London. Altogether there are between 3 million and 20 million Ismailis in the world, according to different estimates.[54]

The history of Twelver Shi'ism in India is split up into several periods when officially Shi'ite kingdoms were formed, strongly influenced by the Safavid model in Iran.[55] In the Deccan, the state of the Qotbshāhis (1512–1687) was founded by an Iranian Turcoman adventurer from Hamadān, who had numerous mosques built where the Friday prayers were said in the name of the Twelve Imams and the Safavids, and where the martrydom of Imam Hoseyn was commemorated. That tradition was perpetuated in the capital, Hyderabad, until the time when that fell at the hands of the Sunni Moguls. The Shi'ite interval of the Nezāmshāh of Ahmadnagār was shorter: in this western part of India Shi'ite influence was maintained for about a century, before the absorption of this kingdom into the Mogul Empire under Shah Jahān in 1633. The 'Ādelshāhis (1490–1686) of Bijapur in central India, who had Shi'ism as their official religion in the sixteenth century, received a large number of Shi'ite Iranians, notably horse dealers; they also recognized the formal sovereignty of the Safavids of Isfahan. Nowhere were these victories for Imamism definitive, as in Iran, but they show the relatively tenacious entrenchment, sometimes under Safavid influence, of convinced Shi'ites in Muslim India.

In the north of India, it was necessary to wait for the breakdown of the Mogul Empire and the repeated thrusts of the Iranian Emperor Nāder Shah (1736–47) in order to see the appearance of a Shi'ite state between Delhi and Benares – that of Awadh (Oudh) at the foot of the Himalayas, with Lucknow as its capital (*Lakhnow*, today the capital of the Indian state of Uttar Pradesh). The *nawāb* (lords) of Awadh were Shi'ite Iranians from Khorasan, the Nishāpuri, at first regarded as governors in the service of the Moguls, then as independent rulers. In fact, under the Emperor Aurangzeb (d. 1707), the Moguls had shown themselves to be tolerant towards the Imamis immigrating in large numbers, that increased as political instability persisted in Iran. The school of Farangi Mahall, in Lucknow, founded by a Sunni theologian and richly endowed by the Moguls, spread its influence

---

54   For the history and doctrine of the Ismailis, see DAFTARY, *The Isma'ilis*; Heinz HALM, *Shiism*, Edinburgh, Edinburgh University Press, 1991 (German text: pp. 192–243); relevant articles in *Encyclopedia of Islam*, 2nd edn, and *Encyclopaedia Iranica* ("Aqa Khān/Agha Khan," "Ismailiyya," "Khodja," "Bohora" by H. Algar and W. Madelung).
55   J. R. I. COLE, *Roots of North Indian Shi'ism in Iran and Iraq*, Berkeley and Los Angeles, University of California Press, 1989, pp. 22ff.

throughout India and trained learned men and administrators who were just as often Sunnis as Shiʾites or Hindus. From the middle of the eighteenth century, the Nishāpuri were in direct confrontation with the British who were already settled in Bengal.

Lucknow became the "Home of Shiʾism" (*Dār ash-shiʾa*), in competition with Faizābād, which was briefly the capital. An ambitious programme of urban development attracted workers and craftsmen from all over India. In pure Indian style, the great *Imāmbāra*, the equivalent of the *hoseyniya* in Iran, was built there: a place for the solemn celebration of Shiʾite mourning. After the building was completed in 1791, the *nawāb* laid out astronomical sums for its adornment. Hundreds of gold and silver replicas of Imam Hoseyn's tomb at Karbalā were placed in the edifice as ex-votos, as were innumerable candlesticks and candelabra, so that the weeping mourners and spectators were no longer able to sit in the great hall. A traveler noted the profusion of blazing lights everywhere at the time of the mourning for Hoseyn and observed that "every evening, all unbelievers and disciples of Omar, Osmān and Abu Bakr were anathematized, for the greater edification of the Hindus who gathered there in large numbers."[56] The Moharram demonstrations reached such fever pitch that in 1784 the *nawāb* himself bled profusely after flagellating himself, and was gravely ill at the end of the mourning celebrations for Hoseyn . . .

Starting in 1796 the princes of Awadh made an alliance with the British East India Company; soon they were to grant the British vast economic advantages before becoming their vassals – a source of great embarrassment to the Shiʾites. Some of them resigned themselves to working in the service of the British. A Lucknow *mojtahed* published a decree around 1830 banning the holding of any office in the service of the iniquitous rulers (the colonial administration); however, he conceded the permissible nature of such work if it could improve the lot of Shiʾites, which in reality allowed it to be justified. When the East India Company began its costly war against Nepal, it borrowed from the *nawāb* Ghāzioddin Heydar (1819–27), who collected the resulting interest. A large part of these profits was reinvested in building religious edifices and making grants to the pious foundations of Shiʾite towns in Iraq. In 1856 Awadh was quite simply annexed by the British. The occupiers continued to pay stipends and pensions to the *mojtaheds* and Shiʾite *ulema* as well as the income on the loan granted by Ghāzioddin Heydar, but were unable to prevent the Shiʾites from taking part in the Great Mutiny of 1857.

---

56   Vicomte G. Valentia, quoted by COLE, *Roots of North Indian Shiʾism*, p. 96.

As early as the 1830s, the Awadh revenue (known as the Oudh Bequest) which British agents distributed to the Shi'ite *ulema* in Iraq on behalf of the Awadh government, allowed the colonial power to intervene directly in Imamite clerical matters in their historic centres at Najaf and Karbalā.[57] (The Iranians who made religious endowments to the Mesopotamian sanctuaries also did so at the time through the intermediary of British agents.) The *mojtaheds* of Iraq – mostly Iranians – who received these funds obviously profited from the British administration services, but by so doing gave a rather dubious image of their relations with the colonial power. Even if the East India Company's agents, technically better equipped to make these financial transfers, carried out their task most scrupulously, they could always be suspected of interfering in the payments they effected on behalf of the Shi'ites. At the request of the Indian sleeping partners who themselves belonged to the *Osuli* tendency, this system chiefly favoured the dominance of the *Osuli* over the *Akhbāri* and *Sheykhi ulema*.[58] The image of perfect independence *vis-à-vis* any political authority, often presented of the *Osuli* Shi'ite *ulema*, is seriously altered by these financial manipulations, even if they originated in the Shi'ite kingdom of Awadh. The institution of Supreme Guide (*marja' al-taqlid*) of the Shi'ite Muslims, established in this period and confirming the strengthening of the Shi'ite hierocracy, certainly benefited considerably from the power imparted by the sums of money at his disposal.[59]

The history of Shi'ism in India gives us a glimpse not only of its extreme wealth but also of the stronger ties it enjoyed than those of the Sunnis with Persian culture and Iran. Even nowadays there are many Iranians who still believe – perhaps it is just a paranoid obsession? – that the British are continuing to manipulate Shi'ite *ulema* by way of large sums paid in the name of Indian Shi'ites. The historic example of the clergy's sensitiveness to this suggestion was given in the defamatory article published on 8 January 1978 in the Iranian newspaper *Ettelā'at* under the title "Iran and Red and Black Colonialism": in it, the author, a top civil servant in the Shah's Ministry of Information, disguised under a pseudonym, accused Khomeyni (whose father had lived in Kashmir) of having Indian origins and being a paid agent of the British. As its appearance provoked

---

57   J. R. I. COLE, "Indian Money and the Shi'i Shrine Cities of Iraq 1786–1850," *Middle Eastern Studies*, 22 (1986), pp. 461–80; H. ALGAR, *Religion and State in Iran, 1785–1906*, Berkeley and Los Angeles, University of California Press, 1969, pp. 237ff.
58   See above, ch. 3.
59   COLE, "Indian Money," p. 476.

demonstrations in Qom that were violently put down, this article was the spark that caused the Islamic Revolution to explode in Iran.

Despite some compromises with the colonial order, Indian Shi'ism took an active part with all Muslims in national struggles, notably starting in 1919 in the great mobilization to safeguard the Ottoman caliphate which Mustafa Kemal showed signs of shedding: the *khelāfat* movement was more one of protest against the dismantling of the Muslim world by colonial powers than it was concerned to restore a Sunni institution which had never governed any other than the Ottoman world. It was also the start of a mobilization for independence.

For Muslims the dilemma soon became one of knowing whether the partition of India, so desired by the Indian poet Iqbal and others, would allow the formation of a society more equitable toward Muslims, who feared domination by the Hindus.[60] The plan of the Shi'ites, who emigrated *en masse* to Pakistan in 1947, was to create a democratic and secularized society where religious differences would not penalize them as a minority. Actually, the Sunnis dominated the new state, whose true nature, after the deep wound of partition, was revealed only very much later. In the 1980s certain Sunnis went as far as to demand that the Shi'ites, like the supporters of the *Ahmadi* sect, should no longer be regarded as Muslims . . .

The principal demand of the Pakistani Shi'ites was to be able to enjoy a personal status based on the Ja'farite legal system and freely practise their religious rites. As regards the legal question, problems began in the school programs where specifically Shi'ite needs were not recognized (there was no teaching of the history of Islam according to Imami interpretation). When General Zia ul-Haqq became president in 1977, a period that coincided with the Islamic Revolution in Iran, greater Islamization of the state provoked interdenominational conflicts: for example, the question of religious taxes, the *zakāt* (legal alms) and the *'oshr* (tithe), which were to be levied from 1979 on owned wealth (bank accounts) and agricultural production. The Shi'ites protested that Ja'farite laws imposed less heavy payments on them, and that they should not make them to the state but to freely selected *ulema* who would receive them on behalf of the *marja'-al-taqlid* (literally "sources of imitation"), themselves acting as delegates of the hidden Imam . . . A certain degree of equilibrium in the political machinery of Pakistan had been reached with the premiership of General Yahyā Khān, a Shi'ite, and equally under the government of his successor, Zulfiqar Ali Bhutto, whose wife was Iranian.

---

60   M. D. AHMED, "The Shi'is of Pakistan," in Kramer, *Shi'ism, Resistance, and Revolution,* pp. 275–88.

The Pakistani Shi'ites, embittered by the harassment they endure from the majority, chiefly during the annual Moharram celebrations, when they try to organize spectacular mourning ceremonies that shock the Sunnis, are strongly attracted by Iranian protection. On this point they are in an equally difficult situation in regard on their own country which, above all after the unleashing of the Afghan crisis, came under very heavy pressure from the Americans and Saudis.[61]

In India where, for historical and sociological reasons, the Shi'ites have a tendency to hide their religious differences, tension builds up again each year at the time of Imam Hoseyn's mourning celebrations. In the town of Lucknow, the only one where Shi'ites have inherited from the pre-colonial era a duly recognized status and where they have their own mosques, disturbances between them and the Sunnis reached such proportions that from 1977 the government had to step in and ban all processions during Moharram.[62] Khomeyni, while he was still in France, told journalists that these bloody scuffles would stop on the day when Indian Muslims enjoyed better education. But the problem lies much deeper, in the inferior social status of the Shi'ites, who can hold no demonstrations, except on just a few isolated occasions like that of 'Āshurā, during which they elevate their grief to the level of a universal value and are then prepared to go to any lengths, however excessive.

61 M. LODHI, "Pakistan's Shia Movement: An Interview with Arif Hussaini," in Gauhar, *Third World Quarterly: Islam and Politics*, pp. 806–17.
62 K. HJORTSHOJ, "Shi'i Identity and the Significance of Muharram in Lucknow, India," in Kramer, *Shi'ism, Resistance and Revolution*, pp. 289–309; D. PINAULT, *The Shi'ites: Ritual and Popular Piety in a Muslim Community*, London, I. B. Tauris, 1992.

6

Shi'ism, Women, and Pleasure

PREAMBLE

There is no intention here of dealing exhaustively with a highly sensitive subject treated (or mistreated?) so often since the Islamic Revolution – that of the condition of women. On the whole, Shi'ism differs little on this plane from Sunnism, except that the situation of women is certainly more enviable in Tehran than in many countries dominated by Sunni Islam, which are spoken of far less, starting with Saudi Arabia. A basic bibliography will enable readers more easily to get their bearings on the matter: – Fariba ADELKHAH, *La Révolution sous le voile: Femmes islamiques d'Iran*, Paris, Karthala, 1991; Farah AZARI, ed., *Women of Iran: The Conflict with Fundamentalist Islam*, London, Ithaca Press, 1983; Erika FRIEDL, *Women of Deh Koh: Lives in an Iranian Village*, Washington and London, Smithsonian Institution Press, 1989; Ziba MIR HOSSEINI, *Marriage on Trial: Study of Islamic Family Law*, London, I. B. Tauris, 1993; Guity NASHAT, ed., *Women and Revolution in Iran*, Boulder, Colo., Westview Press, 1983; Eliz SANASARIAN, *The Women's Rights Movement in Iran: Mutiny, Appeasement and Repression from 1900 to Khomeini*, New York, Praeger, 1982. It would be useful to add various writings by 'Ali Shari'ati and ayatollah Motahhari mentioning the status of women in the ideological perspective of Islamic renewal (see the general bibliography).

In this chapter I have tried to present a perspective that differs slightly from these books and the numerous articles on the women question published after the Islamic Revolution. I am not taking a sociological point of view. A marginal practice and the discourse by which it justifies itself seem to me as instructive as the norm in giving an understanding of the gap between the historical forms of religious behaviour and theological principles. In the case of *temporary* marriage, we are speaking of an exceptional practice, yet one which obsesses minds: an abomination for some, a useful trick for others. A study of this original form of religious law and the way in which sexual morality is made use of, justified, or explained enables a few stereotypes of sexuality and Islam to be overturned. When all is said and done, it becomes apparent that sexist customs depend not so much on religion as on an attitude of mind. The defence of family honor certainly takes different forms in Corsica (or Sicily) and Iran, but the heart of the problem is the same. Between the monogamous family, which is the *de facto* norm for most Muslims as it is for societies in the western Christian world, and polygamy, which is a frequent alternative, legislations have adopted varying solutions.

There is no direct political interference here, although masculine power is often a metaphor for power within the state. There are actually profound differences between the concept of the family held by progressive Shi'ites, who lean toward the abolition of polygamy and repudiation of the wife, and that of more traditional thinkers who justify these juridical forms to defend the patriarchal family against detractors influenced by western individualism or materialist doctrines. Where there is agreement, in reality it hides differing intents. One defends temporary marriage by emphasizing the authority of the paterfamilias and husband, the other by stressing the equality of men and women. From this one gains an impression of utilitarianism: doctrines are sought in order to respond to pressing questions. Religion is closer to humanity than to God.

Unlike Christianity, which sets great store by celibacy and chastity as a foretaste of the angelic state in the Kingdom of God, and which places great value on the spiritual symbolism of marriage, Islam encourages men to take pleasure in carnal love. It condemns fornication in order to avoid social disruption, not to restrict men's sensual desires, since according to Islam the sex drive is a good thing because it conforms with nature. Copulation is thus regarded as good in itself, and even if legal restrictions render its legitimate practice difficult outside marriage, the possibility exists. Furthermore, it is necessary for anyone who wishes to denounce an illicit union "to have seen the stiletto in the pot of eye lotion"[1] (as it is picturesquely expressed), which it will be admitted is a reassuring protection for lovers (without, however, sheltering them from the immediate reactions of the seduced girl's parents who, in the majority of Muslim countries, have the power of life and death over her). The Muslim paradise is not asexual. On

---

1   P. VIEILLE, *La Féodalité et l'état en Iran*, Paris, Anthropos, 1975, p. 141.

the contrary, it is filled with doe-eyed houris of modest gaze, eternally young, nubile virgins as beautiful as rubies and coral, cloistered in pavilions and purified (i.e. ready for love) at all times.

One of the most frequent criticisms leveled against Islam is that it has thought only of man's pleasure, and is unfair toward women. Islamist militants, obsessed as they are with things sexual, the seclusion of women, and their thousand and one rules about coitus and modesty, do nothing to alter the macho stereotypes. Their veneer of asceticism, however, conceals concupiscent eyes; they are caught between an apologia for virtuous restraint, justification for the most unbridled possible masculine sexual activity (in order to avoid psychological disorders), and the rarity or inaccessibility of the women who are lawfully available for this exercise. Once in power, in every country they humiliate women, no doubt less than their unacknowledged model, the harsh Wahhābi rigorists of Arabia, who have never known *emancipation* or the egalitarian demands of the feminists: they impose the obligation to veil the hair and entire body, with the exception of hands and face, in public places; various professional restrictions; sexual discrimination in public places; fairly rigorous confinement in areas within the home; increased surveillance and unfair treatment within marriage, where the woman is her husband's servant, intended to provide him with sexual pleasure and children, and also to act as unpaid domestic servant. As a reward, at the slightest whim of the male, the woman can be rejected without right of appeal and separated from her children. Not to mention her legal inferior status, one man counting for two women as court witnesses, as for shares in an inheritance. (Also not to mention female circumcision, which has nothing to do with Islam as a religion, and which to my knowledge is scarcely practiced in any Shi'ite region, although the matter was debated by theologians in the seventeenth century.)

Of course, Islamist apologists put forward arguments claiming that Islam *liberates* women, even if that brings a smile to the lips of militant feminists in western countries. First of all, they say – and this is recognized historically – Islam considerably improved the lot of women in Bedouin society who, at the time of Mohammad, underwent every kind of torment, starting with the ritual slaughter of little girls, rejection from a marriage without any compensation, virtually generalized slavery. Islam guarantees women an advantageous personal status compared with that of women only a few decades ago in many so-called developed western countries: the right to personal property, economic independence (for example, to hold a bank account), inheritance, respect for their dignity in public life, etc. For Islamists, the horror of the commercial exploitation of feminine nudity reveals the lack of respect that westerners have for their wives, the veil, on the contrary, being a salutary form of protection that guarantees privacy, modesty, and thus the whole person. A rejected wife can, in theory, demand the repayment of her dowry in its entirety, and that price is often fixed, at the time of marriage, at such a high level that the man must give up the idea of divorce: rejection or not, in both cases the legitimate interest of the woman is preserved.

The pertinent idea here for Muslims, that of the *nāmus*, is difficult to translate or explain for westerners (although one may recognize in it the Greek word *nomos*, law). It is a matter of both the virtue of women and the reputation of the family, realities that are invisible yet so sensitive and vulnerable that they immediately trigger reactions should danger threaten. It is what those who live on the northern shores of the Mediterranean call *honneur*, in its absolute sense: a moral value defended by men but of which women are the repositories. The more this honor is in danger, the more the male sensibilities of husbands and brothers are agitated, and they are ready to commit murder or suicide if necessary. The chador (veil) that appals our feminists is a form of protection against the irrational fear of losing the *nāmus*. The permissive society of Iran before the Revolution exposed this fragile treasure by increasing the chances for meetings, touchings, relations that were quite contrary to the jealous and puritanical severity of well-guarded homes, or the seclusion of wives and daughters that gave such a sense of security. Anyone who fails to watch over the *nāmus* of his family is a man without shame, without decency, and thus ill-bred. The prospect of the *nāmus* being violated, or even of a simple immodest glance, is thought of as a catastrophe which the preachers keep alive in the fearful imagination of their flock. Over and above the implications aiming to preserve the severity of family and sexual morals, they make use of these emotive images to stigmatize an attempt by foreigners to get their hands on the Islamic homeland: any incursion, even purely cultural, is the equivalent of an impure penetration, a rape.[2]

Apart from these debates on Islam in the role of women's liberator, which, from Tjakarta to Rabat, rouse preachers and militants of all shades of Islam, Shi'ism also offers several particular points regarding the status of women and marriage. To start with, it must be remembered that this branch of Islam originated from a *woman*, Fatima, the Prophet's daughter, filled with all the supernatural qualities that were then transmitted to her

2   G. THAISS, "The Conceptualization of Social Change through Metaphor," *Journal of Asian and African Studies*, 1–2 (1978), pp. 1–13.

descendants, the Imams. Her intercession, like that of other holy women, is invoked at Qom and elsewhere. If a woman inherits the prophetic charisma, and her descendants – for want of a male line – win the rights to succession from the male descendants of parents in the indirect line, how then can one fail to respect the rights of women in matters of inheritance? Hence arises the originality of Imami law in comparison with Sunnism: when there are no male heirs, it grants the entire patrimony of a dead man to his daughters.[3]

THE MARRIAGE OF PLEASURE: THE MYTH

Shi'ite particularism is marked notably by an institution of early Islam condemned by Sunnism, that of the temporary marriage or – more precisely – the marriage "of pleasure" (*mot'a*). Although this doctrinal and ethical peculiarity is known as Shi'ite, and as such contributes to the theological discourse and polemics between Shi'ites and Sunnis, it seems to be practised officially only in Iran. Some people have even speculated that it may be a survival of pre-Islamic Persia. The custom of temporary marriage is perhaps admitted – but as an anomaly – among Shi'ites in Iraq, where the law does not recognize it; in Lebanon, Shi'ite *ulema* recommend it, even if it is not officially *legal*.[4]

But sexual life cannot be mentioned without immediately entering realms of meaningful fancies:

> A man is approached by a woman who is totally cloaked in a black veil and is unrecognizable. She asks him whether he would want to *sigheh* her (i.e. make a temporary marriage) for a month . . . He is hesitant yet does not want to miss his chance. He asks her to remove her veil and to allow him to see her. She refuses, saying that if he is willing to *sigheh* her, he should do so without seeing her unveiled. She assures him that he would not be disappointed. He agrees to a *sigheh* of three nights.
>
> The black-veiled lady takes him to a house that is as beautiful as a palace and instructs her servants to bathe him, give him fine clothes to wear, and

3   Y. LINANT DE BELLEFONDS, "Le Droit imāmite," *Le Shī'isme imāmite* (Strasbourg Symposium), Paris, PUF, 1970, pp. 197ff.
4   See W. ENDE, "Ehe auf Zeit (*mut'a*) in der innerislamischen Discussion der Gegenwart," *Die Welt des Islams*, 20, 1–2 (1980), p. 20 (Irak) and p. 36 (Lebanon). See also O. CARRÉ, "La 'Révolution islamique' selon Muhammad Husayn Fadlallāh," *Orient*, 29, 1 (1988), p. 78.

then bring him to her room. Washed, perfumed and clothed, he is brought
to a most charming room where the black-veiled lady is expecting him. She
is still in her veil, and though he is excited, congratulating his own good
fortune, he is impatient to see her face. When they finally perform the *sigheh*
ceremony and the woman takes off her veil, he is enthralled by her beauty
and charm. When after three days and nights their contract is over, the man,
regretting his own time restriction, begs her to extend their temporary
marriage longer. But she refuses, saying that he had his chance in the
beginning. She then asks her servants to see him off.[5]

Such is the myth of the temporary marriage as dreamed up by men in
the manner of a tale from the *Thousand and One Nights*, encountered many
times by an attentive female anthropologist during a survey conducted in
Iran. In keeping with Islamic tradition, the plot of this story begins with
man and his sexual desire. Blind desire (the man cannot see the woman he
is "marrying"), which is normal and forms sufficient justification for temporary marriage. But in fact, and astonishingly, the hero of the tale is
matched by the woman's initiative: noticeable here is the feminine role in
the choice of companion (whom she can see), and her rejection of him after
the consummation of their pleasure, either because she has obtained the
satisfaction she desired or because she wants to make the point, by her
refusal to extend the marriage, that man's pleasure is not paramount.
Equally noticeable is the dreamlike quality, removed from material and
temporal constraints: no baby appears as a result of this union, justified
only by the search for unbridled enjoyment; even money gives rise to no
embarrassment or dispute in this contract, since the woman appears to be
well provided for and . . . free!

THE THEORY

On the other hand, only the man's satisfaction is taken into account in the
traditional justification for temporary marriage. The only limit set on that
satisfaction – and not very restrictive – is the prohibition on carnal relations
between sunrise and sunset in the thirty days of Ramadhan. Ascetic celibacy is an outrage against nature, and Muslims in general proscribe it,
getting their support from a famous *hadith* attributed to the Prophet, "No
monasticism in Islam" (*lā rahbāniya fi'l-eslām*), which seems to echo a verse

5   I take this account from the excellent book by Shahla HAERI, *Law of Desire: Temporary
Marriage in Iran*, London, I. B. Tauris, 1989. Here, p. 154.

from the Koran: "In the hearts of those who follow him [Jesus] we have put compassion and mercy, and the monastic way of life they instituted – we did not prescribe it for them – was solely because they were driven by the desire to please God" (LVII, 27). It is true that Louis Massignon, examining the oldest Koranic exegeses and rejecting the authenticity of the *hadith*, concluded for his part that the vow of chastity was accepted by certain Muslims and was condemned only much later.[6] But his efforts as a Christian orientalist to justify ascetic practices are repudiated by the majority of Muslims, and particularly Shi'ites.

According to Shi'ite tradition, the fact that Sunnis are banned from practising temporary marriage stems from the caliph 'Omar, because of his personal animosity toward Imam 'Ali. Here is the fine story piously related by the theologians:

> 'Omar b. al-Khattāb (the second caliph) was holding a grudge against his Holiness Imam 'Ali because of his claim to have intercourse with one of his wives every night. Deciding to prove the Imam boastful, 'Omar invited him to come to his house for dinner. 'Omar instructed his servants to delay serving the dinner, scheming to oblige 'Ali to spend the night at his house. His Holiness 'Ali played into 'Omar's hands and agreed to sleep over. At dawn, under the pretext of awakening him for his morning prayers, 'Omar rushed to 'Ali's chamber. Addressing His Holiness 'Ali, 'Omar said, "Do you remember to have claimed to do such and such act every night?" Imam 'Ali says, "Yes." 'Omar says, "Well, last night you were at my house and had none of your wives with you." Imam 'Ali disagrees and says "Ask your sister." 'Omar becomes so enraged that he rushes out of the house and immediately orders the banning of *mut'a* marriage and the stoning of those who continue to practise it.[7]

As Shahla Haeri suggests, the many dimensions of this anecdote, which is probably without historical foundation, lead us to the heart of the rivalry between Sunnism and Shi'ism: 'Ali's sexual potency (thus, by a metaphorical shift in meaning, his political strength), his failed symbolic emasculation by his enemy 'Omar, and lastly the humiliation suffered by the caliph in return when his sister, without however violating religious law, escapes the rigorous surveillance of family honor. We may observe here the complete non-existence of feminine dignity: had the caliph's sister not been

6   See L. MASSIGNON, *Essai sur les origines du lexique technique de la mystique musulmane* new edn, Paris, Vrin, 1954, pp. 148ff.
7   *Law of Desire*, p. 170.

there, any maidservant would have served the purpose, if it had not been necessary to humiliate 'Omar's contemptible memory by reducing his sister to the level of mere release for the virile Imam's sexual drive. The perfectly irrational justification for the marriage of pleasure and refusal to punish its abuses would be strengthened in Shi'ite eyes because the ban emanated from the despised caliph.

The practice of temporary marriage is not merely a survival of folklore or a barbarous custom shamefacedly marginalized by society as a disgraceful deviation from accepted standards of good behaviour. Classic Shi'ite theologians hold it to be entirely legitimate, if not commendable, and the Iranian civil code, since there has been one, has recognized the legality of such a union, and guaranteed the reciprocal rights of the partners "in pleasure" and those of any children which may result (a fundamental element, bearing in mind Muslims' excessive fear of any illegitimate offspring and the base status reserved for children conceived out of wedlock). What does the civil code of 1985 (which resumes that of 1928) have to say?

Article 1075: The marriage is held to be temporary when its agreed duration is specified.

Article 1076: The duration of the temporary marriage must be clearly specified.

Article 1095: The temporary marriage is null and void if the amount of the dower is not fixed in the contract.

Article 1097: In the temporary marriage, if the man gives up his right definitively before consummating the union, he must nevertheless pay one half of the agreed dower.

Article 1113: In the temporary marriage, the wife has no right to maintenance allowance unless this condition has been fixed in the contract.

These legal provisions are relatively tenuous and do not establish a precise definition of the "temporary" marriage (*aqd-e monqate'*), a term that the Iranian legislator obviously prefers to marriage "of pleasure" (*mot'a*), as used by the theologians. Is it possible to have several temporary wives at a time? No restriction is set for the man, but the wife, in religious Law as in the civil code, can dispose of her body only if it is free from engagement with any other man, according to the same conditions as for the so-called "permanent" (*dā'em*) marriage. At the end of the union, death of the husband, or divorce, she must observe a waiting period: three menstruations or, after the menopause, three months, in the case of permanent marriage (article 1151); but only two menstruations or forty-five days in the case of temporary marriage.

Note the realism of the civil code, which does not waste time on the bizarre nature of the temporary marriage or try to set limits on an institution that functions by force of circumstance and the goodwill of the mullas – the same thing occurred in the secular system prevailing before the Islamic Revolution, when personal status defined in the 1920s already came under religious Law.[8]

A clearer appraisal is given in a legal manual intended to guide Shi'ites through the meanderings of the Iraqi law of 1959 for everything regarding their personal status:

> Temporary marriage is an exception from the general rules of permanent marriage and it is found for particular circumstances, therefore it is stated by the Scholars of Shi'it [*sic*] School that:
>
> 1 It is detestable for a virgin girl to make contract of temporary marriage. And the man is forbidden to tempt a virgin woman to be his wife for a specified period of time.
>
> 2 If a man is able to offer a living of well-to-do standard for a wife and children it is preferable, and it is his duty, for society to choose a wife to live with for all his life.[9]

The Iraqi jurist, who goes on to introduce a moralistic commentary on human frailty and the realism of Islam, is no fool as regards the quality of the cut-price marriage provided by the marriage of pleasure. It should therefore be reserved for widows or divorcees, those second-hand women, whereas young virgins should be able still to dream of the handsome and noble knight coming across the desert to carry them off to the fortunate land of those who live happily ever after. How can the reduced waiting period be justified, however, when this precaution of the jurists is intended to establish paternity clearly should there be a remarriage? Are wives "of pleasure" less likely to conceive, or is their status closer to that of slaves with whom their master has coupled before reselling them? In a classic compendium I read: "A divorced slave of an age to conceive, who does not menstruate, will undergo a trial period of one and a half months, whether her husband is a freeman or slave."[10]

---

8   See ENDE, "Ehe auf Zeit," p. 12.

9   M. H. al-NAJJAR, *Islam-Jafari Rules of Personal Status and Related Rules of Iraqian Law*, 2nd edn, Tehran, WOFIS, 1978, pp. 66ff.

10   A. QUERRY, *Droit musulman: Recueil de lois concernant les musulmans schyites*, part 2, Paris, Imprimerie Nationale, 1872 (trans. of the *Sharāye' ol-eslām* of Mohaqqeq al-Helli, d. 1277), p. 33.

Looked at from a rational viewpoint, the reduction in the waiting period is difficult to understand: if recognition of paternity is necessary, does it not obey biological laws that are the same whatever the legal status of the parents? There is, however, an explanation that brings in the subtle provisions of the legislator in favour of the woman: permanent marriage (*nekāh*), says a contemporary Iranian theologian, is brought to an end by repudiation, and the husband can always have second thoughts during the waiting period, throughout which he continues to pay his rejected wife a complete allowance (*nafaqa*), so the longer the period the greater the woman's protection; in the case of temporary marriage, with a term agreed in advance by common consent, as the waiting period is not accompanied by any allowance, it is in the woman's interest that it should last as short a time as possible so that she may have the opportunity to remarry.[11]

Muslim lawmakers, who readily envisage the most scabrous situations and reply to the most preposterous questions, have anticipated cases in which the waiting time is purely and simply suppressed. First, obviously, if there has been no penetration. Others will maintain that coitus interruptus (*àzl*) is the equivalent of the absence of sexual relations. Some even affirm that sodomy, because it cannot lead to conception, authorizes the suppression of any "trial period." Lastly, again because of the impossibility of conception, a woman past the menopause is exempted from a waiting period by easygoing mullas.

Still other features render temporary marriage of interest to Shi'ites, according to the situation in which they find themselves: if the man is not financially very stable, he is not obliged to pay a living allowance. Thus, unlike permanent marriage, in which the wife is entitled to demand a decent standard of living, the temporary husband is not forced to maintain his wife – unless the partners have expressly included a clause to the contrary in their contract. Moreover, it is not foreseen that the temporary wife shall inherit from her husband, which may be of some reassurance to the children of a former marriage who may see their father remarry with an adventuress. (On the other hand, the inheritance of children remains the same, whatever the matrimonial contract – temporary or permanent – of their parents.)

For the wife, the formalities of the marriage of pleasure are simplified, and a young virgin can contract one without having to produce the express permission of her father or guardian, as is the case in the first "definitive"

11   M. SHAFĀ'I, *Mot'a va āsār-e hoquqi va ejtemā'i-e ān*, 6th edn, Tehran, Heydari, 1352/1973, quoted by HAERI, *Law of Desire*, p. 58.

marriage. This greater liberty is challenged, however, by certain jurists who think of the considerable devaluation of a deflowered woman, and save the piercing of the hymen for a union reputedly more noble and lasting, or at any rate make it subject to authorization.[12] Today, under Iran's Islamic Republic, the authorities mostly try to have temporary marriages registered in order to avoid abuses, but the practice is more easygoing, notably leaning on the fact that a contract "for pleasure" does not require a witness, so no registration or notarized deed. This similarly simplifies "fiddles" over the waiting period . . .

In theoretical terms, but ones that are used in a very direct and and blunt manner by Islamic jurisprudence, marriage is compared to a transaction in which what is traded is the sex of the woman, over whom the husband acquires control for his pleasure and the procreation of children; looked at from this angle, *temporary* marriage is a sort of rental contract, in which the woman hires out her vagina (*boz'*) for a specified period and an agreed rent, so that the husband can enjoy it as he pleases, avoiding procreation if he wishes.[13] In Shi'ite law, a woman in this case is considered as "hired" (*mosta'jera*), in the same way as a workman who hires out his labour. The rental agreement may include clauses that are *a priori* absurd, such as the absence of sexual relations between the couple, or the number or frequency of such relations (on condition that the total period planned at the beginning for the validity of the contract is not dependent on the number of copulations), or a period of 99 years. In the last case, the marriage is deemed to be agreed until death, but does not imply – unless there are express stipulations to the contrary – any obligation upon the man to provide the woman with board and lodging, or any rights of inheritance between the spouses, and divorce is comparable to a simple remission of the time limit, without any legal formality.

THE IDEOLOGICAL JUSTIFICATION

It appears that originally temporary marriage occupied only a marginal position in Muslim law and practices; it was justified by the need to relieve the sexual distress of the Prophet's warriors when they were campaigning

12 Mohaqqeq HELLI, *Sharāye' ol-eslām*, Persian trans. by A. b. Ahmad Yazdi, ed. M.-T. Dānesh-Pajouh, 2nd edn, vol. II, University of Tehran, 1358/1979, p. 523.
13 HAERI, *Law of Desire*, pp. 33ff, 52ff; *boz'* properly speaking means, according to Dozy's dictionary, "the *hymen*, membranous fold ordinarily found, in virgins, at the entrance to the vagina."

far from their wives. Later, and right up to the present day among the Shi'ites, any occasion giving rise to a man's prolonged stay far from his home, whether for business or pilgrimage, justifies his finding a casual companion whom he does not expect to present him with a family.

However, a new type of justification has appeared over the last 100 or so years. Most often quoted on the subject are recent Iranian authors like ayatollah Motahhari (d. 1979), but the arguments one reads in them contain nothing very original in the polemic aiming to reinstate temporary marriage in the face of feminist objections. Even in Sunni areas, theoretically hostile to temporary marriage, the institution preserved by the Shi'ites has aroused envy in some, who propose to imitate it.[14]

First of all, it was noticed that in regions where Shi'ites and Sunnis lived together, as in Iraq, certain Shi'ite missionaries were succeeding in attracting Sunnis to their mosques by painting a glowing picture of the possibility of licitly copulating with venal women. A violent campaign against such practices was unleashed in the journal of Egyptian reformist Muslims, *al-Manār*, in 1900. But the competition between Shi'ism and Sunnism soon seemed derisory compared with the seduction exercised by the modern western world over those elites who temporarily left their homeland to complete their university training. The sight of unsecluded women often provoked a rejection of Islam, as if the young Muslims were discovering that all the rules of purity and modesty they had been taught were no more than an embarrassing and useless set of shackles. They found themselves faced with two irreconcilable positions: either the West was right to throw off the yoke of religion, and the key to its success came from a powerful rationalist and agnostic source (sexual relations having to be considered from the point of view of hygiene, demography, or amorous desire, but in no circumstance from that of a theological justification or prohibition); or the West was utterly rotten, corrupt, satanic, and its use of carnal seduction to turn Muslims away from their religion was seen as part of a plan to enslave dominated nations.

Islam's religious authorities, whose flocks were deserting the mosque for the cinema or cabaret, looked on the attractions of western culture, which disgusted them, as so many dishonest and accursed lures, saying that a child of parents who drink alcohol will be born with a defect and that the sexual promiscuity of westerners is utterly to blame for all the incurable illnesses of our times, syphilis, AIDS, multiple sclerosis, muscular

14   M. MUTAHHARI, *The Rights of Women in Islam*, Tehran, WOFIS, 1981, pp. 25–7; W. ENDE, "Ehe auf Zeit."

dystrophy, cystic fibrosis, rickets, etc. Not to mention the social disorders that irrationally obsess them, as if the child born out of wedlock receives less affection from its mother than one whose parents get divorced or row from morning till night, and will sink into delinquency while all the others become little angels. What really upsets Islam's ideologists is the image of the free, unveiled woman, who challenges their complacent virility and threatens the equilibrium of the home.

Here I am taking up the argument of a westernized Iranian intellectual who attained the highest honors under the Pahlavi monarchy, Hossein Nasr.[15] For him, the abandonment by the West and its imitators of a traditional patriarchal structure guaranteed by the authority of men over women was the beginning of social ruin. According to Nasr, the family as conceived by Islam goes beyond the modern fragmented form, but is no longer the oppressive tribal structure: it is a broad social unit willed by religion, headed by the male, father, defender, provider and "priest" . . .

> The Muslim family is the miniature of the whole of Muslim society and its firm basis. In it the man or father functions as the imam in accordance with the patriarchal nature of Islam. The religious responsibility of the family rests upon his shoulders. . . . In the family the father upholds the tenets of the religion and his authority symbolizes that of God in the world. The man is in fact respected in the family precisely because of the sacerdotal function that he fulfils. The rebellion of Muslim women in certain quarters of Islamic society came when men themselves ceased to fulfil their religious function and lost their virile and patriarchal character. By becoming themselves effeminate they caused the ensuing reaction of revolt among certain women who no longer felt the authority of religion upon themselves.

Contact with western culture, which offered a radically different picture of the family and the role of women, if we are to believe Nasr, destabilized the Islamic "family unit" guided by the authority of the father. In another passage where he tries to justify the licit nature of temporary marriage in Shi'ite jurisprudence, our author begins by using arguments internal to Islam, drawn from the revelation or early Islamic history; then, as if admitting that supernatural argument is not enough to convince, he adds:

> The legitimization of marriage among mankind from the beginning until today is an answer to the instinctive urge for sexual union. Permanent

marriage has been continuously practised among the different peoples of the world. Yet despite this fact, and all the campaigns and efforts at public persuasion that are carried out against it, there exist throughout the countries of the world, in large and small cities, both hidden and public places where illegitimate sexual union or fornication takes place.[16]

Taking this fact into account, Nasr goes on, Islam, which detests adultery and fornication as the sources of impurity and moral corruption, has made legitimate a form of sexual union in which certain conditions are demanded of the woman (to have only one man at a time and observe the necessary waiting period after the union). "The legitimizing of temporary marriage in Islam [*here Nasr means 'in Shi'ism'*] is done with the aim of allowing within the sacred law possibilities that minimize the evils resulting from the passions of men, which if not channelled lawfully manifest themselves in much more dangerous ways outside the structure of religious law."

Foiling fornication because the man has every right to satisfy himself and the woman is his servant sums up the Shi'ite case for justifying temporary marriage. Becoming a seductress – that is, provoking man's irrepressible desires – and a potential mistress, a woman loses her utilitarian and calming function, overturns the order of things, and entices man towards the whirlpool of the senses and passions.

In no case can the sexual need of the woman be taken into consideration here, and the search for such satisfaction on her part would be regarded as an intolerable insubordination. The sole right granted to a woman is to give her consent at the time of the contract that binds her. (In permanent marriage, and notably in cases of polygamy where a wife may be deserted, certain jurists grant the woman the right to demand that her husband must couple with her at least once every four months to ensure that she has the chance of becoming a mother . . .)

Here one could take up the reasoning put forward by ayatollah Mortaza Motahhari in his famous book (quoted earlier), in which with fresh arguments, in order to reply to objections against Islam raised in a feminist women's magazine published in Iran during the time of the Shah, he set out the traditional view of Shi'ite theology on *the rights of women in Islam*. One could repeat the quibbles of certain Sunni theologians tempted by the

16 'A. TABĀTABĀ'I and S. H. NASR, Appendix II, "Mut'ah or Temporary Marriage," in *Shi'ite Islam*, London, George Allen & Unwin, 1975, pp. 229–30, from which also the preceding and following quotations are taken.

idea of reinstating temporary marriage. One could reread even in the discourses of the last Shah of Iran all the invective against the "permissiveness" of western society. One could quote *ad infinitum* the Friday sermons from the mosques in Iran and elsewhere denouncing the depravity of morals and the failure of Christianity in western countries. In every case one would meet the same anguished fear of the West and its seductions, the same obsession with protecting young people from the dissolute morals that endanger the tranquillity of the home and, without altering the demands of social and religious order, tempering the effects of nature on young men who cannot marry before months and years of frustration.

MARRIAGE OR PROSTITUTION?

What exactly are the possibilities, licit or not, of obtaining sexual union? Permanent marriage remains the most common solution for Shi'ite Muslims. Adulterous relations are rare, usually hounded down by families who feel destabilized by a change of woman not controlled and sanctioned by a contract. Resorting to a female slave who could be used as one pleased would presuppose a return to an institution that has been abolished. Classic prostitution, officially banned in Iran today, still exists there in a risky fashion, though it arouses not only a bad conscience but also fears for public health. In Iran's Islamic Republic there is little likelihood that an institution such as the brothel, so far removed from the ideal of purity, could achieve legal status. There remains temporary marriage, and its very flexible formula theoretically allows "simplified access" to women.

Paid sex is organized differently in every society according to moral values and the constraints of both hygiene and the market. Whatever the context, Christian or Muslim, prostitution is regarded with contempt by official morality, but tolerated, even organized, by society to meet a need and avoid a greater evil.

Islam detests the idea of a succession of sexual unions with different partners for the same woman, whose child may be of uncertain paternity, whereas it regards as perfectly normal a man having a limitless number of women to appease his desires, provided he has the means. Nevertheless, there is evidence of prostitution in the majority of Muslim countries. Notably so in Iran in the Safavid period, when Shi'ism became dominant: according to the detailed description of their customs by the Chevalier Chardin, the courtesans of Isfahan in 1666 set a high price on their charms for the men who made them come and dance at their feasts and enjoyed them later in some little hideaway. At that time there would seem to have been some 14,000 officially registered prostitutes in the kingdom's capital.

> Although this abominable profession is so widespread [comments Chardin], I do not believe there is any other country where women sell themselves so dear; for during the first few years of their debauchery they may not be had for less than fifteen or twenty pistoles; this is incomprehensible when one considers that in Persia, on the one hand, their religion allows every man to purchase female slaves and to have as many concubines as he pleases – which should reduce the price of public women; and on the other hand, young men have little money, and are married at a fairly early age. The cause must be attributed to the lustfulness of these hot countries, where the urge is sharper than in other places, and the art of these creatures, which is a kind of sorcery.[17]

At the close of the old Iranian regime (1979), that oldest profession continued to prosper in the capital of the ultra-Shi'ite empire, in the red-light district of Shahr-e now ("new town"); today it is resurfacing, so it is said, against a background of poverty, but in a scattered and uncontrolled manner. This suggests that the Shi'ite institution of the marriage of pleasure does not do away with commerce in the oldest profession in the world.

Temporary marriage greatly resembles it, however, and may be said without exaggeration to compete with it easily in reputedly "holy" places. "Free" love is offered by women who rent themselves to good Muslims while at the same time imparting to their trade an extremely conventional and religiously licit air: they exercise it in the sanctuaries (for purposes of soliciting), clad in a black chador, in exchange for money, and repeatedly. This last point seems hard to justify in an Islamic context, when the law appears to impose a strict waiting period between each union. But that would doubtless be to forget the easy exceptions that can be made use of to annul the waiting period: apart from the exemptions of easygoing jurists mentioned earlier, when there is no risk of conception, a current legal ruse (*hila-ye shari*) consists of contracting with the same person a fresh temporary marriage of very short duration following the one that has just expired, and not consummating it: the second marriage cancels out the waiting

---

17 *Voyages du chevalier CHARDIN en Perse et autres lieux de l'Orient*, new edn by L. Langles, Paris, Le Normant, 1811, vol. II, pp. 208ff. On prostitution in modern Iran, see the references made by W. FLOOR, "Some Notes on Mut'a," *ZDMG*, 138, 2 (1988), pp. 25–331, and chiefly Jakob E. POLAK, "Die Prostitution in Persien," *Wiener medizinische Wochenschrift*, 2, nos. 32, 35, 39 (1861).

period after the first and, as it is not put into effect, it does not carry a "waiting period" itself; women can thus contract a series of temporary marriages . . . (a ruse already pointed out by the orientalist Edward G. Browne in Kermān in 1888).[18]

MARRIAGE . . . UNCONSUMMATED

I have indicated the possibility of contracting a marriage with a non-consummation clause. In reality, it is surely the most frequent form of the marriage of pleasure. (I am not speaking of a pseudo-union with the intention of flirtation and sexual amusement without copulation, a form that is certainly practised, sometimes recommended by mullas and made licit by temporary marriage.)[19] The secondary benefit sought in this unconsummated marriage is to take advantage of a link of kinship automatically created by a marriage contract in order to rub shoulders with the close companions of the so-called "wife" of a few hours, without obliging them to respect the stringent rules about veiling and distance: any and every one are henceforth considered as kin through family connections (*mahram*), and can thus be approached without causing problems. This practice, commonly known in Persian as *siqa-ye mahramiyat*, seems farcical only to those who are unaware of the dilemmas posed by the scrupulous segregation of the sexes in traditional Muslim circles, and the daily problems of promiscuity, poverty, or quite simply, proximity.[20]

Another reason for such a false temporary marriage, in very religious circles, is to give young people destined to marry the opportunity to see each other more freely, for a few hours or days, without however unveiling anything more than the face; negotiations between families can subsequently begin for the real marriage, which will be permanent. In certain cases – ayatollah Motahhari recommends this formula to young people who want to flirt – engaged couples discover each other's body in a sort of "trial" marriage (*ezdevāj-e āzmāyeshi*), if possible without going as far as defloration, which would devalue the ultimate discovery that should be reserved for the following stage, permanent marriage . . .[21]

---

18 See E. G. BROWNE, *A Year amongst the Persians* (reprint), London, Adam & Charles Black, 1970, p. 506.
19 HAERI, *Law of Desire*, pp. 98ff; ENDE, "Ehe auf Zeit," p. 33.
20 HAERI, *Law of Desire*, pp. 89ff.
21 Ibid., pp 97ff: MUTAHHARI, *The Rights of Women*, p. 31.

WOMEN'S REVENGE?

In a society entirely dominated by men, a law such as that of the marriage of pleasure can thus have some utilitarian aspects: it is no longer for the exclusive and selfish enjoyment of the man, but for reasons of convenience and social opportunity.

Going further still, in Shahla Haeri's remarkable survey, one finds situations which turn upside down common stereotypes of sexuality in Islamic society: women who practice temporary marriage are not passive objects or pieces of merchandise, and still less purely venal partners. Mahvash, one of the ethnologist's informants, confided that as she had no permanent husband she sought her pleasure among the men she met around the sanctuary at Qom, and did not deny her reputation as *siqa-ru*, in other words, a "professional;" her only regret was that this reputation closed the door of the "godfearing" against her. It was *she*, as in the story with which I began this chapter, who chose her partners. For Foruq, innocent and with all that she could wish for, who married for love a rich and pious merchant (*hājji*), regardless of the fact that he had another family elsewhere, marriage whether temporary or permanent did not matter to her: she simply observed that it was at her place that her lover performed his daily post-coital ablutions, and that he was thus saving the best of himself for her . . . For her part, Fati admitted that despite the misfortune which turned her into a professional *siqa*, she experienced pleasure with men who were all the more amorous because they had paid for a set time and wanted to get the most out of it, unlike their relations with their wives who were always within reach, and of whom they had grown weary.

Apart from these cases in which the desires of women (interviewed by a female compatriot in whom they felt able to confide) could be freely expressed instead of being submerged in the deceptive silence of sexual segregation, mention must be made of those women who see temporary marriage as a means of fulfilling a vow, and who seek out the most handsome *sayyed* in Shi'ite sanctuaries, to propose that they spend a night with them or their daughters, *paying them to do so*. Possibly this is a form of latent masochism sublimated into a dream of coupling with men with the prophetic charisma, rather like the daughters of Israel who dreamed of giving themselves to a descendant of David in the hope that it would result in a glorious lineage. It will be agreed that this kind of erotic proposal, in a sacred place, bears no comparison with those sorry brothels where love is reduced to a series of rapid and nasty exchanges, but rather recalls some ancient rite of sacred copulation. It is obviously possible that the mullas take advantage of the situation, when they are solicited, and one might even think that sometimes they are the ones who give rise to such ideas.

RELATIONS BETWEEN THE SEXES

Compared with the Christian doctrine of the indissoluble conjugal bond, Islam knows no truly *definitive* marriage, and authorizes the pure and simple repudiation of the wife without any other form of proceedings. Certain Sunni practices, in the guise of a permanent marriage in which the contracting parties come to an agreement in advance about the date of divorce, apart from a few details, boil down to the temporary marriage of the Shi'ites.[22]

Despite the purely contractual nature of marriage and the facility with which the celestial Legislator allows the Muslim to dismiss his wife or take a new one (up to four at a time, but with certain restrictions, not counting slaves or temporary wives), it is noticeable that Muslim society is no less attached than our own to a monogamous family set-up and a permanent matrimonial union with mutual faithfulness of husband and wife. Instability among couples threatens alliances between families, which are the warp and woof of the social fabric. The worst upsets occur if the monogamous preference of the wife's family is assailed, as they will always seek to ensure a stronger position for the offspring of their clan. Today, apart from some exceptions encouraged by the clergy (in the case of war widows who should not be left to fend for themselves, but also because of the lechery of certain mullas, whose example is often denounced in popular culture), the model of the Iranian family is fairly close to that of a French provincial family prior to the urban and industrial explosion of the 1950s. In any case, town life, with its constraints caused by cramped housing, has limited enlarging the family beyond the classic monogamous nuclear family.

In spite of the economic difficulties besetting the parents of a large family in Muslim countries today and the almost voluntary limits placed on the number of their progeny by urbanized parents, procreation remains one of the fundamental aims of marriage. A childless couple is an anomaly, probably smitten by a divine curse. "Children are the economic and defensive power" of the family, and the arrival of the firstborn, after the marriage, is awaited impatiently, any delay being lived through as a kind of

---

22   See D. VON DENFFER, "Mut'a – Ehe oder Prostitution? Ein Betrag zur Untersuchung einer Institution des Schi'itischen Islam," *ZDMG*, 128 (1978), p. 305.

torment; sterility is often the immediate cause of the rejection of the wife, humiliation, and a fall in status; in short, children are the guarantee of a stable home, of the eminent role that will be played by the mother, and her insurance against being dethroned by a second wife.[23]

This also explains the marginal nature of temporary marriage among Shi'ites, where the practice is licit and easily obtainable: as this kind of union does not usually have procreation as its end, it can satisfy nothing more than a sexual urge. Temporary marriage, in which the man has the canonical right, even without the consent of his partner, to practice coitus interruptus so as to avoid being pursued by a mother asking for allowances and subsidies, and which may contain a strict contraception clause (the man or the woman demanding that the marriage shall be childless), has no chance of attracting a young woman of childbearing age in an Islamic society such as those we know today.

We are talking here of two very different kinds of sexual union. In the first, which is the norm, all lustful fantasies are extinguished with the light at the conjugal bedside.[24]

The other union, the one that takes wing toward heavenly delights and is blessed by the mullas with their legal phrases, does not give a fig for marriage, children, or the rights of women. It comprises notably aspects that offend common sense and reduce the partner to a clearly inferior status – that of a person who hires out a part of her anatomy for the enjoyment of another.

The last word belongs here to an Iranian cleric who had temporarily abandoned his mulla's turban and garment to visit relatives in France and Sweden: having met young men and women there who were living together peacefully and without scandal, sometimes with happy children in their "family home," he realized that the Shi'ites' marriage of pleasure, which has caused so much ink to flow because it is practised in a traditional society, is nothing other than concubinage with a less ugly name, registered as such in some western countries between young people who for various reasons have chosen not to legalize their situation in too restrictive a fashion . . .

23 VIEILLE, *La féodalité et l'état*, pp. 90, 130ff.
24 Ibid., p. 143.

7

Islamic Revolutionary Thinking

Two simplistic explanations of the Iranian revolutionary movement are frequently heard: it is said to be the result of a classic political mobilization hijacked by a better-prepared social category (the clergy); or on the other hand, in the culturalist and elitist view, the clergy and their agents are credited with "awakening the consciousness" of the masses – because they are supposed to have been more aware of the distance between the nation's aspirations and the oppressive realities imposed by the West – and the clerical domination is *de facto* justified. On the one hand, a devilish manipulation, with the probable connivance of an external power (United States, Soviet Union . . . ?), on the other, the providential miracle out of the magician's hat. Things were probably far more complicated, although the evolution of the Iranian revolutionary movement sometimes seems to prove both interpretations right, each in its turn.

When many thought that religion would lose its hold over the people, the social movement – for want of anything better – adopted the language of Islam; doubtless because, at a time when dictatorship stifled all opposition, that is where it found a means of self-expression.[1] Religious sensitivity and a rejection of the West were not the only factors in the Iranian uprising of 1978–9, but the religious coloration eventually prevailed. So what new ideas had germinated in Muslim circles, clerical or not, to channel the discourse of the revolutionary movement? What is the ideological posterity of the Revolution? Is it an Islamist, i.e. radical Muslim, or Shi'ite revolution?

1 B. HOURCADE, "Iran: Révolution islamiste ou tiers-mondiste?" *Hérodote*, 36 (1985), pp. 138–58.

CLERICS AND LAYMEN: SAME STRUGGLE?

Political mobilization in pre-revolutionary Iran was not the act of a homogeneous category of militants. When the fruits of modernity were becoming more and more visible and less and less attainable, intellectuals sometimes lagged behind a general awareness that combined a rejection of cultural dependence and a growing economic frustration. In that quest for a direction, there was rivalry between different kinds of intellectuals, the traditional educated men (*ulema*, specialists in theological learning), westernized intellectuals (specialists in knowledge of and about the West) and "new intellectuals." The latter, having a modern speciality (knowledge of at least one European language), sought to legitimize a non-traditional discourse on religion: instead of having climbed the ladder of religious learning in traditional theological schools (*madrasa*), they studied in a more or less secular system of education and, having access by their own means to a corpus of religious knowledge (the Koran, tradition), they claimed to give it a new interpretation, not distorted by centuries of torpor.

Until the 1970s no one had seemed to expect a great renewal of Islam, and in any case no major political challenge disturbed the peaceful path of Muslim countries toward progress and development. The few known incidents that cropped up *en route* were regarded as exceptions, or at the most as resistance of a reactionary nature: in 1909 the opposition of Sheikh Fazlollāh Nuri – the most erudite of the *ulema* in Tehran at the time – to the democratic Iranian movement terminated with his public execution, in the capital, without anyone daring to protest. Later, the two parallel movements of the Muslim Brotherhood in Egypt and the Near East, and the "Devotees of Islam" (*Fedā'iyān-e eslām*, Shi'ite extremists active between 1946 and 1956) in Iran were harshly repressed by Nasser (from 1954) and the Shah (in 1956) without the populations involved making the slightest attempt to rebel.[2] The rebellions that took place in Iran in 1963 could easily be presented to the press as backward-looking resistance in which Islam did not play a very enlightened role; all of which justified their brutal crushing as, in 1964, a new repression of the Egyptian Muslim Brothers and the execution of their intellectual leader, Sayyed Qotb.

---

2 See Y. RICHARD, "L'Organisation des Fedā'iyān-e eslām, mouvement intégriste musulman en Iran (1945–1956)," in O. Carré and P. Dumont, eds, *Radicalismes islamiques*, vol. I, Paris, L'Harmattan, 1985, pp. 23–82; G. KEPEL, *The Prophet and Pharaoh: Muslim Extremism in Egypt*, London, al-Saqi, 1985.

In effect, from that date onwards everything changed. The new Muslim theorists henceforth knew where their enemy lay, and intended to combat it on the intellectual plane as well. They took up the challenge of modernity and showed that they had plans for society for our day and age. On the Shi'ite side, isolation was broken by the religious wing of the Mosaddeqist National Front. Dr Mosaddeq, who was Prime Minister from 1951 to 1953 and nationalized the British-owned Anglo-Iranian Oil Company, had failed, after the defection of religious support, to overthrow the Shah's autocracy.[3] Nevertheless, among those who had supported him to the very end, there existed convinced Muslims who sharply criticized ayatollah Kāshāni's volte-face against the nationalists, discussed above, and tried to define a new route where Islam would be openly demanded together with political values. They rejected the simple secular nationalist fight and, in their Muslim militancy, accepted liberal and democratic values. Often their chief fear was realizing that if they did not express themselves with their religious references, the sole alternative to the Shah's autocratic rule would be Marxism.

While retracing here the broad lines of the ideological development of Iranian Shi'ites, I am by no means forgetting the parallel renewal that took place in Iraq and Lebanon.[4] The fact that Iraq also played a pivotal role, thanks to the meeting in Najaf of clerics from different geographical and political horizons, in no way alters the originality of the Iranian situation. Islam in Iran, greatly reduced in its public expression for half a century, resurfaced in spectacular fashion from the years 1960–70. And since, against all expectation, it was in Iran that the Islamic Revolution took place, it is important to examine the reason.

Within the sphere of influence of Mosaddeq's National Front Muslims began to think politically. Among the most eminent let us mention the "father" of liberal political Islam, the engineer Mehdi Bāzargān.[5] The

---

3   Y. RICHARD, "Ayatollah Kashani: Precursor of the Islamic Republic?" in N. Keddie, ed., *Religion and Politics in Iran*, New Haven and London, Yale University Press, 1983, pp. 101–24.

4   On these two countries and chiefly on Mohammad-Bāqer al-Sadr, see above, ch. 5.

5   H. E. CHEHABI, *Iranian Politics and Religious Modernism: The Liberation Movement of Iran under the Shah and Khomeini*, Ithaca, Cornell University Press, and London, I. B. Tauris, 1990. Chehabi writes "Liberation Movement of Iran," a coinage used by the *Nahzat-e āzādi-e Irān* in its documents in English. The translation used here, *Movement for Liberty in Iran*, avoids the inaccurate suggestion that there would be a struggle against an occupying enemy (in Persian, *āzādi-bakhsh*).

founder, in 1965, of the Movement for Liberty in Iran (*Nahzat-e Āzādi-e Iran*), this graduate of the École centrale in Paris was the inspiration, as he himself claimed in 1981, while he was at the lowest point of his political position, both for the founders of the Islamic Republic and for its keenest enemies, the People's Mojāhedin. In the beginning – a fruitful innovation – his movement gathered together just as many non-clerics as eminent clerics like ayatollah Mahmud Tāleqāni, and the two brothers, ayatollahs Rezā and Abo'l-Fazl Zanjāni. But the political strategy of the Movement for Liberty in Iran suffered from a flagrant contradiction: it chose the parliamentary and legal route while the regime it was seeking to reform allowed it no means of expression, put its leaders in prison, and systematically stifled all its demonstrations. It is true that, even while in prison, the stubbornness of Bāzargān's friends turned them into shining beacons of an energetic discourse on Islam and society.

Ayatollah Tāleqāni, a committed theologian who became one of the principal leaders of the Islamic Revolution in 1978–9, is one of the most striking personalities in this movement. Born in 1911 into a clerical family, Mahmud Tāleqāni had studied theology at Qom and Najaf, notably under the iron rule of a progressive teacher of the era of Rezā Shah, Mirzā Khalil Kamara'i, whom he later followed to Tehran. He was first arrested by Rezā Shah's police because he was not carrying the certificate authorizing him to wear the turban. Beginning as early as the 1930s to turn his attention to the young, whom he was worried to see growing further away from Islam, throughout his life Tāleqāni preserved this dual quality of a man who could hold a dialogue with young people, and a militant against dictatorship: with the nationalists in Mosaddeq's era, but close to the *Fedā'iyān-e eslām*, with Bāzargān's liberal nationalists from the 1960s, but equally close, notably in prison and after the Revolution, to armed combat groups inspired with revolutionary ideas, whether Marxist or left-wing Muslims. Those were the qualities that brought Tāleqāni great popularity and allowed him to take crucial positions in the young Islamic Republic. Symbolically, in the (Constituent) Assembly of experts of 1979, he decided to sit on the ground rather than use the well-padded chairs previously used by the senators of the Shah's era. His death on September 10, 1979, of a heart attack, a mere six months after the establishment of the new regime, removed an obstacle to the setting up of a theocracy that had little respect for fundamental liberties.

Two ideological lines dominate Tāleqāni's work: the struggle against absolute power and a concern for social justice.

In order to fight dictatorship, in 1955 Tāleqāni republished a treatise by Mirzā Hoseyn Nā'ini on the theological justification of parliamentary constitutionalism, a treatise that its author himself had withdrawn from circulation shortly after its initial publication in 1909.[6] With his preface to this fresh edition, and taking up on his own account a Shi'ite justification of democracy, Tāleqāni reconciled the clergy and the liberal tradition that had emerged from the constitutionalist Revolution. Of course, he was taking few risks, since he defined the government of men by saying that it was firstly a matter for God, divine Law (*shari'a*), the Prophets and the Imams whose thinking and spiritual strengths are entirely at the service of those laws, and who seek no royal title, and lastly for the righteous *ulema* and righteous men among the faithful . . . But he clearly reaffirmed the limits of any human entitlement.

Tāleqāni developed his conception of social justice in a book on Islam and property in comparison with the economic systems of the West, which is a kind of refutation of Marxism in the name of a social and "progressive" vision of Islam. As Chehabi shrewdly points out, the gestation period of this book coincided with the Shah's efforts to impose land reform: the landowners rejected the reform on the grounds, among others, that it undermined the sacrosanct principle of property.

> Ownership [replies Tāleqāni] is relative and limited. . . . No person should consider himself the absolute owner and complete possessor. Absolute power and complete possession belong only to God who has created man and all other creatures and has them constantly in his possession. Man's ownership then is limited to whatever God has wisely willed and to the capacity of his intellect, authority and the freedom granted to him . . .[7]

Starting from that premise, it is easy to say that land belongs primarily to whoever uses it to good account. There is no condemnation of landownership, but of the speculative monopolizing of wealth. Tāleqāni goes further: he seeks to refute Marxist arguments by replying to the problems posed by the Marxist criticism of capitalism. Our author did, in fact, have experience of communism, first during the Anglo-Soviet occupation of Iran in 1941–6, a period that saw the birth of a Stalinist Communist Party

6 A.-H. HAIRI, *Shī'ism and Constitutionalism in Iran*, Leiden, Brill, 1977, pp. 124, 158. On Tāleqāni, see M. BAYAT, "Mahmud Taleqani and the Iranian Revolution," in M. Kramer, ed., *Shi'ism, Resistance and Revolution*, Boulder, Colo., Westview Press, and London, Mansell, 1987, pp. 67–94.

7 Sd M. TĀLEQĀNI (trans. A. Jabbari and F. Rajaee), *Islam and Ownership* Lexington, Mazda, 1983, p. 88; Persian text, *Eslām va mālekiyat*, p. 143.

in Iran, the Tudeh party (*Tuda*, "of the masses"). In 1946 Tāleqāni, sent as an observer by the Qom clergy, accompanied Iranian troops who were going to drive the Soviet occupiers out of Iranian Azerbaijan. Later, in prison, he became closely acquainted with Marxist militants, and one of his sons took part in an extreme left activist organization. For him that was a chance to get a concrete view of how communists behaved, notably towards religion. Hence his interest in refuting Marxism and making an apologia for Islam that would reach young intellectuals.

In *Islam and Ownership*, Tāleqāni tackles questions that are quite new for a turbaned cleric:

The development of the principle of ownership, the division of labour and the first economic theories, the industrial revolution.

The abuses of capitalism, the class struggle, and Marxist arguments on the dictatorship of the proletariat and the advent of a classless society.

The economy seen from an Islamic viewpoint, a transhistorical look at the economy: human laws are incomplete, limited by historical experience, subject to change, easily thrown off course by tyrannies, influenced by the upsets of passions, whereas the Law of Islam sheds a timeless light, and transforms the man "possessed" by his passions into a "possessor" of himself.

In Islamic tradition, where God is held to be the absolute Owner of all possessions, there is no "feudalism" (*toyuldāri*), properly speaking, the phenomenon of large-scale landownership being, according to Tāleqāni, one of the consequences of western penetration.

Islam of course forbids usury and the amassing of riches, but it encourages trade, which means the distribution of wealth: from each must be taken according to his abilities and to each must be given according to his needs.

In Islam economic activity is unrestricted, whether in the production or distribution of wealth, and natural resources belong to whoever turns them to good account, but with limits, over which control is ensured by the state.

The economy is not, as Marxists sometimes say, the one dimension of inequality: Islam recognizes that there are differences between men, but rejects those that derive from privilege of situation, as often happens in monarchic regimes, or under the influence of the military. It is hypocritical, declares Tāleqāni, to carry the banner of the Declaration of the Rights of Man and at the same time violate it in the name of the interests of a nation or a particular class (he is chiefly criticizing the double-talk of colonial powers, and here makes a direct reference to France during the Algerian war).

As may be seen, Tāleqāni had a "modern" turn of mind. On some occasions he spoke out against the existence of a clerical class in Islam, and for a decentralization of the office of spiritual guide (*marja' al-taqlid*), but his thinking is not dominated by anticlericalism.[8] Similarly, although Mehdi Bāzargān, his fellow traveler from the beginning of the 1940s, studied thermodynamics in France and wore a hat and tie, in 1979 he facilitated the setting up of a political system dominated by the clergy. Their moderate idea of Muslim progressivism, seeking to protect individual and collective liberties and restore the Muslim ethic without breaking with modern cultural and industrial development, in fact accepts clerical authority, even if both men try to relegate it as much as possible to the spiritual sphere. As for the rest, they tend to juxtapose their religious faith and their political commitment in the service of liberty, national independence, and social justice: they state clearly that there is no incompatibility, and even a correspondence, between the two, but they keep their political action at a certain distance from their religious conviction.

NON-CLERICAL SHI'ITE THINKING

The ideology of the Movement for Liberty in Iran draws on two of Shi'ism's fundamental inspirations: respect for tradition, notably in its clerical form (like the heritage of the Imams), and a profound democratic aspiration. In fact Shi'ism is neither more nor less "democratic" or "egalitarian" than Sunnism, as far as such an anachronistic evaluation has any sense. The Imams 'Ali and Hoseyn had combated the iniquity and violence of the Omayyads, who had forgotten social and ethical virtues and were practising a generalized nepotism. Their struggle was later taken as an example by non-Arab "followers" who expected to be treated with justice by the religion to which they had given their adherence. They thus represented a more "popular" trend, despite the legitimist principle of blood succession, which they defended against the Sunni rule of electing the caliph by a council (*shurā*). In the period of the Imam's Occultation, Shi'ites fulfill their political authority to the extent that there come into force the principle of *ejtehād* (interpretation, at any time, of the application of the Law by authorized theologians) and the tradition of free choice among believers of their religious leader (*marja' al-taqlid*).[9] In this dual power lies the essence

8   Cf. A. K. S. LAMBTON, "A Reconsideration of the Position of the *Marja' at-taqlid* and the Religious Institution," *Studia Islamica*, 20 (1964), pp. 125ff.
9   H. ENAYAT, *Modern Islamic Political Thought: The Response of the Shi'i and Sunni Muslims to the Twentieth Century*, Austin, University of Texas Press, and London and Basingstoke, Macmillan, 1982, pp. 134, 160ff.; reviewed by N. Keddie, *Middle East Journal*, 37 (1983), pp. 489ff.

of democracy: control by the nation (or community) over authority and the application of fundamental laws.

Such was 'Ali Shari'ati's inspiration. This writer and orator has already been quoted here several times in connection with his contentious interpretations of Shi'ite themes and his politicized vision of Islam.[10] It was in Paris, where he met the militants struggling for an independent Algeria, Frantz Fanon, Louis Massignon, and Jean-Paul Sartre, that Shari'ati learned to associate Islam with a revolutionary set of themes. Returning to Iran, he clashed with the political police, who several times stopped him from speaking, tried to involve him in anti-Marxist propaganda and finally imprisoned him (1973–5). He died in 1977, when his writings were being clandestinely distributed, recopied by hand using carbon paper (photocopying was still dear and risky), and his fame was enormous, his photograph being borne aloft almost as much as that of ayatollah Khomeyni in the great revolutionary processions of 1978–9. After the easing of censorship restrictions in Iran, which occurred at the time of his death, his books were gradually published, at first under pseudonyms, then openly but in rough, typescript form; they reached a circulation previously unknown in Iran, reputedly several million copies for certain titles.

In the 1990s that popularity seems to have died down. Why? The "outdating" of a committed line of thinking whose author vanished on the eve of the Revolution is not surprising. Those who reject that thinking in the name of a pretended doctrinal "purity" guaranteed by the *ulema* are today trying to emulate Shari'ati, in their own way, by making Islamic ideology fit any situation: Shari'ati embarrasses them because he posed deeper problems than the simple adaptation of educative structures to the Islamization of the modern world and he was not interested in patching up the clerical system. Those who have laid claim to this line of thought in order to justify their political activism have certainly distorted it by transforming its ideas into slogans: Shari'ati was against hasty actions, and wanted first of all to shape minds.

Refuting Dr Shari'ati, a polemical book published in 1983 by an institution (subsidized by the Islamic Republic) linked to the theological schools at Qom put an end to the unspoken misunderstanding which implied that Khomeynism was in ideological harmony with Shari'atism: it made a formal attack on him, expressly linking him with the reformers of the earlier era (Hakamizāda, Sangalaji), all accused of being agents manipulated by imperialism to destroy the unity of the Muslim community. The book's

10 See above, ch. 4.

author, a mulla named 'Ali Monzer, praises Motahhari for having thwarted this conspiracy against Islam . . .[11] (It was the precise intent of Motahhari's murderers to punish him for having criticized Shari'ati at the Ershād Hoseyniya in Tehran.)

Despite other similar attacks, it cannot be said that Shari'ati's influence has been ruled out: numerous militants on the revolutionary committees or Guardians of the Revolution (*Pāsdārān*) were shocked by the publication of Monzer's book, and there are doubtless some who still dream of ridding the Revolution of the mullas' domination; a number of indications in the official discourse of the Islamic Republic, and notably in school books, indicate the persistence of Shari'atist ideas, his terminology ("ideology," "Islamist vision of the world") and of his efforts to define a progressive and anti-imperialist Islam.

On the other hand, Shari'ati's work has certainly "aged" today: it was addressed to young intellectuals seeking an Islamic path between submission to the pro-western imperial regime and the revolt inspired by Marxism. Arguments in favour of a return to Islamic values find less echo in an atmosphere saturated with re-Islamization and weary with religious propaganda. The nature of the problems has changed, but the impetus given by Shari'ati could still be taken up again and actualized. In any case, the ban on reprinting certain volumes of his works because of their virulent criticism of the clergy shows that the potential impact of his writings is still feared by those in authority in the Islamic Republic.

Among the activist organizations which had adopted Shari'ati's anticlerical stance as a guideline, one recalls the clandestine group *Forqān* which, just after the Revolution, claimed responsibility for some spectacular attacks, such as the murder of Dr Mofatteh, a cleric, former pupil of Khomeyni, teaching Islamic philosophy at the University of Tehran, and ayatollah Mortazā Motahhari (*ulema* accused of obstructing Shari'ati's influence). *Forqān* was disbanded and its leaders executed in 1979, but the "Ideal of the Underprivileged" group (*Ārmān-e mostaz'afān*), inspired by the same hardline Shari'atist ideology, survived for several years. Today there is no association in Iran that can openly boast of Shari'atist ideology. The Center for publishing Dr Shari'ati's thinking (*Kānun-e nashr-e afkār-e doktor Shari'ati*), which directed the publication of the master's works, has been officially dissolved and some of Shari'ati's important books have

11   'A. ABO'L-HASANI (Monzer), *Shahid Motahhari efshā-gar-e towte'a*, (The Martyr Motahhari Unveiler of a Conspiracy), Qom, Daftar-e enteshārāt-e eslāmi, 1362/1983.

been banned, as, for example, the first volume of his collected works (containing letters to his father) and the famous book on *Alavid vs Safavid Shi'ism*, which harshly criticizes the clergy. On June 19, 1981, a meeting of his friends for the commemoration of the fourth anniversary of his death was attacked in his widow's home by an armed commando group who scattered and wounded the participants. One last group survives in Iran, clandestinely, with a branch in France, the "Monotheists of the Islamic Revolution" (*Movahhedin-e enqelāb-e eslāmi*), trying to continue the work of "the Doctor" (Shari'ati) by acting and speaking in the same spirit of a progressive Islam that used to be his own, rather than making an idol out of the man who inspires them.

The Iranian People's Mojahedin (Fighters) of the Iranian People (*Sāzemān-e mojāhedin-e khalq-e Irān*), a revolutionary group displaying the opinions of a progressive Islam, came into being after the massive demonstrations against the Shah in 1963, but only existed as a reality from 1971 (terrorist activities, training in the Palestinian camps in the Lebanon). It fell out with the greater part of the Shi'ite clergy in 1975, when it became obvious that it was largely inspired by Marxism. Its best protector after the Revolution was ayatollah Tāleqāni: with his death in September 1979, the Mojāhedin were left orphaned. At this time they were removed from power by Khomeyni and the Islamic Republic Party (IRP, in Persian *Hezb-e jomhuri-e eslāmi*), then on June 21, 1981, after the dismissal of Bani-Sadr, with whom they had made an alliance, they passed to open rebellion. For over a year, with bloody attacks and suicidal demonstrations, they spread a climate of overt political violence. Finally, after a last desperate offensive in Kurdistan which preceded the cease-fire between Iran and Iraq (August 1988), this extremist organization, whose leaders had withdrawn to Baghdad when obliged to leave France in 1986, virtually disappeared until it reemerged in Western Countries in 1993.

The way the Muslim militants of the People's Mojāhedin made use of Shari'ati is an old misunderstanding.[12] Shari'ati himself took a stand on the subject of the Mojāhedin, and he was not gentle with them: he denounced those who mistook agitation for action and who tried to add names to the Shi'ite list of martyrs without reflecting in any way on the immaturity and uselessness of this blood cult, in an era when the martyred Imams and their

---

12 E. ABRAHAMIAN, *The Iranian Mojahedin*, New Haven, Yale University Press, and London, Tauris, 1989, errs by making the Mojāhedin disciples of Shari'ati, chiefly pp. 122ff.

descendants were still used by popular beliefs for magic acts of piety. In place of that agitation, Shari'ati asked for a true Islamic doctrine to be formed.[13]

As for the Mojāhedin, they always kept at a certain distance *vis-à-vis* Shari'ati, whom they tried to place at the very most as a brilliant essayist, and never as their ideologist. In 1974 they suspected him of being a SAVAK agent. After the Revolution, in a little work published in Tehran in 1980, they indirectly attacked Shari'ati's thinking as "a *petit-bourgeois* understanding of Islam." It was only much later, when the leaders of the organization were in exile in Paris, that the bluntest criticisms and rejection of Shari'ati were expressed in the Mojāhedin publications: they blamed him for turning aside from action and wanting to transform the superstructures without changing the balance of power within society.

Some of the ideas that were the strength of the People's Mojāhedin could return one day, because of their Islamic expression and their very powerful social inspiration. Such was the case notably for their principles of Koranic exegesis summed up in these lines taken from "How to Learn the Koran":

In the practice of "ideology," our Organization insists for various reasons on the use of the original texts of Islam, in particular the Koran and the *Nahj ol-Balāgha*. Of course the method used by the Organization to interpret those texts differs qualitatively from that of the traditionalists. To achieve success in this scheme, the Organization developed, among others, a "scientific-realistic" approach . . . No ideological work can reach its goal if it is not in accordance with the evolution of society and with the social-revolutionary movement . . . Many people express their own beliefs under the name of the Koran, and we can easily detect the differences and the evident contradictions between them. And beside the justifications and commentaries that have been made deliberately by the ideologues tied to those regimes – apparently Islamic regimes, but in fact anti-Islamic – their exegesis in order to defend and legitimize the present order and enable it to last, are devoid of the true meaning of the Koran. A book that was giving life and liberty – and should be doing so – was put to the service of tyrannical powers exploiting the people and depriving them of their life and liberty . . . Some people would probably say that the Koran bears its own
' clear meaning and has no need of further commentary: but if you look at

13 'A. SHARI'ATI, *Bā Makhāteb-hā-ye āshenā*, (Correspondence, Collected Works, vol. I), Tehran, Hoseyniya Ershād, 1356/1977, p. 210. Numerous negative allusions to the Mojāhedin are to be found in various works and letters, mostly without actually naming them because of censorship.

what has happened in our times to Marx, and the way his doctrine has been so distorted that Lenin, only a few years later, in *State and Revolution*, was obliged to reply vigorously to the revisionists, accusing them of turning his radical ideas into harmless banalities, and that even Marx himself said he was not a *Marxist*, so you must realize why we must interpret the Koran today . . .[14]

This dynamic interpretation allows the People's Mojāhedin to politicize religion very strongly. They change the meanings of words. Thus the "Community of believers" (*ommat*) becomes a "dynamic society in dialectic movement toward perfection;" monotheism (*towhid*) becomes "egalitarianism;" *jehād* is a war of liberation and the "holy warrior" (*mojāhed*) a guerrilla; the martyr is less a witness to the faith and more of a revolutionary hero . . . One can see what inheritance this group left to the Islamic Republic. The Mojāhedin were the first to make use of the Koranic term *mostaz'af* in the political sense of oppressed masses, which traveled the road we know in Khomeynist discourse. As Abrahamian remarks, for the Mojāhedin the wait for the Twelfth Imam is the expectation of the coming of a classless society, freed from need, war, injustice, oppression, corruption, and alienation.[15] There is certainly an eschatological dimension, but one no longer knows if it refers to the other world or this one.

Any outcome from these deviations was not dependent on the continuance of the People's Mojāhedin, whose childish behaviour wiped out any chance of their having a political future: suicidal demonstrations against the Islamic Republic in 1981–2, spectacular attacks but without results, a political agreement with Baghdad at the height of the Iran–Iraq war, a simplistic cult of the leader, etc. These failures might be likely to prompt a possible imitator of the Mojāhedin and alert him to the pitfalls: one might then see the rebirth of a Shi'ite militant organization. Different structures in the Islamic Republic, moreover, have been inspired by this example, and the style of militant clad in a parka, trained in guerrilla warfare and stereotyped responses to any question, or his sister in trousers covered by an "Islamic coat," her head covered with a broad scarf, has become the general reference of young people since the Revolution, and the norm defined by the state. That is the one triumph – slender, it is true – of the People's Mojāhedin.

14 Sāzemān-e Mojāhedin-e khalq-e Irān, *Cheguna Qor'ān biāmuzim*, 2nd printing, [Tehran] 1358/1979, pp. 9–18. Freely paraphrased by E. ABRAHAMIAN, *The Iranian Mojahedin*, p. 95.
15 ABRAHAMIAN, *The Iranian Mojahedin*, p. 96.

THE "ORGANIZED SPONTANEITY" OF PRESIDENT BANI-SADR

Among the notorious failures of the Islamic Republic, that of its first President, Abo'l-Hasan Bani-Sadr, must be recalled. Before becoming an unlucky politician, this sociologist (and economist), who was born in 1934, the son of an ayatollah, had been a political militant and disciple of Mahmud Tāleqāni. Exiled in France after the repression of the uprising in June 1963, he pursued his economic studies and in particular, with the collaboration of the French sociologist Paul Vieille, published a manifesto denouncing the workings of the Shah's regime, "Oil and Violence."[16] Fame reached Bani-Sadr in October 1978 when he welcomed ayatollah Khomeyni first to his home in Cachan in the Parisian suburbs, and then at Neauphle-le-Château. Despite faltering French, he became for some months one of the ayatollah's interpreters and at all events one of his close associates, together with two other Iranian liberal opposition members, Sādeq Qotbzāda (Sadegh Ghotbzadeh, executed in 1982 after the failure of an attempted *coup d'état*) and Ebrahim Yazdi (close to Bāzargān, without office since November 1979).

At the time of his return to Iran with Khomeyni in February 1979, Bani-Sadr was known to only a handful of intellectuals who had read his dense treatises in which he set out in Persian his ideas on Islamic government. He continued to gain the confidence of public opinion by placing himself in Imam Khomeyni's immediate entourage and, in the Constituent Assembly or his newspaper "Islamic Revolution," criticizing the clerical turn deliberately taken by the new regime. Elected in January 1980 to the presidency of the Republic – in the first and perhaps the only truly free and democratic election of the new regime – rapidly confronted with the political power of the Party of the Islamic Republic, and externally with the war with Iraq, Bani-Sadr showed himself to be a weak politician and was in the end forced to go into exile in France after being put out of office thanks to a violent *coup d'état*.

In a little work written in Persian on the "Fundamental Principles of Islamic Government," published in Paris in 1974 and widely circulated in Tehran during the winter of 1978–9, Bani-Sadr develops a theoretical construction of the future state in the manner of the great nineteenth-century

16   P. VIEILLE and A.-H. BANISADR, *Pétrole et violence: Terreur blanche et résistance en Iran*, Paris, Anthropos, 1974.

European ideologists.[17] His method consists of dealing systematically with the principles of Shi'ite Islam: (1) the uniqueness of the divinity (*towhid*), i.e. the destruction of all idols; (2) "sending on mission" (*ba'sat*), or the dynamic permanent movement within Islam; (3) the Imamate, i.e. the direction of the movement according to the divine plan by the Imam (or "Guide") and his successors; (4) divine justice, or the negation of the absolute and arbitrary all-powerful God: it is a balancing force that keeps the movement within precise limits; (5) the "return" (*ma'ād*), i.e. the return to God, the resurrection, salvation, the ultimate aim of the movement.

It is the principle of the oneness of God that really guides Bani-Sadr's analysis. Thanks to the purification of the idea of God, freed from all idolatry, one can condemn all the forms made absolute by man which play an oppressive and divisive role: "The principle of the *towhid* brings with it the negation of any kind of economic, political, ideological or other stronghold in which power could be concentrated" (p. 24). Guided by this principle, the believer must strive to achieve unity everywhere so that society may reflect the community willed by God. Devotions are training in the struggle to achieve this ideal: communal prayer, fasting, pilgrimage (a kind of universal annual congress), and holy war (against evil impulses) prepare us for the fight against oppression by turning daily life into a permanent movement of rejection of all that is not God. Thus we must adore no earthly master, neither Stalin, nor Hitler, nor de Gaulle, nor Mosaddeq, nor Khomeyni . . . (p. 22), for making a cult of men brings enslavement and totalitarianism. In Bani-Sadr's thinking this principle goes a very long way, since all power, all authority, inasmuch as it comes from men, is condemned, even if it attempts to justifiy itself by means of religion: Bani-Sadr strongly protests against the idea of God as an arbitrary and absolute will, an idea which, according to him, Muslim theology developed in the imperialist period of the caliphate, and which would allow a government to impose its authority despite its illegitimacy and irreligiousness.

All these false human authorities, which are there to divide men, must be overthrown. The principle of the *towhid* enables one to combat the mythicizing of the past, an idol of which totalitarian regimes (that of the Pahlavi in particular) have always made use. Social dynamism must not

17   A.-H. BANI-SADR, *Osul-e pāya va zābeta-hā-ye hokumat-e eslāmi*, [Paris], 1353/1974; trans. Md Qanoonparvar, *The Fundamental Principles and Precepts of Islamic Government*, Lexington, Mazda, 1981.

be compartmentalized into classes where the community is divided into the dominant and the dominated: so property must not become an absolute value, for taken to excess it becomes a negation of God (Koran XVIII, 32–42). Economic resources must be controlled, therefore, so that they do not give rise to the concentration of power to the advantage of great powers, depriving the majority of men of their ability to think and be productive: human slavery in the form of the organized mass migration of workers from poor countries to rich ones must be abolished. In Islamic government, only work justifies the ownership of the produce of that work, which rules out capitalism. The economy must be planned to serve everyone, not just one class. It is necessary to weed out the luxury and combat the opulence of one group, which brings about the poverty of the greater number.

To Marxists, who say that religion has prevented an awareness of alienation by turning the rebellious cries of the exploited into prayers, Bani-Sadr replies that the differences between men come from God, and are not to be denied: their giving rise to classes may be avoided by placing the most gifted (or advanced) qualities at the service of society. This is the meaning of the Imamate. Bani-Sadr himself criticizes ideologies which, after being used by certain people to win power, are then employed as an instrument of domination; every belief used for purposes of domination is an opiate for the people. Islamic government does not make use of belief, but aims to serve it; Islam was established on the basis of universal laws and human nature (*fetrat*): there is no danger that it can be turned into an ideology of enslavement. The end must not justify the means.

The aim of Islamic government, in Bani-Sadr's view, is not merely to prevent one person or one group from monopolizing power, but to do away with power, to do away with the state as a means of domination. Nationalism is a pretext for dividing and oppressing peoples: the offensive army must purely and simply be abolished. Only a defensive army should be organized, but it must be organically based in society. Holy war means the fight against idolatry: "We must liberate, that is, restore others to their original nature" (p. 55). This holy war is in reality a permanent revolution in which there is no "model to imitate" (*marja al-taqlid*): each man must discover for himself the cause for which he is fighting.

As may be seen, this surprising political reflection is in truth anarchistic (in the true sense of the word). While stoutly maintaining belief in God and in the revelation, it denies and rejects any domination of man by man, no matter what the pretext: Bani-Sadr declares himself in favour of *spontanéité organisée*, a term that he himself coined to sum up his thinking in the

French language.[18] It was certainly a daring ideology, by which the 1979 constitution was partially inspired in its efforts to put the brake on a slide towards the dictatorship of a man or a group. In his quality of elected expert Bani-Sadr played an active part in drawing it up, but refused to sign the final text of that constitution because of the exorbitant powers granted to the Guide in the chapter on the "Power of the Religious Jurisconsult" (*velāyat-e faqih*).

The practical application of this pro-spontaneity ideology, however, leaves something to be desired: Bani-Sadr cannot be blamed for inciting his supporters to violence, since his rejection of oppression and repression led him on several occasions to take the side of non-violence, and the setting up of the Islamic Republic caused him much vexation in this area. Unfortunately, his refusal to go through the mediation of a mass organization and his overconfidence in his popularity weakened the first Iranian president, who was notably in confrontation with the Islamic associations gathered around the Party of the Islamic Republic and its leader, ayatollah Beheshti. Alternately hostile to Bāzargān, then his ally against the radicals, Bani-Sadr ended by surrounding himself with the worst political support that a non-violent man could have chosen by associating himself, from September 1980 and up till eighteen months after his exile to France, with the People's Mojāhedin and their chief, Mas'ud Rajavi. From his brief passage across the scene there remains the clear illustration of the difficulty of controlling a large country by means of dreams dreamed on the golden campuses of European universities and a noble ideal of liberty, in the face of ayatollahs who are realistic, determined, and solidly entrenched in the population.

THE IDEOLOGY OF A GREAT SHI'ITE PARTY

The Party of the Islamic Republic represents precisely the opposite of Bani-Sadr's political practices. It was founded shortly after the victory of the Revolution (February 1979) by *ulema* who had been students of ayatollah Khomeyni at Qom – the ayatollahs and *hojjat ol-eslām* Mohammad Beheshti, 'Abd ol-Karim Musavi Ardabili (who succeeded Beheshti as president of the High Court of Justice), 'Ali Khāmena'i (Khamenehi, President of the Republic from 1981 to 1989, then "Guide of the Revolution"), 'Ali-Akbar Hāshemi-Rasfanjāni (president of the parliament until 1989, then President of the Republic) and Mohammad-Javād Bā-Honar (Prime Minister,

18 Personal conversation, Tehran, February 1979.

assassinated in 1981). It also included several "laymen," none of whom rose to positions of major responsibility, such as Hasan Āyat, Jalāloddin Fārsi, Habibollāh 'Asgar-Owlādi.

Several distinct ideological currents were associated with the founding of the PIR, and those tendencies were to be seen in the internal divisions following Beheshti's death on June 28, 1981. First, the Federation of Islamic Associations (*Jami'at-hā-ye mo'talefa-ye eslāmi*), which came into being at the beginning of the 1960s and took an active part in encouraging the uprising of June 1963. Among its members were the organizers of the assassination of the Prime Minister, Hasan-'Ali Mansur, in January 1965. Ayatollahs Beheshti and Motahhari were among the leaders of these Islamic Associations. The PIR also inherited the remainder of an activist party, the Party of Muslim Nations (*Hezb-e melal-e eslāmi*), founded in 1961 by Kāzem Musavi Bojnurdi with armed struggle against the Shah's dictatorship and the unification of Islamic countries as its program. This party had been disbanded, and nearly all its surviving members were in prison. After the Revolution the majority, for example 'Abbās Duzduzāni (Minister of Islamic Guidance in the Rajā'i cabinet in 1981), entered the PIR, but some, like Hojjati-Kermāni, preferred Bani-Sadr's line. A third large organization, the Hojjatiya group, created around 1955, had as its aim the ruthless battle against Bahā'ism. (For a time this association had been manipulated by the Shah's regime to harness the anti-communist and anti-Bahā'i tendencies of religious circles.)[19] Breaking with the association's line, an influential splinter of this group, including notably ayatollah Abo'l-Qāsem Khaz'ali (member of the Supervisory Council of the Constitution) and Dr Velāyati (Minister of Foreign Affairs from 1981), rallied behind the principle of clerical power (*velāyat-e faqih*) and the PIR. Among the non-clerical leaders of the party, there were also a few ideologists, certain of whom had inherited from the Mosaddeqist experiment a fierce hostility to liberal nationalism, and belonged rather in the wake of ayatollah Abo'l-Qāsem Kāshāni (d. 1961): the ayatollah's own son, Mahmud Kāshāni, or his friend Hasan Āyat (murdered in July 1981), both connected with the former "Workers' Party" (*Hezb-e zahmatkeshān*) of Mozaffar Baqā'i Kermāni.

This confluence of currents and the backing of respectability imparted by the participation of known theologians explain why the PIR carried off

---

19   A. VALI and S. ZUBAIDA, "Factionalism and Political Discourse in the Islamic Republic of Iran: The Case of the Hujjatiyeh Society," *Economy and Society*, 14, 2 (May 1985), pp. 139–73; C. VERLEUW "L'Association Hojjatiyye Mahdaviyye," in B. Badie and R. Santucci, eds, *Contestations en pays islamiques*, vol. II, Paris, CHEAM, 1987, pp. 81–116.

a victory in the first "free" elections of the Assembly of experts entrusted with the task of drawing up the Constitution. Ayatollah Beheshti was elected its vice-president; it was he who presided at most of its meetings and took it upon himself to act as arbiter every time the debates became bogged down. In January 1980 the PIR appeared to be declining, and lost the presidential elections for want of a suitable candidate, but in the following spring it achieved a crushing victory in the "free" parliamentary elections. Taking advantage of the revolutionary strength of its fiercest militants, who diverted to their own benefit the occupation of the American Embassy by the "Muslim students loyal to the line of the Imam" (November 1979– February 1981), the PIR eliminated its most threatening enemies, one after another, notably those calling for a liberal or progressive Islam.

Profoundly weakened by two spectacular murderous attacks which cost the lives of its most eminent members, in the party headquarters on 28 June 1981 (Beheshti, Mohammad Montazeri, Duzduzāni), then on the offices of the Prime Minister on August 30 (Bā-Honar, Rajā'i), and by individual attacks (Āyat), the PIR managed to surmount difficult hurdles and maintain an apparent cohesion. In 1986 it dissolved itself at the request of Khomeyni when he had succeeded in giving a coherent ideological framework to the institutions of the Islamic Republic. (If it disappeared without any trouble, it was also because it had never been a true party: that type of militant association is not suited to the customary ways of thinking and relations of the Shi'ite clergy.)

The "brain" behind the PIR, who died prematurely in the terrible attack that destroyed the party headquarters and 100 or so of its most important members on June 28, 1981, deserves special attention. The martyr ayatollah Sayyed Mohammad Hoseyni Beheshti, frequently known as *Dr* Beheshti because he held a doctorate in theology, was born at Isfahan in 1928 into a modest clerical family.[20] He did the traditional religious studies but at the same time attended the upper grammar school, including the study of European languages – French and, mainly, English. After the Second World War, at Qom, he became a disciple of ayatollah Borujerdi, the great Shi'ite thinker 'Allāma Tabātabā'i (d. 1982), and ayatollah Khomeyni. Enrolled for a theology degree course at the (state) University of Tehran, he funded his studies by teaching English. Caught up in the whirlwind of the nationalist movement, Beheshti, dressed in clerical garb, took part in the demonstrations in favour of Mosaddeq, whom he did not repudiate.

---

20 See the posthumous autobiography of Beheshti published in the PIR organ, *Jomhuri-e eslāmi*, 13 Tir 1360/July 4, 1981.

After the *coup d'état* of August 1953 against Mosaddeq, he became aware of the urgent need to train good executives to resume and organize the movement: that would be his life's work.

Henceforward, Beheshti was simultaneously teacher, writer, educationalist, and lecturer. That was how he saw his role as a cleric. In 1963 he took part from a distance in the revolt led by ayatollah Khomeyni, and afterwards played an important clandestine role, together with the Islamic Associations, in organizing the struggle during his master's exile. At the same time, with the help of several theologians (including Mohammad-Javād Bā-Honār), he recast for the Ministry of Education the catechisms taught in official schools. The Secret police (SAVAK) kept a close eye on him when he was in contact with the founders of the Organization of the People's Mojāhedin and the assassins of Prime Minister Mansur. It was at that time, in 1965, that he was invited to run the mosque in Hamburg, and he left Iran. For five years he busied himself with the chaplaincy for Iranian students and traders in Germany: he learned German and travelled widely in Muslim countries, among other places visiting Najaf where Khomeyni was in exile.

On returning to Iran, Beheshti continued to exercise his talents as an organizer, notably in the heart of the Militant Clergy (*Ruhāniyat-e mobārez*), and found his natural place among the elites of the Islamic Revolution. He was handicapped in political action by his use of an abstract clerical language that lacked warmth (as opposed to that of ayatollah Tāleqāni), which hampered his popularity. His most noteworthy work was the creation of the PIR, and he may be said to have been its principal inspiration. The document setting out the party's direction, entitled "Our Positions," was very probably written by Beheshti himself: the style conveys as much a political report giving the official ideological line as a theological treatise on politics as seen by Islam. It contains dogmatic positions and practical orientations for both the short and the long term.

The work begins with an anthropological definition: according to Islam, man, who is more than mere matter, endowed with the knowledge of good and evil, responsible toward his natural environment which he must use without becoming its slave, is also responsible toward himself, destined for salvation thanks to the gifts of God, and toward society in which he must blossom forth by overcoming hostile historical and social currents. There follows a theoretical exposition of the revelation, the role of the prophets in telling us of salvation, the justification for the authority of the Prophet Mohammad and his heirs, the Imams: as it is the divine doctrine that saves us, we need the authority of those to whom the doctrine has been passed on. And today the specialists in the application of the Law are the heirs of the Prophet and the Imams, they have the knowledge and understanding (*feqh*) to reply, in the light of Islam, to the questions facing men in every era, whence their name *foqahā* (plural of *faqih*). Moreover, this is what the Islamic constitution has stipulated in its fifth article: the *velāyat-e faqih* (governorship of the jurist-theologian) allows the assurance of Islamic doctrine over all social strata, as both Sunnis and Shi'ites have to submit to it in the name of reason, in order to achieve the "oneness" of society (*towhidi*); "doctrinal politics" (*siyāsat-e maktabi*) causes society to progress towards the "rule of God," putting a check on the colonialist argument for the separation of the political and the religious.[21]

Here may be seen the systematic justification of the new regime's principles: it was Beheshti who had the famous article 5 and chapter 8 on the *velāyat-e faqih* included in the 1979 constitution. In actual fact, he did not take the initiative in it and would originally have settled for the more democratic arrangements of a first version of the constitution. But he rallied round with conviction and made clear the apparently contradictory double reference to a transcendent principle and popular legitimacy:

Islamic society is "democratic," says the PIR text, since the greater number of the people have chosen the Islamic doctrine, the constitution, the Guide (*rahbar, faqih*), the parliamentary members, and other eligible persons. But as only the authority of the doctrine guarantees man the power to be master of his own destiny, there must be no yielding to demagogy and, without rushing things of course, the desires of the people that would not be in keeping with Islamic doctrine must be resisted.

Democratic, Islamic government is based on a "council-oriented" system (*shurā*), by virtue of the Islamic character of the collegial administration of power. Elections are secret in order to respect freedom of choice, but as the political maturity of the people grows there should be a trend toward making them public. The clergy will play a special role in the councils, as they are a protection and refuge for the people against dictatorship, as has been shown in recent history. It is the duty of the *ulema* to be present wherever their theoretical or practical qualifications predestine them for public service. But that does not give them any special privilege. Liberty is respected in Islamic society, the PIR program goes on, unlike what is to be seen in the totalitarian regimes of the communist bloc or in capitalist countries, where an uncontrolled permissiveness, without any

21 "Mavāze'-e mā," Tehran, PIR, 1981, previously published in *Jomhuri-e eslāmi*, March 1981 (in Beheshti's lifetime). Here, I am giving an analytical résumé.

criterion, removes the very meaning of liberty. Anti-Islamic opinions may be published, as long as they are accompanied by "sound" (Islamic) views, so that the reader may analyze both and make his choice. Parties are free, even if they have no reference to Islam. Those that are against Islam must not be prohibited unless they threaten Islam: reason, not violence, should be used to combat them.

Different nationalities and minority cultures must be respected, according to the PIR program, but the Islamic connection takes precedence over all the others, and enables national and racist fanaticism to be neutralized: all peoples are equal in the Islamic community.

The PIR approves wholeheartedly of the cultural revolution undertaken in the Islamic Republic, beginning in spring 1980: its aim is to wipe out the traces of an anti-religious and hegemonic western culture which has sidetracked Muslims from an awareness of their identity. In all instances, technical specialization must not be the sole criterion for the recruitment of the country's executives: favor should even be shown to those who, although less educated in their field, are Islam's fervent militants.

The last two delicate areas dealt with in the PIR programme are justice and the economy. Apart from the independence of the judiciary authority, the Islamic justice desired by the PIR and western justice have few points in common: the party's program does not extend far over this problem, which is tackled elsewhere in a projected penal code put forward to parliament by the PIR and based on the law of an eye for an eye (*qesās*). In this law, which was accepted in broad outline by the Islamic Republic, reliance is placed on the dissuasive effect of the principles literally set out in the Koran and in classical Islamic jurisprudence: victims must be compensated in kind, in camels, sheep, measures of corn, or various tortures ... The establishment of the talionic or retaliatory law in Iran is in contradiction not only with the history of justice in that country, since Islamic precepts have never been applied in such a literalist spirit, but also with the very wording of the 1979 constitution which, in chapters 3 and 11, tries to harmonize the principles of Islamic justice with a modern conception of the law; in particular, the constitution guarantees every citizen the help of a lawyer before the courts (article 35). The talionic bill makes provision for corporal punishment, such as public flogging, amputation of a hand, a foot, gouging out an eye ... stoning, or simple execution by hanging; but in certain cases these penalties may be paid, with the agreement of the plaintiff, in the form of money. The bill also assumes that the testimony of women, as in Islamic tradition, is worth only half that of men. Lastly, let us note that in its program the PIR disapproves of the perpetuation of an exceptional "revolutionary" administration of justice and wants the judicial system to be unified without delay.

As regards the economy, the PIR is inimical to extreme solutions: it refuses to make absolute the right of property-ownership, since that really applies only to God, according to the theory of contemporary Islamic ideologists. Beheshti always took a close interest in the problem of property and the distribution of wealth: the wording of the program resumes his subtle distinctions over the sources of private property. He also gives us a vigorous apologia for individual enterprise and recommends the subsidizing of all family-sized businesses or those with a cooperative system. Here the PIR clearly assumes the class character of the *petite bourgeoisie* of the bazaars, whose ideal of a liberal and protected economy it shares.

Finally, it will be noticed that, with regard to its foreign policy program, the PIR takes up on its own account the official slogan "Neither East nor West – Islamic Republic;" by doing so it tries to define Iran's position from the starting-point of Islamic revolutionary ideology, setting aside the history of that nation. Furthermore, Iran is named in the text only when followed by the paraphrase "liberated part of the country of Islam" (*qesmat-e āzād-shoda-ye mamlekat-e eslām*). Was the Iranian entity no longer adequate to define a political program? Such omission and theoretical negation of the historic nation openly mocked by the party leaders did nothing to suppress the tensions with Iranian nationalism that the war with Iraq would have sufficed to awaken, if there had been any need.

A THINKING CLERIC AND THOSE WHO ARE "CLEAR THINKERS"

Beheshti's example is interesting on two counts: firstly, because of his efforts to give a systematic definition to the government set up after the Revolution. Although the new leaders were feeling their way, with many hesitations, this program proves that there was also a general line that had been deliberated upon. Secondly, a cleric with a university degree who organizes political action is far removed from the ideal type of Islam's *ulema*, whom one visualizes seated on the ground in the midst of their students, teaching them the Law of Islam and its perfect paradigm, the life of the Prophet.

Beheshti was no longer a mulla hunched over traditions, but already a true *intellectual*, if the sociological meaning is applied to this word: the designer of the central values in his society, offering the public models and clues so that it can take its place in the modern world. This English- and German-speaking mulla, who had traveled the world and had himself addressed as *Doctor*, had no cause to be jealous of a Europeanized Iranian intellectual. They are both rivals but equal in the ideological market. Permeability between the category of clerics and that of westernized intellectuals works in the other direction as well: there are academics and writers who do not wear a turban but who nonetheless claim sufficient competence to hold a discourse on religion and ethics. Facing the modern cleric is the theologian-intellectual. Here purists denounce the somewhat "do-it-yourself" handiwork of those who present themselves as established producers of discourse on religion and the world.

Whereas, formerly, the stability of traditional institutions guaranteed an unfailing credibility to those holding a monopoly of authorized religious discourse, today there is competition and overbidding, for on all sides there is talk of precepts, principles, interpretation, exegesis, the purity of the message, and the danger of eclecticism. Two intellectuals, university graduates – Rezā Dāvari and 'Abdolkarim Sorush, for example, who have each received a solid foundation training in religion, but have continued their theological careers as autodidacts – today debate serious questions, such as the government's conformity with Islam, the danger of fascism arising from the absolutism of clerical power, the threat to Islam of an insidious westernization . . . And at the same time, in scarcely different venues (university campus or mosque), clerics speak *ex cathedra* of the depraved sexuality of westerners, the illusions of American leaders or the distress of the Palestinians.[22]

THE SERMON: IDEOLOGICAL MEDIUM

Because of its overtly secular inspiration and lack of an ideological basis, the Pahlavi regime had not been able to persuade the Shi'ite clergy to use their talents to preach collaboration with the state. But the Islamic Republic, dominated by *ulema*, inspired by an eminently clericalist doctrine and the desire to promote religion as the central value of society, had no difficulty in mobilizing its troops. During the Revolution, the great phases of the popular movement matched the periods when the faithful most assiduously attended the mosques to listen to the preaching: Ramadhan

22   See Y. RICHARD, "Clercs et intellectuels dans la République islamique d'Iran," in G. Kepel and Y. Richard, eds, *Intellectuels et militants de l'Islam contemporain*, Paris, Le Seuil, 1990, pp. 29–70.

(August 1978) and Moharram (December 1978). The place for clerical discourse is the sermon, and the most solemn sermon, the one that carries the most political meaning and weight, belongs to the Friday prayers.

On July 27, 1979, the first Friday in Ramadhan, a few months after the victory of the Revolution, Imam Khomeyni entrusted ayatollah Tāleqāni with the task of leading and preaching at the Friday prayers in Tehran. The place symbolically selected for this gathering was not a mosque. In any case what covered building could have allowed several tens of thousands of the faithful to sit down on a clean floor to listen to the preacher, and then to prostrate themselves in rows, turned towards Mecca, on a surface as rigorously flat and clean as tradition prescribes? Necessity forced the authorities to make certain arrangements: the prayers were held on the campus of Tehran University. The material drawbacks (sloping ground, the impossibility of seeing the preacher and prayer-leader from all points of the campus, and of protecting the faithful from the sun, wind, rain, etc.) were minimal compared with the symbolic gain: the University of Tehran was a central place, well situated in the town, where all the values of "secular knowledge" and the social promotion of the old regime were henceforward overturned, rendered accessible to the lower classes and dominated by a rite formerly proscribed within its enclave. It was the Islamization of a profane place.

To attract attention and maintain dynamism, one must create an event. The organizers of the Friday prayers understood this very well, at the same time carrying on an ancient tradition. The head of the Community, by virtue of his qualities, is in fact the Friday prayer-leader; he is the spokesman and, in his role as preacher, from the height of his pulpit, not only does he deliver edifying speeches, but also gives orders, takes decisions, hands out advice on political matters and in general on matters concerning the Community.[23] Thus, in post-revolutionary Iran, political leaders who come to speak during the course of Friday prayers bring the event itself with them. They comment, usually in the second sermon (*khotba*) before prayers, on the various happenings of the week, summing them up methodically. In the course of the *khotba* important decisions are announced regarding the government's programs, the war, international relations, negotiations with Iraq or the West. Coming from some wretched suburb, how can one fail to be fascinated by this rhetoric, which can be listened to live and free of charge, and which is addressed to the whole world?

There is something to suit all tastes in the Friday prayers: it often

---

23   J. PEDERSEN, "Masdjid," *Shorter Encyclopaedia of Islam*, s.v.

happens that the moral exhortation contains unexpected elements of modern culture. On one such occasion, Hāshemi-Rafsanjāni conducted a sort of inquiry into sexuality in the West which served to confirm all conjectures on the corruption of morals in "Christian" countries. The scabrous details about these sensitive issues – homosexuality, AIDS, permissiveness and the catastrophes involved for the family and upbringing of the children – allow the orator to hold the attention of the faithful, to dramatize the urgent need for an awakening of consciousness, and to justify at one and the same time all the invective against the enemy and the solutions provided by Islam.

Sexual morality is an inexhaustible topic which seems to haunt Islamic preaching. Metaphors of rape, defloration, prostitution, impurity, adultery, or incest carry the strongest emotions and immediately transfer to a social and political content: unassuaged desire, violence, domination, penetration, suppression, corruption, and disorder.[24] Without obvious transition, one can pass from sexual morality to the political domain, to the need to uphold the government's efforts, to protect Islam, all the concomitants of the aspiration toward security and purity. The preacher will then have little trouble in tackling economic problems and necessary hardships, or in commenting on world news. He advises the Americans to change their policies if they want their hostages in the Lebanon to be freed. For the listener there are always interesting items in this panorama of current events: it is as pregnant and engrossing as reading a magazine. The most mundane matters of everyday life can also be found there – for example electricity or water cuts, the consequence of immoderate consumption.

In a world where the caliphate no longer existed and the mosque ceased to be at the centre of things, the *khotba* lost the connotations and function that it enjoyed in classic Islam, where it had no competition. The diversification and secularization of knowledge and general culture deprived the preaching of the *ulema* of its central and normative character. Political discourse in Parliament or meetings reached a wider audience (through the press or radio), and responded more satisfactorily than a sermon to the expectations of modern citizens, for whom the mosque was a marginal place, belonging to the culture of the past.

Although modern media, the press, but chiefly audiovisual media, radio, tape recordings, cinema, television, have quickly come to occupy an important place in today's Iran, as in many third-world countries, their acceptance

24   See the remarkable analysis, dating from before the Revolution, on preaching in Iran, by G. THAISS, "The Conceptualization of Social Change through Metaphor," *Journal of Asian and African Studies*, 1–2 (1978), pp. 1–13.

has given rise to various theological problems (they didn't exist in the Prophet's time! They are often used and controlled by anti-religious elites, broadcast exciting music or indecent variety shows and, on this account, many *ulema* hold them to be works of the devil . . .); pro-development sociologists or functionaries of the Iranian old regime, however, had seen them as instruments of the secular trend of westernization and had been in favor of their more general spread. For the intellectuals, ever eager to break down the incomprehension and inability to communicate that separated them from the masses, these media offered only advantages even if, at best, for want of reaching a wider public, they ensured only an increased reproduction of translated culture. The clerics were not hampered by the same inhibitions when it came to holding forth in public, and if they made full use of audiovisual media it was because they had been thoroughly prepared for it by the sermon, which they managed to restore in part to the position it had enjoyed in the past.

The power and influence of the clergy, notwithstanding the negative prognostications of westernized intellectuals, had not been diminished by the modernization process; on the contrary, they had been accentuated. The ineffectualness of a *translated* and imported discourse really came to light when the mullas, abandoning their traditional reserve, came out into the streets of Iranian towns at the head of imposing processions. Closer to the people, they spoke their language and, above all, they knew how to *speak*, for they had been trained in that art in their first years in theological schools and Iran. The man with the "silver tongue" thus easily won the day as opposed to the bookish man trained in the university.

Well-read men (intellectuals or clerics) and the public meet in specific places. The distinction in connotation between sacred and profane places is an important parameter of the Islamic Revolution. The mosque is not only a place of prayer (its supreme purpose), but also an integrated gathering-place where the cleric teaches. There are mosques in all towns, all districts of towns and even in isolated villages. Their architecture traditionally comprises an *eyvān* opening on to a courtyard with the basin for ablutions in the centre. Other walled rooms, sheltered from the cold and rain, allow meetings to be held in winter weather. The use of the mosque's space is relatively flexible and versatile: mats and carpets spread on the floor and folded up when required allow people to carry out the ritual prostrations, sit in rows to hear a sermon or in a more restricted circle to listen to a master's teaching. Apart from meetings for prayer or teaching, the mosque is an oasis of silence and tranquillity in the midst of busy streets and noisy bazaars.

By contrast, the university presents a modern and complex architecture, linked with imported (translated) culture, accessible to a handful of the privileged, with precise and complicated rules, situated in specific places to which access is controlled. It encloses space adapted to precise uses, leaving little room for improvisation. The public has little chance of being welcomed there outside the rare programs that may be organized for it. Even more than school, university evokes a place where one opens one's intellect on to the world, chiefly to knowledge and progress coming from the West, but loses contact with spontaneous popular culture. In short, to resume the former schematization, where the mosque and its ministers in charge seem to welcome the public (the nation, Muslims, and their socio-economic problems), the university opens its arms to the outside world, claiming to be the only body in Iran to have knowledge of it and to impart that knowledge. The university looks at another world, but one that is immediate and material; a world beyond the seas rather than beyond death. When the university indulges in philosophy or metaphysics (i.e. the world beyond this one, religion, spiritual and transcendent phenomena) it does so less like the mosque, answering spiritual questions and holding a dialogue with the divine, but rather to address intercultural matters concerning the West, in the perspective of a dialogue with a geographical "beyond."

One can therefore understand why the new regime gave priority to mosques as centres for the diffusion of values and socialization. By becoming almost institutional administrative centres (distribution of rationed goods, surveillance of the population), they were partly removed from their pedestal but efficiently supervised the nation. At the same time, Friday prayers organized in non-sacred places opened a breach of Islamization in a world formerly turned exclusively toward the West.

This redistribution of talking-places is instructive. After the Islamic Revolution there was no longer the same chasm between "clear-thinking" intellectuals (according to the sense of the Persian expression *rowshan-fekr*, recalling a connection with our eighteenth-century Enlightenment, the liberating of the intellect) and clerics who were thinkers. Several reasons explain this change: the new offices to which the clerics were invited by the Islamic regime allowed them once more to occupy a central place in society and to rediscover the world; on the other hand, a new generation of intellectuals, who had emerged from traditional circles but had been educated in the school of modernity, acquired a mastery of intellectual discourse without giving up their links with Islamic culture; for both sides the world was there to be reconquered.

It is not quite the same world as in the nineteenth century, dominated by the Enlightenment of the West, but a world where the West is in retreat, Islam is becoming aware of its importance, and the third world has a full existence. The existence of the third world was no novelty for intellectuals who, for several decades, had followed the struggles of decolonization, the Vietnam war, the Palestinian problem, the rise of the non-aligned movement, and the fight against underdevelopment. On the other hand, for the clerics freshly come to power who had to redefine Iran's position in the world, the discovery of Nicaragua or Angola, the struggles of Muslims in the Lebanon, the Philippines, or Afghanistan, to name but a few "hot spots," came as something quite new. They had not waited until they were leading the country in order to find out about them: since his Iraqi exile, how could Khomeyni have been unaware of the Palestinian or Lebanese movements, some of whose protagonists were already resorting to Islamic reference? *Ulema* awareness of third-world struggles, when they suddenly found themselves in command of a country in conflict with the United States, allowed them to hold their own against "modern" Iranian intellectuals. After all, the latter were only specialists on the West.

The anti-establishment prestige of the clergy disappeared in the Islamic Republic: the *ulema* who had enjoyed great independence in relation to political power have today partially merged with it. The Friday prayer-leader is not only the representative of power, he is himself the holder of that power. The result is an inversion of positions: intellectuals' relations with the West lose their ignominious aspect of complicity with a repressive world order and assume a positive dimension of participation in modernity, rendered more tempting by its "forbidden fruit" aura. At the same time, the strait-jacketed ideology of the clergy and their excessive recourse to the opposing categories of deprived/powerful and pure/impure strip them of their militant appeal and turn them into proclaimers of negative values.

In short, whereas before the Revolution clerics and intellectuals lived in separate spheres and only rarely had the opportunity to meet, the Islamic Republic has greatly increased confrontations between them, in university or research areas, in the various media where they express themselves, or in the state's decision-making centres. The institutional links between the clerical educational system (*howza-ye ʾelmiya*) and the modern university system, recommended in 1980 by the "cultural Revolution," have certainly not yielded results, but the frontiers between the two institutions are no longer watertight. Numerous councils and commissions give academics the opportunity to rub shoulders with clerics. The former, if they accept the new conditions, may be invited to speak in mosques. And those who, in total disagreement with the regime, prefer to keep silent, take a greater interest than ever in the discourse of the clerics, analyzing the way they work and keeping a look-out for their weak moments. Lastly, the running of public affairs by certain clerics, their responsibility during the war with Iraq for the organization of the nation's defence, their representation abroad, those collective tasks for which they must surround themselves with the expertise of Iranians who are non-clerical – and sometimes unbelievers – favour an improved reciprocal understanding between the two learned bodies, and occasionally doubtless a greater rivalry, even mutual enmity.

The redistribution of roles and partial disappearance of the stereotype of learned intellectual or cleric are accompanied by the rise of a new category of thinkers who are more men of action than thinkers, the "Islamist Engineers."[25] Bāzargān, a good generation ahead of his time, had already demonstrated that a specialist in factual knowledge could also become a kind of verbal militant. In his wake, numerous students from technical faculties, whose profession brought them into contact with materials rather than ideas, with industry rather than university, became the pivotal points in the overturning of values that accompanied the Revolution. Their technical know-how, which in itself calls for neither values nor tradition, but merely for competence, makes it possible to lend credibility to the unlikely alliance between positive knowledge that transforms the world and supernatural revelation that touches the hearts of men. The discourse of these engineers, which is not truly expert on the subject of either Islam or the West, sometimes appears derisory to us, but their actions outstrip those of clerics or intellectuals. It is thanks to them that, against all expectations, after 15 years of revolution and eight years of war Iran has not collapsed.

IDEOLOGY: A NEW FORM OF RELIGION

Daryush Shayegan denounced the "ideologization of tradition" effected in outstanding fashion by the Islamic Revolution.[26] In the "common Marxism" conveyed in "diffuse ideologies" he saw the essence of what he considered a monstrous phenomenon, the "religious revolution." Shayegan takes the example of 'Ali Shari'ati, the very man who had popularized in Iran the use of the word "ideology" in the sense of a body of doctrines

---

25   For this concept, see N. GÖLE, "Ingénieurs musulmans et étudiantes voilées en Turquie: Entre le totalitarisme et l'individualisme," in Kepel and Richard, *Intellectuels et militants*, pp. 167–92. The phenomenon is equally true in Iran.

26   D. SHAYEGAN, *Qu'est-ce qu'une révolution religieuse?*, Paris, Éditions d'Aujourd'hui, 1982, pp. 179ff and 216ff.

inspired by religious beliefs and guiding social and political action: Shariʾati compared Islam as ideology, an active application of beliefs, with Islam as religious culture, the preservation of a heritage of dogmas.[27] The use of the term "ideology" is today claimed loud and long by the authorities of the Islamic Republic. They do not confuse it with "doctrine" (*maktab*). Through ideology, militant Islam is in rivalry with political doctrines, whether Marxist, nationalist, or other. Shariʾati, the idol of young schoolboys and students before the Revolution, is not quoted one single time in today's school textbooks because of merciless censorship, but his discourse which, in the earlier phase of revolutionary mobilization, filled the hearts and minds of Islamic militants, strongly shapes the philosophical field of the new regime's teachers. By over-politicizing religion, Shariʾati had certainly upset religious order and imposed outlines in which the religious was sometimes reduced to ideology.

An Iranian catechism published in 1988, intended for children in their first year of high school (about 15 or 16 years old), begins with a few interesting definitions which establish the social aim of religious teaching: it is simultaneously *maktab* (doctrine), *jahān-bini* (perception of the world, *Weltanschauung*) and *ideolozhi* (ideology).

> The knowledge and consciousness that each individual has of the world as it exists are called the "vision of the world." The program, the route and the method we choose for ourselves during our life reveal our "ideology." [*Textbook note*: "Ideology" can be used in two senses, particular and general. In the particular sense it is the whole collection of values, duties, obligations, and prohibitions (system of values), and in the general sense it is the equivalent of the term *maktab*. For example, when one says "Islamic ideology," one means the doctrine of Islam. In precise and scientific discussions, "ideology" has the particular sense just mentioned, although in everyday conversation the word has the general sense.] So the vision [or perception] of the world is what each one perceives and knows of the world and its events, the ensemble of our awareness of the world of being and of man, while ideology is the route and method we choose to act in the arena of the world.
>
> The whole created by the vision of the world and ideology is our doctrine [*maktab*]. This view of the world and human life is called a doctrinal view [*maktabi*]. The man who thinks on this basis and knows himself to be committed to realizing the program and ideology of the doctrine is called a *maktabi* man.[28]

27 SHARIʾATI, *Bā makhāteb-hā-ye āshenā*, p. 209.
28 See Y. RICHARD, "L'Enseignement de la religion dans les écoles d'état en Iran," in J.-P. Willaime, ed., *Univers scolaires et religions*, Paris, Cerf, 1990, pp. 107–8.

Does *maktabi* mean "doctrinaire"? I am tempted to translate it as "integrist," a word defining, in Roman Catholicism, the anti-modernist tendency to return to tradition and insistence on clerical authority in the face of humanist values. Here is a fine example of the stiffening of a line of thinking, accentuated by enclosing it in classificatory definitions.

Another religious manual, this time intended for non-Muslim "minorities" (Zoroastrians, Jews, and Christians) but written by the Ministry of Education, also defines monotheistic ideology: life is like a journey, one must know one's destination (that is the "vision of the world"), choose to go there and organize one's trip; the latter stage is the ideology, "the route or the method we choose in what the world offers to us," duties, and prohibitions; the vision of the world and ideology together form the doctrine (*maktab*).[29]

Shayegan's analysis would thus seem justified: we have here, consciously, the reduction of the religious message to a system of thought and action, a closed doctrine reduced to its utilitarian function. The transcendent dimension of religion is not denied, but the room left for meditation, worship, personal prayer, and the personal relationship with God is necessarily diminished by the importance given to the social dimension, to the collective efficacy of religion. Anyhow, this is how the writers of the Islamic Republic's religious manuals justify their unlikely undertaking of publishing common monotheistic catechisms for "minority" (non-Muslim) pupils. Of course, there are similar points in the beliefs of Jew, Christians, and Muslims, and even, if one is loose about definitions, in those of Zoroastrians. But what matters to the authorities of the Islamic Republic is not the rediscovery of an Abrahamic or prophetic ecumenism . . . it is to prevent Iranian "minorities," if left to their own devices, from being tempted to abandon every religious belief and turn to secular ideologies. The Armenian catechism in Iran, if left to the Armenians, would form pan-Armenian nationalists or – worse still – Marxists, as Armenian leaders are suspected of putting religious values well behind national values. They need to be saved from this by having the debased form of religion known as ideology imposed upon them.

RELATIONS BETWEEN SHI'ITES AND SUNNIS

It was not surprising that the regime set up in Iran after the Revolution should have difficult relations with non-Muslims, who had certainly fitted

---

29   RICHARD, "L'Enseignement de la religion," p. 108.

in better with the secularly inclined principles of the Shah's era. But one of the paradoxes of the Islamic Republic is its awkwardness in defining its relations with Sunni Muslims. This in fact was the test of non-sectarianism that all radical Muslims outside Iran were waiting for to rally to the Khomeynist regime: if the new Iranian rulers wanted – as they maintained – to export their Revolution, they must prove that it was not confined to Shi'ites alone, and resume on their own account the efforts displayed since the nineteenth century with the pan-Islamism of Jamāloddin al-Afghani (Asadābādi) to restore a common universal dimension to the various Muslim denominations.

It has already been noted, whether in respect of the 1979 constitution or the program of the Party of the Islamic Republic, that the intent to open out to the Sunnis clashed with the necessities of mobilizing the Shi'ites, and that the latter depended heavily on the use of specifically Shi'ite themes such as the commemoration of Hoseyn's martyrdom or the messianic expectation of the Imam's return.[30] When during his lifetime Imam Khomeyni gave a speech directly centered on a Shi'ite theme, the Arab press, ordinarily reticent toward the Iranian Revolution, happily reproduced it on the front page in translation and without comment: that was enough to discourage from the Islamic Republic any undecided Sunnis who might be dreaming of having a similar experiment in their own country.

Attempts at a *rapprochement* between Shi'ites and Sunnis do not date from the 1979 Revolution.[31] The degree of opposition between the two Muslim sects varies notably as regards schools of law: the Hanbalite Sunnis and, in particular, the Wahhābis are far more closed toward a dialogue with the Shi'ites than are the Shafi'ites or Hanafis; in return, certain Shi'ites (chiefly the Ismailis, the Aga Khan's faithful) are much more reluctant than the Twelvers – with whom this book is concerned – to pray with Sunnis. As early as the eighteenth century, Nāder Shah had attempted to reduce Shi'ism to the level of a fifth legal school of Islam, which he had called *Ja'farite*, after the Sixth Imam, Ja'far al-Sādeq. Was his aim to lessen the tensions between Iran and its Sunni neighbours (Afghans and Uzbeks to the east, Ottomans and Turks to the west), or to make a clear distinction between himself and the Safavid dynasty which he had just supplanted, to

---

30 See above, ch. 4; E. SIVAN, "Sunni Radicalism in the Middle East and the Iranian Revolution," *International Journal of Middle East Studies*, 21, 2 (1989), pp. 22ff; W. ENDE, "Sunni Polemical Writings on the Shi'a and the Iranian Revolution," in D. Menashri, ed., *The Iranian Revolution and the Muslim World*, Boulder, Colo., San Francisco, and Oxford, Westview Press, 1990, pp. 219–32.

31 ENAYAT, *Modern Islamic Political Thought*, pp. 30–51.

which Iranians owed their Shi'ism? It seems chiefly that, in purely pragmatic fashion, he saw the need to erase his Shi'ite origins the better to
establish his legitimacy as sovereign among the Sunni populations of his
vast empire, where Shi'ites were only a minority.[32] Of his great reform,
which he had solemnly ratified in 1743 by theologians from all the Muslim
schools, nothing remained, after his assassination in 1747, except the ban
on the invectives against the first three caliphs, which had become ritual in
Iran since the time of Shah Esmā'il at the beginning of the sixteenth
century. Henceforward Shi'ite authorities would officially recognize the
legitimacy of Abu Bakr, 'Omar and 'Othmān as caliphs, i.e. the Prophet's
successors.

European interference, starting from the nineteenth century, made Muslim
divisions seem ridiculous and, according to anticolonial militants, sought to
make use of those divisions and sectarianism in order to achieve greater
domination over the population. The first to realize this danger and apply
a remedy was Jamāloddin Afghani: born a Shi'ite (as he was Iranian from
the region of Hamadān), he had no hesitation in posing as a Sunni Afghan
and carrying on from Istanbul, capital of the Ottoman Empire, a lively
propaganda campaign for the unity of Islam and the strengthening of
caliphal power. This activity was inspired not so much by the desire to
bring Muslims spiritually closer, to reflect on the errors of the past and the
unity of the Community of believers, as by the urgent political need to
gather all Muslim forces together to face up to colonial enterprises.

The most fruitful line of Muslim reformism, begun by Afghani himself
and his Egyptian disciple Mohammad 'Abdoh (d. 1905), did not lead in the
direction of a reconciliation between Sunnis and Shi'ites, but rather in the
direction of an anti-Shi'ite fundamentalism, a return to the beliefs held by
the "ancestors" of the faith (*salaf*, whence the name of the movement, the
salafiya) and a stripping away of everything, in the later tradition, that gets
in the way of reason, thus notably some beliefs that encumber Shi'ism.

Rashid Ridha, an eminent successor to Afghani and 'Abdoh until his
death in 1935, wrote a work in two volumes on "Sunnism and Shi'ism."[33]
He believed, says Hourani, that it was essential to unite Shi'ites and Sunnis,

---

32 'A. EQBĀL, "Vasiqa-ye ettehād-e eslām-e nāderi" (Nader's Commitment to the Unity
of Islam), *Yādegār*, 4, 6 (esfand 1326/1948), pp. 43–55; L. LOCKHART, *Nadir Shah*,
London, Luzac, 1938; H. ALGAR, "Shi'ism and Iran in the Eighteenth Century," in T.
Naff and R. Owen, eds, *Studies in Eighteenth Century Islamic History*, Carbondale and
Edwardsville, Ill. and London, Austin, 1977, pp. 288–302.
33 See A. HOURANI, *Arabic Thought in the Liberal Age, 1798–1939*, Oxford, Oxford
University Press, 1962 (new edn, 1970), pp. 230ff.

and that it was possible on two conditions: that both parties collaborated on the points over which they were in agreement and forgave each other for those on which they diverged; that when a member of one Community offended another, a member of his own group should respond. Alongside these fine sentiments, each time a problem cropped up to tarnish inter-denominational harmony, Rashid Ridha was quick to blame the Shi'ites and attribute infamous motives to their leaders. In his eyes, Shi'ism was a jumble of legends and illicit innovations; its leaders prevented the unity of the Islamic world by their cupidity and desire for fame; this sect came from a doctrinal divergence that did not exist in the era of the "ancestors of the faith" – therefore suspect – and from the manipulations of the first "converted" Jews (who "denatured" Islam . . .). As Hourani notes, one guesses that despite his theoretical attempts at *rapprochement*, Rashid Ridha had rather strained relations with the Shi'ites.

However, lines of communication between the two great families of Islam were not altogether blocked. In fact, the best flow of understanding passed through this fundamentalist reformism of the *salafiya*. Little known because it was rejected by the majority of the Shi'ite clergy and had difficulty in making itself heard in a period of intense secularization in Iran, a brilliant Shi'ite reformism, indirectly influenced by Mohammad 'Abdoh and Rashid Ridha, left its mark on a whole generation of Iranian intellectuals between 1921 and 1941. Its best representative is Shari'at Sangalaji, a Shi'ite theologian who had read the works of the Egyptian reformers and had been impressed by Hanbalite Wahhābism, several of whose rules he adopted (the rejection of graves protruding above ground level, minarets . . .).[34]

It is doubtless dangerous to put 'Ali Shari'ati in the same line as Sangalaji, but his desire to declericalize Islam draws them closer on more than one count. For him, agreement with Sunni Islam stems from opposition to a degenerate form of Shi'ism – what he terms the "Shi'ism of the Safavids." He gives a caricatural example of the latter, where a Shi'ite author goes so far as to drag the caliph 'Omar through the mud, calling him the offspring of an incestuous line . . . This infamy is broadly the same as that inflicted elsewhere on Shi'ism by a triumphant Sunnism: a destructive contempt that slams the door on dialogue. In the face of this Safavid clericalism, so Shari'ati tells us, there are Shi'ite theologians who have won the respect of

34 See above, ch. 4 and Y. RICHARD, "Shari'at Sangalaji: A Reformist Theologian of the Ridā Shāh Period," in S. A. Arjomand, ed., *Authority and Political Culture in Shi'ism*, Albany, SUNY Press, 1988, pp. 172ff.

the Sunnis. Beside ayatollah Hoseyn Borujerdi (a great Iranian spiritual leader, d. 1961), he mentions notably Iranians ('Abd ol-Hoseyn Amini, ayatollah Māzandarāni), Lebanese (Mohsen Amin Jabal-'Ameli, Javād Maqniya) and Iraqis (Mohammad-Hoseyn Kāshef ol-Qetā). A book published in Persian by an institute for the *rapprochement* of Muslims (*Dār ottaqrib*) gives large extracts from books written by these personalities on the same ecumenical theme.[35] The craftsmen of the *rapprochement* praised by Shari'ati include, on the Sunni side, eminent sheikhs such as Sheikh Shaltut, Grand Mufti of Cairo and rector of al-Azhar, who in 1959 made the study of Ja'farite (Shi'ite) jurisprudence permissible in that great Sunni university. According to our author, the significance of working in that direction was obvious in an era when the Muslim world, divided in the face of colonialism and neo-colonialism, was no longer conscious of its unity as a Community of believers.

Shari'ati thus desired a *rapprochement* with Sunni Muslims, which is not to say that he had abandoned or underestimated the essentially Shi'ite arguments with which his work teems: the need of the Community to have an Imam at its head, the exemplary value of Imam Hoseyn's martyrdom, Imam 'Ali's outstanding sense of justice, the dynamic wait for the return of the Imam . . . Certain Muslim translators have had little compunction in rendering Shari'ati insipid and hardly recognizable: with the probable intention of acting as apologists, they have tried to present an image of him that would be acceptable to Sunnis, glossing over the too explicitly Shi'ite aspects of his work and keeping only the general writings on Islam. Such distortion must not lead astray anyone seeking to understand those aspects specific to pre-revolutionary Shi'ite thinking.[36]

The *rapprochement* of Shi'ites and Sunnis therefore has a history. Even if it still clashes with age-old customs, it was not invented in 1979 by the Iranian Islamic Republic.[37] Khomeyni himself, moved by a desire to unify

---

35   'A. SHARI'ATI, *Tashayyo'-e 'alavi va Tashayyo'-e safavi* (Collected Works, vol. IX), Tehran, Tashayyo', 1359/1980, pp. 72–88, 248ff; M. M. J. FISCHER, *Iran: From Religious Dispute to Revolution*, Cambridge, Mass. and London, Harvard University Press, 1980, p. 178.

36   See for example 'A. SHARI'ATI (trans. H. Algar), *On the Sociology of Islam*, Berkeley, Mizan Press, 1979.

37   SIVAN, "Sunni Radicalism," *IJMES*, 21, 2 (1989), pp. 1–30; W. ENDE, "Sunniten und Schiiten im 20. Jahrhundert," *Saeculum* 36, 2–3 (1985) pp. 187–200; *idem*, "Sunni Polemical Writings on the Shi'a and the Iranian Revolution," in D. Menashri, ed., *The Iranian Revolution and the Muslim World*, pp. 219–32; *idem*, "Die Azhar, Šaih Šaltut und die Schia," in W. Diem and A. Falaturi, eds, *XXIV. Deutscher Orientalistentag (vom 26. bis 30. September in Köln): Ausgewählte vorträge*, Stuttgart, Franz Steiner, 1990, p. 308–18.

the Muslim Community, appreciably cooled the interdenominational polemic by acknowledging (something the Shi'ites had not done since the eighteenth century) the virtues of the first two caliphs, Abu Bakr and 'Omar: "His first two successors maintained the Prophet's line of conduct in their personal and public life, although in other aspects they infringed that rule to the point where the patent deviations of 'Othmān's era became manifest, deviations that have today forced us into this dreadful situation [the division of Muslims and the meddling of colonial powers]."[38]

The third caliph was not reinstated: was it not his government that had brought about the conflict between his clan (the Omayyads) and 'Ali's? But Khomeyni did not stop there. In order to make contact between Shi'ites and Sunnis easier, he gave his imitators permission to pray behind a Sunni Imam. That apparently harmless reform facilitated an interdenominational *rapprochement* at the very time of the annual pilgrimage to Mecca and later on the occasion of visits by Sunni personalities to the Iranian Islamic Republic.

Mention has already been made of the insoluble contradiction between discourse of universal scope, aiming to gather together all Muslims into one Community of which Khomeyni was to be the first head, and the mobilization of the people over sometimes exclusively Shi'ite subjects. Those contradictions, for the Iranian regime having to shoulder them, brought both internal and external political difficulties: the difficulty of integrating into the national community ethnic groups which for the most part were Sunni, such as the Baluchi tribe in the south-east, certain Arab tribes of Khuzistan and a large part of the Kurds and Turkomans in the north. Cultural centralism and leveling out by means of the Persian language in these poor provinces thus now assumed a denominational hue. Obligatory declarations of allegiance preserved bitternesses that Shi'ite triumphalism could not appease. It is in these peripheral regions, notably between the Turkomans and Kurds that the bloodiest clashes since the victory of the Revolution have taken place.

Apart from the strictly political and ideological implications, there is more direct interference in private life that can only hurt the Sunnis. On the political level, it is the recognition of a government which proclaims the supremacy of the hidden Imam and agrees to govern only while awaiting the return of this Imam – a heresy for the Sunnis. The supreme instance of this regime, the "Guide," is defined on the basis of a typically clerical and Shi'ite structure (the *mojtaheds* elected to the Council of Experts are

---

38   R. KHOMEYNI, *Velāyat-e faqih*, new edn, Tehran, Amir Kabir, 1357/1979, p. 56; trans. H. Algar, *Islam and Revolution*, Berkeley, Mizan Press, 1981, p. 57.

charged with the task of designating the ayatollah who will succeed the Guide). In public, are the Sunnites not obliged frequently to pray behind a Shi'ite mulla and respond to a call to prayer to which is added the phrase "'Ali is next to God" (*'Alian vali-ol-Lāh*, in which *vali* can just as easily express one who is close to divine love as one who is close to the power of God)? In school, are their children not bound to learn religion from textbooks that have certainly been produced with Sunnis in mind, but have been emended, if not written, by Shi'ites? These books say nothing on the historic foundations of the caliphate or the origin of sectarian dissensions at the time of the Prophet's death.[39]

Outside Iran, those contradictions made it difficult to carry out the Revolution's ambitious programme of ideological exportation. The constitution explicitly states that Iran will defend "the rights of all Muslims" (article 152) and "will give its support to the legitimate fight of the underprivileged for their rights against the powerful in every region of the world" (article 154). Despite the overall favorable response that the Revolution received in Muslim countries, at least in the heart of Islamist movements, it must be admitted that the outcome is not as brilliant as the Iranian leaders had wished, and that their influence has been exercised mainly in Shi'ite regions.

It is not that the basic inspirations lack points in common: denouncing the compromise of elites professing to be Muslim (including the *ulema*) with governments giving their allegiance to the West or materialist ideologies, replacing nationalist ideologies and corrupt potentates with the sovereignty of the Islamic Law (the *shari'a*), working toward the return of a political structure common to all Muslims, restoring the rights of Muslims wherever they have been subjected by violence to a foreign law, notably in Palestine . . . Common ideological writings, however, are restricted by the incompatibility of respective references, which explains the slowness or rarity of translation of these authors from Arabic into Persian or vice versa. How can one call upon 'Ebn Teymiya, the destroyer of the Shi'ite "heresy," if one wants to join forces with the Shi'ites? How can one take 'Ali and Hoseyn as models *par excellence* if one wants to associate with those who fought against them?

PILGRIMAGE AND ITS IDEOLOGY

The place for testing out the policy of exporting the Khomeynist revolution was the annual pilgrimage that Muslims make to Mecca, the *hajj*.

---

39 RICHARD, "L'Enseignement de la religion," p. 97.

Most Islamist authors recommend, as did Shari'ati, that this gathering should be transformed into a kind of annual political congress for Muslim peoples.[40] The essence of its justification, they say, is to bring together at the same time believers from all parts of the globe so that they can get to know and help one another. As early as January 1971, from his Iraqi exile, Khomeyni had had tracts distributed to Iranian pilgrims to Mecca, saying:

> O dear Muslim nation gathered together here in the place of the revelation to fulfil the rites of pilgrimage, it is up to you to seize this opportunity to take counsel together and find solutions to resolve the community's problems [the interference of colonial powers] . . . Open your ears to the problems of each Muslim nation as it sets them out itself, and leave no stone unturned in your efforts to resolve them together . . .[41]

Khomeyni next inveighs against those who, on the occasion of the pilgrimage, distribute defamatory anti-Shi'ite pamphlets and seek to divide Muslims. He then presents problems peculiar to Iran, the reasons for his struggle against the Shah's regime. This new approach, which did not seem to call the Saudi dynasty into question and provoked no police clampdown, was a precedent. After the setting up of the Islamic Republic messages intended for the pilgrims were more of a threat to the equilibrium of the region and in particular the Saudi kingdom. The traditional discipline of mental dissimulation or discretion (*taqiya*), which had allowed Shi'ites to pass through unremarked, was over and done with. The first direct clashes with the Saudi police occurred in 1981, leading to the death of an Iranian. But more serious troubles with the forces of order erupted in 1987, when over 400 pilgrims lost their lives, at least half of them Iranian. For Iranian Shi'ites, boycotting this pilgrimage in the years following the tragedy up to 1990 made contact and propaganda among non-Shi'ite Muslims no easier. Redoubled propaganda against Wahhābi Saudis suddenly revived the isolation of the Shi'ites: other Muslim militants certainly have more than one reason to reproach the dynasty that guards the holy places, but the specifically Shi'ite grievances put forward by the Iranians here contribute little to obtaining a good reception for their arguments from the Sunnis.

40 See for example on Sayyed Qotb, O. CARRÉ, *Mystique et politique*, Paris, Presses de la FNSP/Cerf, 1984, p. 200.
41 Text in Sd H. RUHANI, *Nahzat-e Emām Khomeyni*, vol. II, Tehran, 1364/1985, pp. 995ff; trans. H. Algar, *Islam and Revolution*, pp. 195ff. On the problem of the *hajj* under the Islamic Republic, see M. KRAMER, "La Mecque: La Controverse du pèlerinage," *Maghreb-Machrek*, 122 (October–December 1988), pp. 38–52.

Khomeyni directly challenged Saudi control over Mecca and Medina which, in his opinion, belonged to all Muslims and should remain freely accessible to everyone. Something else was at stake here, apart from the quarrel between Sunnis and Shi'ites: the upsurge of non-Arab Islam and the role that Iran, together with other Muslim countries in Asia, is entitled to play in organizing the pilgrimage. In the Indian subcontinent there are 250 million Muslims, more than in all the Arab countries put together, and Indonesia, with 150 million Muslims, is the largest Muslim country in the world . . . In 1979 28 percent of pilgrims to Mecca came from Asiatic non-Arab countries, and 41 percent in 1984. In 1987, although they are relatively close to Mecca, the Arab countries had only 401,000 pilgrims in all, that is, fewer than half the total, and this disproportion is becoming more pronounced.[42] So even if the revolutionary message was no longer getting through, because of the temporary boycott on the pilgrimage by the Islamic Republic, the challenge to Saudi Arabia's role as custodian of the holy places could well be resumed with even more virulence after the war of winter 1991. The geopolitical development of Muslim peoples is heading in this direction. Saudi legitimacy, upheld by the American military, has lost its prestige, and guardianship of the holy places, for which one imagines there will soon be a vacancy, is a coveted position.

Confirmation of the Iranians' hegemonic stake in their misfired operations in Mecca arrived belatedly, some months before Khomeyni's death, when the Imam published his famous religious decree (*fatvā*) on *The Satanic Verses*, causing such an upset in the West. It was above all to those Asian Muslims that the condemnation of Salman Rushdie was addressed, in February 1989: it was less a matter of an anti-western operation than of an astute maneuver to recover a movement that had gone elsewhere and that the *ulema* of Saudi Arabia did not dare to touch. By anathematizing the "apostate" author of *The Satanic Verses*, Khomeyni was killing two birds with one stone: he was proving, contrary to Saudi propaganda, that Shi'ites were truly strict Muslims, concerned with defending the integrity of the Koran and the respect due to Mohammad. He was equally setting himself up – and this was confirmed at the Islamic Conference in Medina where only the Iranian representative dared to uphold the traditional point of view – as the sole effective protector of the Islamic faith in the face of the West's intrigues.

42　S. ZEGHIDOUR, *La Vie quotidienne à La Mecque de Mahomet à nos jours*, Paris, Hachette, 1989, pp. 438ff.

IS SHI'ISM REVOLUTIONARY?

Revolutionary Shi'ism is increasingly taking on the appearance of an ideology: since it was in this denomination of Islam that the most spectacular revolution inspired by Islam triumphed, one is entitled to wonder if that revolution in a Shi'ite country was a mere chance of history, or whether an intrinsic connection really exists between this religion and the idea of violent political change. Is Shi'ism – in a word – revolutionary?

We must first of all dispose of an ambiguity: one is revolutionary when one wants to upset a social order to change the structure of its ruling power; in this sense, every militant who tries to realize his ideas to the very last is a revolutionary, whether Marxist, Muslim, or Buddhist. We know that the most revolutionary, even the Stalinists, sometimes behave worse than the Tsars as soon as they are in power themselves. But among those who do not hesitate to upset social relations completely, and turn economic structures upside down, some, paradoxically, fear the disrupting of order because, in their view, revolution means restoring to natural order the disorder created by man. Muslim revolutionaries belong rather to that second category: they seek to restore the order of nature made by God and sent astray by man's ingratitude (*kofr*). Among them the Shi'ites stand out, certainly, on more than one point.

Some distinctive theological features of Shi'ism take on a particular emphasis as soon as they are used in a political context: the eschatological wait for the saviour-Imam (the "great evening"), the justification of rebellion against an iniquitous government, secrecy and clandestinity, obedience to a religious leader chosen by oneself. Not one of these elements exists in Sunnism, and each is liable either to a completely mystic interpretation, or to become laden with emotion and acquire an irresistible force, even in politics. And as the example of Khomeyni himself bears witness, are not revolutionary effectiveness and charismatic value amplified by the mystic aspect of belief? Khomeyni blessing the crowds literally fascinated his public, and any words uttered by him when he was thus stretching out a pacifying hand took on the importance of an oracle. At the very beginning of the revolutionary disturbances in 1978, a friend of mine, one morning before dawn entering a mosque in the south of Tehran ('Abd ol-'Azim's mausoleum) where he had a family tomb, was surprised to find in the prayer hall believers who appeared to be meditating; discreetly drawing near, he heard them murmuring political slogans hostile to the Shah. How could it have occurred to any police to track down at that hour of the morning, in a mosque, such well-behaved and inoffensive demonstrators, who nevertheless were preparing for the most merciless battles?

The paradox of Shi'ism is that this revolutionary potential is not left to its own devices, but channeled as much as possible through the clergy. Among all the radical Islamist groups, the Shi'ites are the only ones to accept *ulema* into their ranks and give them a deciding role.[43] The persons most hostile to clerical power, like Shari'ati, are the first to want the *ulema* to be replaced by enlightened guides who will lead the people, for the latter are supposed to be incapable of emancipating themselves by their own efforts. In this sense, if the ultimate aim of the Islamic movement is to hand over power to a social category concerned first and foremost with order, in no way can it be called revolutionary. It is true that not all Shi'ite militants desire this rerouting, and some long for the continuation of a social revolution that they consider unfinished. Far from being a mechanism for revolution, Shi'ite theology is a tangle of themes of social break-up and glimpses of transcendency.

Can it be said that the leaders of the Iranian Revolution "have the same conception of the Shi'ite Community as Marx had of the proletariat: a particular group realizing the emancipation of the whole of humanity"? Is Shi'ism, "in thought as in practice, the avant-garde of the global Islamic revolution"?[44] It is certain that Khomeynist discourse does not stop at Iranians or Shi'ites, and that the internal logic of the movement he unleashed seeks to enlarge the circle of those who will be saved by his message. It is a universal doctrine, of which Khomeyni felt himself to be the guardian, and his desire for hegemony flowed from the liberating cause whose servant he claimed to be.

A NEW FORM OF NATIONALISM?

Outside Iran, revolutionary Shi'ites were obliged to admit that their "Persian connection" hampered them on two counts: as an ethnic barrier (their Iranian, as opposed to Arabic or Islamic, nature) and as a denominational barrier (Shi'ism versus Sunnism). One of the most fruitful effects of the Iranian revolution was indeed the effacement of classic nationalist ideology, ousted by Islamism.

---

43   SIVAN, "Sunni Radicalism," pp. 9–11.
44   O. ROY, "Le Facteur chiite dans la politique extérieure de l'Iran," *Central Asian Survey*, 9, 3 (1990), p. 59.

Relations between nation-states and transnational ideologies are by their very nature strained. They are even more so with Islam, which since its origins has dreamed of gathering together all believers into one united political entity. For two centuries colonization and then chiefly decolonization have continued to distance Muslims from this dream. The term *mellat*, which originally meant a religious community to distinguish it from others (the community of Islam compared with that of Christians or Jews, etc.), gradually came to mean, at first in the Ottoman world and then in Iran, ethnic and political groups formed since the nineteenth century in reaction to European interference and by mimicry of western nations.[45] In this context, endless misunderstandings and conflicts set "nationalists" against "Islamists."

The Iranian constitutionalist revolutionaries of the beginning of the twentieth century employed the inexact term *mellat* to designate their identity as a people demanding their share of power, and named their parliament *Majles-e shurā-ye melli*, "National Parliamentary Assembly," recalling that the 1906–7 constitution was concerned with the people's rights. The adjective *melli* created difficulties at that time because of its paradoxically secular connotations: the demonstrators who occupied the gardens of the British legation, for example, rejected the imperial edict convoking an "Islamic" (*eslāmi*) parliamentary assembly, holding that this term allowed the exclusion of so-called "unbelievers" and members of non-Muslim minorities. In their view, the term *melli* therefore integrated them all into one single body without any denominational nuance. Demand for a national identity resulted in a reappraisal of the term *mellat*, the bearer of collective democratic legitimacy in the face of the apparatus of state or interference from abroad. Indeed, that meaning was to prevail, for example to designate "nationalizations" (*melli-shodan*) and the great nationalist struggle (*nahzat-e melli*) of the 1950s against the Anglo-Iranian Oil Company which Mosaddeq, in fact, nationalized.

In 1952 the breakaway of the religious wing of the National Front (*Jebha-ye melli*), which confirmed the one already effected by the radical Islamists (the *Fedā'iyān-e eslām*), was a foretaste of the rivalry that erupted during the Islamic Revolution. But this time, in 1979, the nationalists no longer had the strength to resist. Whereas in the pre-revolutionary phase many western observers – and chiefly the BBC, much listened to in

---

45   Y. RICHARD, "Du nationalisme à l'islamisme: Dimensions de l'identité ethnique en Iran," in J.-P. Digard, ed., *Le Fait ethnique en Iran et en Afghanistan*, Paris, CNRS, 1988, p. 270.

Iran – envisaged an important role for the Mosaddeqists, who numbered some outstanding personalities, from Shapour Bakhtiar to Mehdi Bāzargān, by way of Abo'l-Hasan Bani-Sadr, these representatives of nationalist liberalism were seen to fall one by one. When the Islamic Republic had gained control of all the central institutions and banned the majority of nationalist organizations and their newspapers, the last nationalist public demonstrations were a fiasco: instead of convincing liberals that they represented a sufficient force and ought to unite, they were occasions for violence and a complete rout of the nationalist camp. The final permitted meetings took place in March 1981. The one organized by Mehdi Bāzargān and the Movement for the Liberty of Iran was turned into uproar by young extremists claiming to act for the *Fedā'iyān-e eslām*. The other, arranged by President Bani-Sadr on the campus of Tehran University to commemorate the death of Mosaddeq, was marked by violent clashes that ended in Bani-Sadr's downfall.[46]

The last chance was snatched from the nationalists on Monday, June 15, 1981. On that day the National Front and the Movement for Liberty in Iran, mobilized to defend the rights of man, called for a peaceful demonstration in the centre of Tehran against the bill concerning the retaliatory law, then under discussion in parliament. In reality, they also wanted to show support for President Bani-Sadr by a mass gathering, on the eve of the exceptional parliamentary debates due to commence on the morrow on the matter of his dismissal. Khomeyni immediately opposed the demonstration, condemning as a renegade anyone who obeyed a nationalist ideology. Bāzargān, whose knowledge of Islam had just been called into question in a series of articles by Jalāloddin Fārsi in the PIR's daily newspaper, was the first to surrender by cancelling the call to demonstrate. A counter-demonstration of *hezbollāhi* at once took place and the handful of middle-class nationalists who had timidly prepared to march remained on the pavements, spectators of their own defeat.

The patriotic outburst against Iraqi aggression in September 1980 shows that Shi'ite revolutionaries were not uncomfortable at belonging to a national state.[47] Khomeyni himself set the tone by calling for the defense of the homeland (*vatan*) "dearer than very life," extolling the martyrdom of those who would thus serve the cause of Islam. Since the Law of Islam

46   Y. RICHARD, "The Relevance of 'Nationalism' in Contemporary Iran," *Middle-East Review*, 21, 4 (Summer 1989), pp. 27–36.
47   J. P. PISCATORI, *Islam in a World of Nation-States*, Cambridge, Cambridge University Press, 1986, p. 114.

applied in Iran, was there in fact any difference between defending the homeland and defending the faith?

May your lives be hallowed [declared Khomeyni on March 22, 1982 to encourage Iranian volunteers at the time of the recapture of Khorramshahr], brave fighters and soldiers in the path of God who have safeguarded the honor of Islam, made the Iranian nation illustrious and raised the heads of those committed to the way of God. The great Iranian nation [*mellat-e bozorg-e Irān*] and the children of Islam are proud of you, who have placed your homeland [*mihan-e khod*] on the wings of angels and raised it aloft among all the nations of the world [*melal-e jahān*].

Here we face two realities: on the one hand, the defense of the nation, *per se*, now mobilizes among the population only those elements bewildered by the political evolution, those who are the least dynamic; and on the other, the defense of Islam incorporates that of the nation and goes even further. Mosaddeqist nationalists are overtaken by a discourse stronger than their own, and one which is a better match for the aggression felt: defending the quality of being Iranian when it is not being threatened attracts no one, and turning the struggle for liberties or human rights into a political theme is to relegate to secondary importance the political or economic influence and interference of imperialist powers. When the Islamist militants express scorn they show that, in their eyes, the true urgency lies not in the defense of national feeling or individual liberties, but in the reinstatement of an identity stolen, perverted, subjugated by the world of economics and the world of culture. To confront the stereotype of the arrogant, materialist, depoliticized westerner, with his internationalized mediocre culture, the Islamic Revolution has recourse to parts of the cultural heritage that go deeper than national sentiment and the humanist ideal. This does not mean that attachment to Islam is significant only as regards identity, but religious feeling has more efficacy than an appeal to reason as a means of social mobilization in a revolutionary situation. It is less a matter of a rebirth of faith (which did not cease to exist) than of making use of Islam for self-protection following the weakening of traditional social structures. Confronted with the ideals of the "nationalists," humanist and noble but abstract, Islamists resort to more evocative metaphors to denounce their dispossessed situation *vis-à-vis* imperialism: violator, devourer of the planet, sucker of the nation's blood . . .

Conclusion

More than fifteen years after the advent of the Iranian Islamic Republic, which explicitly claimed Shi'ite Islam as its principle, one may be surprised by the absence of any original thought aroused by that new type of revolution. An event claims to introduce the divine world into history, but Shi'ite thinkers have not put forward any new theology to give it sense: the clerics continue to repeat, comment on and expand the texts of the past, refute the errors and justify the choices of the present. With Khomeyni gone, any innovatory discourse would doubtless be badly received in a Community henceforward more concerned with orthodoxy than with revolution.

After the first bursts of enthusiasm, this stark return of the religious has inspired more invective and sarcasm than calm reflection among westerners. The French philosopher Michel Foucault set the tone of the misunderstanding: even before the victory of February 1979, he was admiring the role played by religion in the Iranian Revolution.

> In that way they had of living the Islamic religion as if it were a revolutionary force (he declared to journalists) there was something else beside the will to obey the law more faithfully, there was the will to renew their entire existence by reviving a spiritual existence they believe they can find in the very heart of Shi'ite Islam. Marx and the opium of the people are forever being quoted. The sentence immediately before, which is never quoted, says that religion is the spirit in an unspiritual world. Let us therefore say that Islam, in this year 1978, was not the opium of the people, precisely because it was the spirit of an unspiritual world.[1]

1   Cl. BRIÈRE and P. BLANCHET, *Iran: La Révolution au nom de Dieu*. Following an interview with M. Foucault, Paris, Le Seuil, 1979, p. 234.

Foucault, who had gone to Iran to follow events, also wrote in autumn 1978, in a weekly with a high circulation: "How sensible for the men living there [Iran] to seek, even at the cost of their life, something of which we in the West have forgotten the very possibility since the time of the Renaissance and the great crises of Christianity: *a political spirituality*. Already I can hear some Frenchmen laughing, but I know that they are wrong."[2]

Foucault – he regretted it himself later – had been carried away by a rebellious movement that had aroused great sympathy throughout the world. After all, many an insurrection of liberation has ended in strong-arm methods of regaining control, and revolutionary forces often become an instrument of state coercion in the regimes they have themselves helped to establish. Another question now arises: would not the mobilization of Iranians around their clerics have been the same if they had been Sunni muftis, bonzes, or Orthodox priests? Is it not the reemergence of the religious, something new and unexpected in the cultural field of 1978, that causes Foucault to marvel, rather than the particular effectiveness of Shi'ism, largely concealed by specificities that elude us?

There is, however, one specific essence of Shi'ism that cannot be reduced to historical contingencies: before being a doctrine of power or counterpower, this religion is also and primarily a way of perceiving the spiritual world and attaining the divine. For Shi'ites there is an unshakable faith in certain truths which exist for them alone and which are beyond argument. In that faith, Muslim belief in one God and in the prophecy of Mohammad is enriched by the expectation of the Imam's return, by the existence of intercessors for prayer, and by the consequent rites, such as participation in the ritual mourning ceremonies for the martyred Imams.

Surprised by the feeble interest shown by researchers in this family of Islam, Henry Corbin deplored the westerners' deafness to Shi'ite spirituality, which he himself had studied with unbounded enthusiasm and erudition, stressing its most ahistorical theosophical dimension. By purest chance, just as the orientalist philosopher died (October 1978) ayatollah Khomeyni arrived in Paris and unleashed an unprecedented interest in another kind of Shi'ism, a Shi'ism firmly anchored in history, militant – and no longer discarnate or resigned like the one studied by Corbin. Should one read into it a sign of the inner transformation of this religion which, from being persecuted, the creator of invisible forms, was becoming triumphant and

---

2   Quoted 11 years later in the *Nouvel Observateur*, no. 1283, June 8–14, 1989; see further L. OLIVIER and S. LABBÉ, "Foucault et l'Iran: A propos du désir de révolution," *Canadian Journal of Political Science*, 24, 2 (June 1991), pp. 219–36.

thereby losing the thread of its justification – rather as, four centuries earlier, by making Shi'ism the religion of Iran the Safavids had taken away its intrinsic quality of a spirituality reserved for the initiated?

In becoming the ideology of a revolution, Shi'ism loses its status as a universal belief in salvation to become the instrument of history, subject to the unpredictability of events. Like all human doctrines, it evolves in time; it is versatile and able to fulfill various functions in the same era. While a learned tradition scarcely touched by modernism was kept alive in the theological schools at Qom and Najaf, the very foundations of the clerical institution were shaken by collusion with political power and the desire to have a hand in the world's destiny. While a great ayatollah at Najaf (Abo'l-Qāsem Kho'i), was very careful not to adopt a stance over the Revolution and the organization of the state, at Qom another great ayatollah (Kāzem Shari'at-madāri, 1904–86) found himself deposed from his rank of "Guide to imitate" (*marja'al-taqlid*) because of his political alliances, as if henceforward clerical status were dependent on relations with the government. Are we to see in this a split, inside Shi'ism, between those who would give allegiance to the Islamic Republic and those who, going "underground," would preserve the traditions of the Imams in all their purity?

In the various, chiefly ideological, avatars of Shi'ism the elements of its foundation are constantly rediscovered: for example, the memory of Imam Hoseyn's rebellion, the obligation to go through spiritual guides to direct the community, or attaining access to the divine by way of a structure of human signs. On the social plane, two features predominate: Shi'ism offers hierocratic or clerical structures ready to form a counter-society; furthermore, it builds man's destiny on the expectation of the great revolution at the End of Time, the triumphal return of the Imam and his reign of justice and truth.

But after the Islamic Revolution and Khomeyni, were those specific points not blunted by the integration of the clergy into the state? As the awaited event took place in 1979, the eschatological concern is no longer the expectation of an unveiling that keeps humanity in suspense, but the unfolding of a logic whose elements are already known and give rise to no dreams.

Let us go further. Shi'ism has contradictory faces: we know now that there is an oppressive Shi'ism and a liberating Shi'ism; one conservative and one anti-establishment; one theocratic and one "democratic;" one "integrist" and one progressive; one inflexible and one open . . . Like Shi'ism, Catholicism has its saintly intercessors, its votive chapels, its pious images, its clergy, its Vatican, its infallible pontiff surrounded by an authoritative body of theologians who are independent of the state and steeped in their own legitimacy, its "integrism," its Jesuits, its theology of liberation, and its boldness in holding out against the way the world is going.

Instead of seeing only clerical discourse misrepresented for purposes of propaganda and distorted by the cultural distance between the West and societies where Shi'ism is in the majority, should we not rather search popular religious feeling to try to understand if the Revolution has really changed something within Shi'ism? Should we not replace the view from on high with a fresh view, from below? Religion would then seem much more real to us, if I am to believe this Iranian sociologist:

> As long as religious studies are confined to picking out the mainly abstruse features of learned religiosity, they will be accomplices of the hegemonic and dominant classes and will remain prisoner of mental outlines that find no echo in popular religious feeling and, by their twisted complexity, express an aristocratic view of social relations; thus, the doctrines so learnedly studied by Henry Corbin are shared by only a handful of erudite Shi'ites who use them to distinguish themselves from the "ignorant" whose religious feeling, allegedly superficial and simplistic, is implicitly reduced to "blind faith" and declared unfounded. The revival of popular religiosity expresses both the protest of the masses against a world order that is crushing them, and the frailty of that protest . . . Institutional Islamology, following straight on from orientalism, perceives nothing but the Islam of the learned. It sees no religiosity *sensu eminenti* but that of the *ulema*; Islam is reflected in its jurisprudence (*feqh*), its mysticism (theosophy, Sufism, etc.), possibly in its architecture that is in itself a reflection of the divine oneness . . . Popular religiosity and its social function are overlooked. Beyond the divisions that separate them, Islamologists and the hierarchy of Islamic clergy are linked by ties of intellectual and spiritual complicity: they enjoy mutual esteem, agree on the essential role of the clergy in the spiritual (if not temporal) guidance of society, on both sides, to varying degrees, employ the same knowledge, share the same mental structure, and are superbly unaware of the evolution of society and the new kind of Islam emerging among the masses: one that is not very intellectualized, but in direct contact with the modern world, with the traumatizing consequences of subordination and the need to shake up old mental structures.[3]

This stern criticism of the orientalists and the clergy seems to have as its ideal a popular Islam, no longer manipulated by its clerics but rejecting all

3 Dj. ATTARI, "Transformations de la religiosité populaire iranienne," *Peuples méditerranéens*, 34 (January–March 1986), pp. 129 and 133–4.

theological discourse, in turn expressing anguish and revolt. Two explanations for political behaviors are in confrontation: the first, *neo-orientalist*, rests on the all-pervasiveness of theology and the past; the second, tending more toward the sociological, on the unequal relations created by the world-wide spread of modernity and trade, or the resultant frustrations aroused among dependent societies. Paul Vieille writes:

> The ideological postulate of the role of elites in revolutions is one con-structed by the elites themselves; when made, it tends to establish its own truth, as history is first of all a narrative, and thus to legitimize the claim of those elites to occupy a role of power in society. Hence its expansion. This poses a subsidiary and specific question . . . in what way is orientalism in-volved in political strategies in the heart of "oriental" societies?[4]

Unfortunately, apart from revolutionary outbursts, the masses reveal only vague expressions of themselves. "Popular religion" knows little else than to copy the snatches of learned religion still available, and blend them, patch them together, syncretize them. From his Iranian village, the Austrian anthropologist Reinhold Loeffler reports only individual professions of faith in which he finds it difficult still to recognize a universal religion.[5] Fragmented, belief cut off from its discursive expression lacks even the means of self-perpetuation. It is obvious that the study of these infra-discursive manifestations is of major importance for an anthropological description; that it can be an effective instrument in tuning into social phenomena where an inarticulate religion sublimates all aspirations and setbacks. But that very inarticulacy cannot exist without reference to a theological discourse, however oblique. The discourse of the elites remains the reference for popular beliefs.

Condemned to follow orientalism, that is to say, to understand Islamic society only through the discourse of its elite, we sometimes have difficulty in grasping the social dynamic. Forewarned of this danger, let us now go to the defence of the elites – even if they are clerical – and of orientalism.

It would be wrong to underestimate the information provided by clerical discourse. Only let us decode it cautiously. It acts on the masses as a central discourse, in competition with that of intellectuals or the media, imported

---

4   P. VIEILLE, "L'Orientalisme est-il théoriquement spécifique? A propos des interprétations de la révolution iranienne," *Peuples méditerranéens: L'Orientalisme*, no. 50 (January–March 1990), p. 161; in the same issue, see F. KHOSROKHAVAR, "Du néo-orientalisme de Badie: Enjeux et méthodes," pp. 121–48, chiefly p. 140.

5   R. LOEFFLER, *Islam in Practice*, Albany, SUNY Press, 1988, pp. 246ff.

or "locally grown." The originality of Shi'ite clerical discourse lies in its very lack of comfort: the heir of a tradition independent of government, impregnated with theology and mysticism, but henceforward itself the holder of power, having become one of the "interfaces" allowing society to communicate with the outside world. Its failures are today more apparent than its successes: it has not managed to be convincing beyond the Shi'ite Community, and ecumenical attempts in the Muslim world seem to be compromised for a long time; even in the strongly Shi'ite Communities of Lebanon and Iraq, the export of the model of a society politically dominated by the clergy has produced no concrete result; liberation from the scourges of economic and cultural dependence seems always to be put off until the morrow, for the most pragmatic and reasonable motives. The symbol of the intransigence of the Tehran revolutionaries appears to be the death sentence on the author of *The Satanic Verses*, Salman Rushdie; they doubtless want him to go on living as long as possible, for with him would vanish one of the last signs of the break with the West.

Are Henry Corbin's writings on Shi'ism taken from the discourse of the elite? So be it! Let us hope that there may always be elites in Shi'ism, and that social problems may one day lose their obsessive character that makes us forget the immaterial truths. Without an elite and esoteric secrets there would be no revolution, no dream, no guide to lead us in such a troubled world! In fact, no Shi'ism . . .

Chronological Highlights

632	Death of the Prophet Mohammad. 'Ali is excluded from the caliphate.
656–61	Caliphate of 'Ali.
661–750	Omayyad caliphate, capital Damascus.
680	Martyrdom of Imam Hoseyn at Karbalā.
750–1258	'Abbāsid caliphate, capital Baghdad.
818	Death (or martyrdom) of Imam Rezā at Tus, near present-day Mashhad.
874–941	Minor Occultation of the Twelfth Imam.
945–1055	The Buyids dominate the caliphate in Baghdad.
1501	Shah Esmā'il founds the Safavid state and proclaims Shi'ism the official religion in Iran.
1722	The Afghans take Isfahan; end of the Safavid kingdom.
1736–41	Nāder Shah in Iran; challenge to Shi'ism.
1779–1925	Qājār dynasty in Iran.
1850	Execution of the Bāb in Tehran.
1891	Protest against British control over tobacco monopoly. Religion versus the Iranian monarchy.
1906–9	Constitutionalist revolution in Iran.
1920	Revolt of Shi'ites in Iraq.
1922	Sheikh 'Abdolkarim Hā'eri Yazdi restores the theological centre at Qom.
1925–41	Rezā Shah Pahlavi.
1935	Violent demonstrations at Mashhad against the laws of authoritarian westernization of clothing.
1941–79	Mohammad-Rezā Shah Pahlavi.
1946	Assassination of Ahmad Kasravi by the *Fedā'iyān-e eslām*.
1951–3	Mosaddeq Iranian Prime Minister; nationalization of oil.
1955	Wave of persecution against the Bahā'is in Iran.
1961	Death of ayatollah Borujerdi.
1963	First mass demonstrations around ayatollah Khomeyni.
1964–79	Ayatollah Khomeyni in exile.

1969–73	Hoseyniya Ershād, Muslim progressivism, 'Ali Shari'ati.	1980–8	War between Iran and Iraq.
1977	Death of Shari'ati in London. Relaxing of censorship in Iran.	1987	Repression of a Shi'ite demonstration during the pilgrimage to Mecca: 402 dead, of whom 275 are Iranian.
1978	Disappearance of Imam Musā Sadr in Libya.	1989	(February 15) Khomeyni condemns the writer Salman Rushdie to death for apostasy.
1979	(February 11) Victory of the Islamic Revolution in Iran. (November 4) Taking of hostages in the American embassy in Tehran.		(June 3) Death of Imam Khomeyni. Khāmena'i succeeds him.
1980	Execution of Mohammad-Bāqer al-Sadr by Iraqi police at Najaf.		

Glossary

Arabic and Persian terms. Most Arabic words in the religious vocabulary are used in the same sense in Persian, sometimes in a Persianized construction (with the *ezafa*). In the simplified transcription used for this book, Persian words are written according to the rules of the classic written language: endings in -a (as in *ejāza*) are pronounced like the "e" in "bell" in the contemporary spoken Persian of Tehran; the *h* is sounded; *qāf* and *gheyn* have been uniformly transcribed as *q*; *'eyn* and *hamza* are shown as an apostrophe; the "e" and "u" should be pronounced as in Italian or German (respectively as in "bell" and "too"). Words marked with an asterisk (*) are Persian or Persianized forms.

Ahl-e Haqq:* "Faithful to truth:" a mystic community that had its origins among the Kurdish Shi'ites, practicing an exaggerated cult of the Imam 'Ali, and rites that sometimes resemble those of the Sufis. See J. DURING, *Musique et mystique dans les traditions de l'Iran*, Paris and Tehran, Institut français de recherche en Iran, 1989, pp. 291ff.

akhbār (sing.: *khabar*): Traditions recorded by the Imams. Commonly known as "hadith" (*hadis*).

akhbāri: Name of a branch of Twelver Shi'ism (opposed to the *osuli* branch) which bases its jurisprudence exclusively on the traditions (*akhbār*) received from the Imams

ākhund:* Originally designated a teaching cleric. In the absolute sense, means the philosopher Mollā Sadrā Shirāzi (1571–1640). Commonly today a pejorative to mean a cleric. *Zedd-e ākhund*,* "anticlerical."

'alam: Banner carried in ritual demonstrations for the mourning of the Imam Hoseyn

'alavi: Those who revere 'Ali. The 'Alavites of Syria and Turkey have a greater veneration for 'Ali than for the prophet Mohammad.

'ālem: (pl. *'olamā*, whence our *ulema*): Well-read, educated. Learning (*'elm*) being *par excellence* that of religious knowledge, *'alem*/*ulema* designates the clerics of Islam.

'allāma: The distinctive title given to a particularly erudite *'alem*, "Doctor" in religious knowledge

āqā:* Commonly used for "Mr." In the absolute sense means the Master, the *marja'-e taqlid*.

'Āshurā: The tenth day of the lunar month of Moharram; ancient Jewish celebration. On this day the battle of Karbalā took place, and Shi'ites solemnly celebrate a day of mourning in its memory.

Āstān-e Qods-e Razavi:* A pious foundation (*vaqf*) connected with the mausoleum of the Imam Rezā at Mashhad

'Atabāt: Sacred "thresholds," or mausoleums of the Imams situated on Iraqi soil

āyatollāh: Literally "miraculous sign from God." Honorary title used to address a high-ranking *mojtahed.*

āyatollāh al-'ozmā: "Great ayatollah," considered suitable to be chosen as a Guide to imitate (*marja'-e taqlid*)

bāzār:* A place, often covered, reserved for trade; Arabic: *suq* (souk). Bazar traders are usually effective upholders of the clergy.

chador: See *hejāb*

dars-e khārej:* Final year of theological studies. Literally "lesson *outside* the book."

dasta:* Procession of flagellants for the Moharram mourning

darvish* (dervish): "Poor" (Arabic: *faqir*), member of a Sufi brotherhood

ejāza: Permission to teach, "license." Delivered individually by a master who judges that a cleric has profited well from his course.

ejtehād:* Effort of interpretation, praticed by the *mojtahed*, to clarify religious law by the use of reason and the principles of jurisprudence (*osul al-feqh*)

emām (imam): He who is in the forefront, the guide (notably for prayer). For Shi'ites, in the absolute sense, one of the twelve spiritual successors of the Prophet Mohammad. Since 1979, the title given by revolutionary Iranians to ayatollah Khomeyni.

emām jom'a: The official leader of the Friday prayers appointed by the local authority in each town. It is he (or his locum) who gives the sermon (*khotba*) before the prayers.

emām-e jamā'at: The prayer-leader directing public prayers

emāmzāda: A descendant of an Imam, or his mausoleum that has become a centre of pilgrimage

'erfān: Gnosis, or mysticism not touched by Sufism (*tasavvof*). Term accepted by the clergy to designate a mysticism taught in official theological schools.

eslāmi: Islamic. Sometimes used today in the non-religious sense of "one who belongs to the Islamic Republic," which is thus different from *mosalmān** (Muslim).

esnā 'ashari: Twelver, referring to the Twelve (*'esnā 'ashar*) Shi'ite Imams

falsafa: Philosophy. Shi'ism has kept alive a philosophical tradition that goes back, via Avicenna, to the neo-Platonists and Aristotle.

fatvā: Religious decree pronounced by a *mojtahed* (by a *mofti* in Sunnism). See *resāla.*

faqih (pl. *foqahā*): Specialist in jurisprudence, *mojtahed.* Khomeyni defined legitimate authority as belonging to the *faqih* inasmuch as he is the heir of the Prophet Mohammad.

feqh (fiqh): Islamic jurisprudence. Literally "comprehension" of the Law.

hadith (hadis): See *akhbār*

hajj: Annual pilgrimage to Mecca during the month of *zo'l-hejja*, in which every Muslim is required to take part – if he has the wherewithal – at least once during his lifetime

hejāb: Veil covering the head and shoulders. May be a chador (large veil covering from head to foot) or a *rusari** (wide scarf covering the head) or even a *maqne'a* (headgear tied under the chin and covering the shoulders, strictly revealing only the middle of the face).

hejri: Of the Hegira. The liturgical calendar of Muslims is determined by a lunar year (*qamari*) of 354 or 355 days, and the computation of the years begins from the Hegira of the Prophet (AD 622). So 1991 is year 1411–12 by lunar computation, or 1369–70 by solar.

hekmat: Wisdom. *Hekat-e elāhi:* theosophy. Another way of designating philosophy.

hezbollāh: Literally "party of God." Name adopted by various Islamist groups, notably Shi'ite, in Iran and the Lebanon. *Hezbollāhi*, in the general sense: "fanatic."

hojjat ol-eslām: Literally, "apodictic proof of Islam." Honorary title given to the *mojtahed*.

hoseyniya (hosseyniyeh): Place where the mourning for Imam Hoseyn is celebrated. Often in the form of a mosque with the four walls surrounding the central courtyard arranged to accommodate the public: a sort of theatre where the stage, in the centre, is surrounded by two tiers of boxes. This name is also given to amphitheatres of more modern construction, planned for religious demonstrations: the Hoseyniya Ershad in Tehran where 'Ali Shari'ati taught.

howza-ye 'elmiya:* Learned circle, centre of theological studies, traditional Islamic university grouping together several *madrasa*

imam: See *emām*

ithnā 'ashari: See *esnā 'ashari*

ja'fari: Referring to the Sixth Imam, Ja'far al-Sādeq. Name of the juridical school of Twelver Shi'ites; see *mazhab*.

jehād: Holy war. The root stresses the idea of effort, and Muslim apologists hold that it is an internal war within the believer against evil impulses. The Islamic Republic institutionalized a Holy War of construction (*Jehād-e sāzandagi*), a body intended to promote development operations in rural zones.

ketmān: Discipline of the arcane, mental dissimulation. When the Shi'ites were persecuted they had to justify lying in order to survive. If they admitted their Imamite faith they risked endangering the very survival of Shi'ism itself. Also called *taqiya*.

khoms: The fifth of excess revenue and certain capital (treasure trove, accumulated gold or silver, pearls found in the sea, etc.) paid to the clergy, generally to a duly accredited agent of the *marja'al-taqlid*

khotba: Sermon, and notably at the Friday prayers when two sermons are delivered, one after the other: the first, general, is a religious exhortation, the second is concerned with political or social problems

madrasa (madrésseh): Traditional theological school, whose premises, rather like the colleges at Oxford and Cambridge, are both places for living and places for teaching. Tutors and students live in neighbouring "cells." *Madrasa* are usually maintained thanks to mortmain foundations (*vaqf*). Students receive allowances in cash or kind. See *howza-ye 'elmiya*.

Mahdi: The "well guided," he who will restore justice and truth to the world. Thus, for Shi'ites, the Twelfth Imam.

majles: Assembly, parliament. Also: assembly to pray or listen to preaching.

marja'al-taqlid:* Literally "source of imitation." Every Shi'ite believer must choose from among the *mojtahed* the one who is the most learned, worthy, and pious, and conform to his legal advice (*fatvā*) for the application of the law. If this *marja'* dies, another must immediately be chosen, as one cannot imitate a dead man.

mazhab: Religion. Legal school within Islam. Shi'ism is sometimes recognized as a fifth school alongside the four schools of Sunnism, the Ja'farite school (*Ja'fari*).

metwali: Traditional ethnic name designating the Shi'ites in the Lebanon. Literally "those who recognize the authority" of the Imam 'Ali.

mofti (mufti): In Sunnism, one who is competent to issue a *fatvā*

Moharram: First month of the Islamic lunar year. On 9 and 10 Moharram (*tāsu'ā*, *'āshurā*) Shi'ites commemorate with very extravagant ritual mourning ceremonies the martyrdom of Imam Hoseyn at Karbalā in 680.

mojtahed: Theologian who has received a good number of *ejāza* from other *mojtaheds*, and is competent to issue legal opinions (*fatvā*) and to practise *ejtehād*

molla:* Vague term derived from the Arabic form *mowlā* (master), used to designate a cleric, with somewhat pejorative connotations

moqaddamāt: Elementary degree in theological teaching in the *howza*

mosalmān:* Muslim. The common Arabic term is *moslem*. "Muslim," which implies adherence to a faith, is distinct from *eslāmi*, which refers rather to a culture.

mot'a: Marriage "of pleasure," of which the time limits and various conditions are defined by contract between the two parties. They can decide notably to practise strict contraception. See also *siqa*.

nabi: Prophet. See *rasul*.

namāz:* Prayer.

omma (umma, oumma): Transnational Community of believers in Islam

osul al-feqh: Principles used as premises for judgement in jurisprudence

osuli: School of Shi'ism, dominant from the eighteenth century, giving *mojtaheds* authority to apply the Law. Is in opposition to the *akhbāri* doctrine.

qeyba (ghaybat): Occultation of the Twelfth Imam. The "minor" Occultation (*q. al-soqrā*, from 874 to 941), a period when the Imam communicated with the faithful through the intermediary of four agents, is distinguished from the "major" Occultation (*kobrā*), during which there is no longer any communication – unless by a mystic path – between the Imam and the Community.

qotb: Mystic Pole in Sufism

Ramadhān: Ninth month of the Islamic lunar year, during which believers must fast totally and abstain from conjugal relations between dawn and sunset. A period of preaching, ascetic practices, conviviality, and thus of great mobilization. In countries where, in the hot season, the day lasts too long, Muslims often adopt an average schedule for their fast. On 21 Ramadhān Shi'ites celebrate the memory of Imam 'Ali's assassination.

rasul: Apostle, prophet. Mohammad is often called *rasul-Allah*.

resāla: Mission. Treatise. Often designates the "practical treatise" (*resāla-ye 'amaliya**) in which a *mojtahed*, when he becomes a *marja' al-taqlid*, gathers together all the *fatvā* he has issued giving advice on legal problems.

rowza(-khāni):* Meeting during which a preacher recounts, chants and sings about the martyrdom of one of the Twelve Imams. The name comes from the collection *Rowzat al-shohadā*, "The Garden of Martyrs," written about 1502 by Vā'ez al-Kāshefi, a Naqshbandi Sufi (Sunni) from the Khorasan region.

ruhāni:* Cleric. Term formed from *ruh* ("spirit") as "spirituality" from "spirit."

ruhāniyat:* Clergy. A social body clearly distinguished by an internal solidarity, and access reserved for those who have completed the curriculum of theological studies and are authorized, at a ceremony held on a day of religious festival, to wear the turban (*'emāma*).

sahm-e emām:* The "Imam's share," half the *khoms* paid by the faithful to the clergy, left to the discretion of the recipient: some say that this share should be distributed among the *sayyed*. The other half must be given to the needy.

salavāt (plural of *salāt*, prayer): Prayer or eulogy particular to the Shi'ites who use the phrase: "*Allāh-omma salle-'alā Mohammaden va-āle Mohammad*" (O, God, bless Mohammad and the Family of Mohammad).

sayyed: Patrilineal descendants of the Prophet beginning with Fatima's two sons. *Sayyed* clerics wear a black turban as a sign of mourning for the Imams. Many *sayyed* lineages are usurped.

shari'a, shari'at* *(charia)*: Canonical law of Islam

sheykh: Old. Respectful title for a mulla (mollā).

shi'a: Clan, party, whence *shi'at 'Ali*, "the party of 'Ali," Shi'ism

sina-zani:* Literally, to beat one's breast. Various flagellations and mortifications of the flesh that Shi'ites inflict on themselves in public on the occasion of mourning for the Imams, but above all for Hoseyn during the month of *Moharram*.

siqa (sigheh): Literally, a form binding spouses to each other. In Iran it commonly means a contract of temporary marriage (mot'a), or even the woman who marries in this way.

sofra:* Tablecloth. Votive meal offered by a pious woman, usually to other women, with preaching performed by a woman.

ta'assob: Fanaticism. Viewed favorably, a strongly motivated commitment.

taqiya: Mental dissimulation. See *ketmān*.

taqlid: Imitation. Applied in particular with regard to the great *ayatollah* whom it has been decided to choose as "Source of imitation" (*marja' al-taqlid*).

tasannon: Sunnism

tasavvof: Sufism, the mystic path of Islam

tashayyo': Shi'ism

ta'ziya (taziyeh): Demonstration of mourning. In particular the religious plays acted to commemorate the martyrdom of Hoseyn or the other Imams during the first ten days of the month of *Moharram*.

tekiya: Place, a special building, where the mourning of Hoseyn is celebrated. See *hoseyniya*.

ulema: See *'alem*

umma: See *omma*

vaqf, pl. *owqāf*: Mortmain foundation the profits of which are generally allocated to an institution of religious nature: hospital, library, mausoleum, school, etc. The director (*motavalli*) of this foundation is often a cleric and can draw a salary from the profits of the sums he administers.

velāyat al-faqih (velāyat-e faqih*): Principle according to which political authority belongs to the *ulema*, and foremost amongst them, the religious jurist *faqih*. This principle became the keystone of the constitution of the Islamic Republic of 1979, revised in 1989.

zakāt: Legal alms which can be paid at the same time as the *khoms*

ziyārat: Visit. Pilgrimage to a mausoleum.

Bibliography

With few exceptions, the books listed are in European languages and refer to the original sources (in Persian or Arabic) with Shi'ism as their principal subject. The numerous articles quoted in the footnotes are not included here. Since 1977 there has been an annual bibliography of studies on Iran, with abstracts mainly in French, published by the Institut français de recherche in Iran, *Abstracta Iranica* (distributed by Peeters, Louvain and Paris); each number includes numerous references to studies concerning Shi'ism, with critical abstracts. Further documentation is to be found in the following encyclopedias: *Encyclopedia of Islam*, Leiden, Brill (from 1960, 2nd edn in progress); *Encyclopaedia Iranica*, Costa Mesa (California), Mazda (from 1982).
SUNY = State University of New York.

SHI'ISM IN GENERAL

As Viewed by Shi'ites

Mohammad Ali AMIR-MOEZZI, *The Divine Guide in Original Shi'ism*, Albany, SUNY Press, 1994.

(Mohammad b. 'Ali EBN BABUYA), *A Shi'ite Creed*, trans. A. A. A. Fyzee, London, Oxford University Press (Islamic Research Association series, 9), 1942 (= transl. of *Resālāt al-e 'teqādāt*).

Asaf A. A. FYZEE, *Outlines of Muhammedan Law*, Oxford, 1949 (4th edn, Delhi, 1974).

Jassim M. HUSSAIN, *The Occultation of the Twelfth Imam: A Historical Background*, preface by Dr. I. K. A. Howard, London, The Mohammadi Trust of Great Britain and Northern Ireland/The Zahra Trust, 1982.

H. M. JAFRI, *Origins and Early Development of Shi'a Islam*, New York, Longman, 1976.

Hossein MODARRESSI TABĀTABĀ'I, *Kharaj in Islamic Law*, distributed by E. J. Brill, 1983.

Hossein MODARRESSI TABĀTABĀ'I, *An Introduction to Shī'ī Law: A bibliographical study*, London, Ithaca Press, 1984.

(Cheikh al-MUFID), D. Sourdel, "L'Imamisme vu par le Cheikh al-Mufīd," *Revue des études islamiques*, 40 (1972), pp. 217–96 (trans. and commentary by K. Avā'el al-maqāl āt).

Shaykh al-MUFID, *Kitāb al-Irshād. The Book of Guidance*, trans. I. K. A. Howard, preface by S. H. Nasr, London, Balagha Books/The Muhammadi Trust, 1981.

M. Javad MASHKOUR, *An-Nawbakhti: Les Sectes shiites*, transl. with notes and Introduction, Tehran, 1980. (Published in 1958– in *Revue de l'histoire des religions*.)

Majeed Hamad al-NAJJAR, *Islam Jafari Rules of Personal Status and Related Rules of Iraqian Law*, reprint, Tehran, "A Group of Muslim Brothers" (= WOFIS), 1978 (Ist edn, 1974).

Seyyed Hossein NASR, *Ideals and Realities of Islam*, London, Allen & Unwin, 1966; new edn, 1975.

Seyyed Hossein NASR, *Man and Nature: The Spiritual Crisis of Modern Man*, London, Allen & Unwin, 1968; reprint, Mandala Books, 1976.

Seyyed Hossein NASR, ed., *Ismā'īlī Contributions to Islamic Culture*, Tehran, Imperial Iranian Academy of Philosophy, 1977/1398.

Seyyed Hossein NASR, *Knowledge and the Sacred*, New York, Crossroad Publishing, 1981 (The Gifford Lectures, 1981).

Nasrollah POURJAVADY and Peter L. WILSON, *Kings of Love: The Poetry and History of the Ni'matullahi Sufi Order*, preface by Sd. H. Nasr, Tehran, Imperial Iranian Academy of Philosophy, Boulder, Great Eastern Book Co., and London, Thames & Hudson, 1978.

A. SACHEDINA, *Islamic Messianism: The Idea of the Mahdi in Twelver Shi'ism*, Albany, SUNY Press, 1981.

A. SACHEDINA, *The Just Ruler in Shi'ite Islam*, New York, Oxford University Press, 1988.

'Allāmah Sayyid Muhammad Husayn TABĀTABĀ'I, *Shi'ite Islam*, trans. S. H. Nasr, London, Allen & Unwin, 1975.

A Shi'ite Anthology, texts chosen by 'allāmah TABĀTABĀ'I, trans. W. C. Chittick, introduction by S. H. Nasr, Albany, SUNY Press; London, Mohammadi Trust of Great Britain and Northern Ireland, 1981.

As Viewed by Orientalists

Le Shi'isme imamite: Colloque de Strasbourg (6–9 mai 1968) (arranged by R. Brunschvig and Toufic Fahd), Paris, PUF, 1970.

Henry CORBIN, *En Islam iranien: Aspects spirituels et philosophiques*, 4 vols, Paris, Gallimard, 1971–2.

Henry CORBIN, *Spiritual Body and Celestial Earth: From Mazdean Iran to Shi'ite Iran*, Princeton, Princeton University Press, 1977. (2nd, revised, French edn: *Corps spirituel et Terre céleste: De l'Iran mazdéen à l'Iran shi-ite*, Paris, Buchet-Chastel, 1979).

Henry CORBIN, *Cyclical Time and Ismaili Gnosis*, trans. R. Manheim and J. Morris, London, 1983.

Henry CORBIN, *Temple and Contemplation*, trans. P. Sherrard, London, 1986.

On Corbin, see Ch.-H. de FOUCHECOUR, "Henry Corbin (1903–1978)," *Journal Asiatique*, 267, 3–4 (1979), pp. 231–7; Ch. JAMBET, ed., *Henry Corbin*, Paris, L'Herne, 1981; *idem*, *La Logique des Orientaux: Henry Corbin et la science des formes*, Paris, Le Seuil, 1983; D. SHAYEGAN, "Corbin, Henry," *Encyclopaedia Iranica*, vol. VI.

Frederick DE JONG, ed., *Shi'a islam, sects and Sufism: historical dimensions, religious practice and methodological considerations*. A collection of papers presented at the 15th Congress of the Union Europeenne des Arabisants et Islamisants (Utrecht/Driebergen, September 13–19, 1990). Utrecht, M. Th. Houtsma Strichting, 1993.

Jean DURING, *La musique iranienne: Tradition et évolution*, Paris, Recherches sur les civilisations/Institut français d'Iranologie de Téhéran (Bibliothèque iranienne, 29, Mémoires 38), 1984.

Jean DURING, *Musique et mystique dans les traditions de l'Iran*, Paris and Tehran, Institut français de recherche en Iran (Bibliothèque iranienne, 36), 1989.

Jean DURING, *The Art of Persian Music*, Washington, Mage Publ., 1991.

Richard GRAMLICH, *Die schiitischen Derwischorden Persiens*, 3 vols, Wiesbaden, Franz Steiner, 1965, 1976, 1981.

Heinz HALM, *Die islamische Gnosis: Die extreme Schia und die 'Alawiten*, Zurich and Munich, Artemis Verlag, 1982.

Heinz HALM, *Shi'ism*, Edinburgh, Edinburgh University Press, 1991.

Christian JAMBET, *La Grande Résurrection d'Alamut*, Lagrasse, Verdier, 1990.

Harald LÖSCHNER, *Die dogmatischen Grundlagen des ši'itischen Rechts. Eine Untersuchung zur modernen imamitischen Rechtsquellenlehre*, Erlangen, and Nuremberg, Carl Heymanns (Erlanger Juristiche Abhandlungen, 9), 1971.

Martin J. McDERMOTT, *The Theology of Al-Shaikh al-Mufīd (d. 413/1022)*, Beirut, Dar el-Machreq (Recherches de l'Institut de lettres orientales de Beyrouth, n.s., A., Langue arabe et pensée islamique, X), 1978.

Wilferd MADELUNG, *Lectures on the History of Shi'ism*, Chicago, University of Chicago Press, 1976.

Wilferd MADELUNG, *Religious Trends in Early Islamic Iran*, Albany, SUNY Press (Bibliotheca Persica, Columbia Lectures on Iranian Studies, 4) 1988.

Moojan MOMEN, *An Introduction to Shi'i Islam: The History and Doctrines of Twelver Shi'ism*, New Haven and London, Yale University Press, 1985.

Matti MOOSA, *Extremist Shi'ites: The Ghulat Sects*, Syracuse, NY, Syracuse University Press, 1988.

James Winston MORRIS, *The Wisdom of the Throne: An Introduction to the Philosophy of Mulla Sadra*, Princeton, Princeton University Press, 1981.

Sd Hossein NASR, Hamid DABASHI and Sd Vali Reza NASR, eds, *Shi'ism: Doctrines, Thought and Spirituality*, Albany, SUNY Press, 1988.

Sd Hossein NASR, Hamid DABASHI and Sd Vali Reza NASR, eds, *Expectation of the Millennium: Shi'ism in History*, New York, SUNY Press, 1989. (Anthology of articles by orientalists on Shi'ism.)

Amédée QUERRY, *Droit musulman: Recueil de lois concernant les musulmans schyites*, Paris, Imprimerie Nationale, 1871–2 (transl. of the *Sharāye' ol-eslām* of Mohaqqeq al-Helli).

Paul E. WALKER, *Early Philosophical Shi'ism: The Ismaili Neoplatonism of Abu Ya'qub al-Sistani*. Cambridge – New York, Cambridge University Press, 1993 (Cambridge Studies in Islamic Civilization) – 219 p.

Montgomery WATT, *The Formative Period of Islamic Thought*, Edinburgh, Edinburgh University Press, 1973.

THE RELIGIOUS SOCIOLOGY OF SHI'ISM

General

Said Amir ARJOMAND, *The Shadow of God and the Hidden Imam: Religion, Political Order and Societal Change in Shi'ite Iran from the Beginning to 1890*, Chicago and London, University of Chicago Press, 1984.

Said Amir ARJOMAND, ed., *Authority and Political Culture in Shi'ism*, Albany, SUNY Press, 1988.

Mahmoud AYOUB, *Redemptive Suffering in Islam: A Study of the Devotional Aspects of 'Āshurā in Twelver Shi'ism*, The Hague, Mouton, 1978.

Peter J. CHELKOWSKI, ed., *Ta'ziyeh: Ritual and Drama in Iran*, New York, New York University Press, and Tehran, Soroush, 1979.

Juan R. I. COLE and Nikki R. KEDDIE, eds, *Shi'ism and Social Protest*, New Haven and London, Yale University Press, 1986.

Hamid ENAYAT, *Modern Islamic Political Thought: The Response of the Shī'ī Muslims to the Twentieth Century*, Austin, University of Texas Press, and London and Basingstoke, Macmillan, 1982.

Shahla HAERI, *Law of Desire: Temporary Marriage in Iran*, London, I. B. Tauris, 1989.

Shi'ism in Modern Iran

Ervand ABRAHAMIAN, *Iran between Two Revolutions*, Princeton, Princeton University Press, 1982.

Ervand ABRAHAMIAN, *The Iranian Mojahedin*, New Haven, Yale University Press, and London, I. B. Tauris, 1989.

Shahrough AKHAVI, *Religion and Politics in Contemporary Iran: Clergy–State Relations in the Pahlavi Period*, Albany, SUNY Press, 1980.

Hamid ALGAR, *Religion and State in Iran 1785–1906: The Role of the Ulama in the Qajar Period*, Berkeley and Los Angeles, University of California Press, 1969.

Hamid ALGAR, "Religious Forces in Twentieth-Century Iran," in P. Avery, G. Hambly, and C. Melville, eds, *The Cambridge History of Iran*, vol. VII: *From Nadir Shah to the Islamic Republic*, Cambridge, New York, Port Chester, Melbourne, and Sydney, Cambridge University Press, 1991, pp. 732–64.

H. E. CHEHABI, *Iranian Politics and Religious Modernism: The Liberation Movement of Iran under the Shah and Khomeini*, Ithaca, Cornell University Press, and London, I. B. Tauris, 1990.

Abdul-Hadi HAIRI, *Shī'īsm and Constitutionalism in Iran: A Study of the Role Played by the Persian Residents of Iraq in Iranian Politics*, Leiden, Brill, 1977.

Michael M. J. FISCHER, *Iran: From Religious Dispute to Revolution*, Cambridge, Mass. and London, Harvard University Press, 1980.

Kurt GREUSSING, ed., *Religion und Politik im Iran: Mardom nameh – Jahrbuch zur Geschichte u. Gesellschaft des Mittl. Orients*, Frankfurt-am-Main, Syndikat (Berliner Institut für vergleichende Sozialforschung), 1981.

Nikki R. KEDDIE, *Religion and Rebellion in Iran: The Iranian Tobacco Protest of 1891–1892*, London, Frank Cass, 1966.

Nikki R. KEDDIE, *An Islamic Response to Imperialism: Political and Religious Writings of Sayyid Jamāl al-Din al-Afghānī* (including a translation of the *Refutation of the Materialists* from the original Persian by N. Keddie and H. Algar), Berkeley and Los Angeles, University of California Press, 1968.

Nikki R. KEDDIE, *Sayyid Jamal al-Din al-Afghani: A Political Biography*, Berkeley and Los Angeles, University of California Press, 1972.

Nikki R. KEDDIE, *Iran: Religion, Politics and Society. Collected Essays*, London, Frank Cass, 1980.

Nikki R. KEDDIE, *Roots of Revolution: An Interpretive History of Modern Iran* (with a section by Y. Richard), New Haven and London, Yale University Press, 1981.

Nikki R. KEDDIE, ed., *Religion and Politics in Iran: Shi'ism from Quietism to Revolution*, New Haven and London, Yale University Press, 1983.

Martin KRAMER, ed., *Shi'ism, Resistance, and Revolution*, Boulder, Colo., Westview Press, and London, Mansell (The Dayan Center for Middle Eastern and African Studies, The Shiloah Institute, Tel Aviv University), 1987.

Reinhold LOEFFLER, *Islam in Practice: Religious Beliefs in a Persian Village*, Albany, SUNY Press, 1988.

Vanessa MARTIN, *Islam and Modernism: The Iranian Revolution of 1906*, London, I. B. Tauris, 1989.

Michel M. MAZZAOUI, *The Origins of the Safawids: Shi'ism, Sufism and the Gulat*, Wiesbaden, Franz Steiner (Freiburger Islamstudien, 3), 1972.

Roy MOTTAHEDEH, *The Mantle of the Prophet: Religion and Politics in Iran*, New York, Simon & Schuster, 1985; London, Chatto & Windus, 1986.

Islamic Revolution

Ervand ABRAHAMIAN, *Khomeinism: Essays on the Islamic Republic*, London, I. B. Tauris, 1993.

Hamid ALGAR, *The Islamic Revolution in Iran* (transcript of four lectures given at the Muslim Institute, ed. K. Siddiqui), London, Open Press, 1980.

Said Amir ARJOMAND, *The Turban for the Crown: The Islamic Revolution in Iran*, New York and Oxford, Oxford University Press, 1988.

Shaul BAKHASH, *The Reign of the Ayatollahs: Iran and the Islamic Revolution*, New York, Basic Books, and London, I. B. Tauris, 1984.

Constitution of the Islamic Republic of Iran, trans. from the Persian by H. Algar, Berkeley, Mizan Press, 1980.

Hamid DABASHI, *Theology of Discontent: The Ideological Foundations of the Islamic Revolution in Iran*, New York, New York University Press, 1993.

John L. ESPOSITO, ed., *The Iranian Revolution: Its Global Impact*, Miami, Florida International University Press, 1990.

Chapour HAGHIGHAT, *1979: Iran, la révolution islamique*, Brussels, Complexe, 1985.

Eric HOOGLUND and Nikki R. KEDDIE, eds, *The Iranian Revolution and the Islamic Republic*, Syracuse, NY, Syracuse University Press, 1986.

Shireen T. HUNTER, *Iran and the World: Continuity in a Revolutionary Decade*, Bloomington and Indianapolis, Indiana University Press, 1990.

Farhad KHOSROKHAVAR, *L 'Utopie sacrifiée: Sociologie de la révolution iranienne*, Paris, Presses de la Fondation nationale des sciences politiques, 1993.

David MENASHRI, *Iran: A Decade of War and Revolution*, New York and London, Holmes & Meier, 1990.

Farhang RAJAEE, *Islamic Values and World View: Khomeyni on Man, the State and International Politics*, Lanham, New York, and London, University Press of America (The American Values Projected Abroad Series, 13), 1983.

Kazem RAJAVI, *La Révolution iranienne et les Moudjahedines*, preface by M. Rodinson, Paris, Anthropos, 1983. (Point of view of the Mojāhedin of the People.)

R. K. RAMAZANI, *Revolutionary Iran: Challenge and Response in the Middle East*, Baltimore and London, Johns Hopkins University Press, 1986.

Daryush SHAYEGAN, *Qu'est-ce qu'une révolution religieuse?* Paris, Éditions d'Aujourd'hui, 1982.

Daryush SHAYEGAN, *Le regard mutilé. Schizophrénie culturelle: pays traditionels face à la modernité*, Paris, Albin Michel, 1989.

Paul VIEILLE and Farhad KHOSROKHAVAR, *Le Discours populaire de la révolution Iranienne*, vol. I: *Commentaire*; vol. II: *Entretiens*, Paris, Contemporanéité, 1990.

Shi'ism outside Iran

Fouad AJAMI, *The Vanished Imam: Musa al Sadr and the Shia of Lebanon*, London, I. B. Tauris and Cornell University Press, 1986.

Juan R. I. COLE, *Roots of North Indian Shi'ism in Iran and Iraq: Religion and State in Awadh, 1722–1859*, Berkeley and Los Angeles, University of California Press, 1989.

Karl-Heinrich GÖBEL, *Moderne schiitische Politik und Staatsidee, nach Taufīq al-Fukaikī, Mohammad Gawād Mugniya, Rūhullāh Humainī (Khomeyni)*, Opladen, Leske and Budrich (Schriften des Deutschen Orient-Instituts), 1984.

John Norman HOLLISTER, *The Shi'a of India*, London, Luzac, 1953.

Pierre-Jean LUIZARD, *La Formation de l'Irak contemporain: Le Rôle des oulémas chiites à la fin de la domination ottomane et au moment de la création de l'état*, Paris, Éditions du CNRS, 1991.

Chibli MALLAT, *Shi'i Thought from the South of Lebanon*, Oxford, Centre for Lebanese Studies, 1988.

Chibli MALLAT, *The Renewal of Islamic law: Muhammad Baqer as-Sadr, Najaf and the Shi'i International*, Cambridge, Cambridge University Press, 1993. (On Iraqi Shi'ites but also on the ideological approach to economics, international Shi'ite connections, and the genesis of the Iranian constitution of 1979.)

Yitzhak NAKASH, *The Shi'is of Iraq*, Princeton, Princeton University Press, 1994.

Augustus Richard NORTON, *Amal and the Shi'a: Struggle for the Soul of Lebanon*, Austin, University of Texas Press (Modern Middle Eastern Series, 13), 1987.

David PINAULT, *The Shi'ites: Ritual and Popular Piety in a Muslim Community*, London, I. B. Tauris, 1992. (On Shi'ites in India.)

Monika POHL-SCHOBERLIN, *Die schiitische Gemeinschaft des Sudlibanon (Gabal 'Āmil) innerhalb des libanisischen konfessionellen Systems*, Berlin, Klaus Schwarz (Islamkundliche Untersuchungen, Bd 117), 1986.

Wilfred THESIGER, *The Marsh Arabs*, London, Longman Green, 1964. (On Shi'ites in South Iraq.)

Modern Shi'ite Ideologists' Writings

Abol-Hassan BANISADR, *The Fundamental Principles and Precepts of Islamic Government*, Lexington, Mazda, 1981.

Abol-Hassan BANISADR, *Quelle révolution pour l'Iran?* pref. by P. Vieille, Paris, Fayolle, 1980.

Abol-Hassan BANISADR, *Work and the Worker in Islam*, trans. H. Mashhadi, Tehran, Hamdami Foundation (Islamic Renaissance Series), [1980].

Abol-Hassan BANISADR, *L'Espérance trahie*, Paris, SPAG Papyrus, 1982.

Ayatullah Dr Muhammad Hosayni BEHISHTI and Hujjatul-Islam Dr Javad BAHONAR, *Philosophy of Islam*, Salt Lake City, Islamic Publications, [1986?].

Ruhollah KHOMEINI, *Islam and Revolution: Writings and Declarations of Imam Khomeini*, trans. H. Algar, Berkeley, Mizan Press, 1981.

Murtada MOTAHHARI, *Polarization around the Character of ʾAli Ibn Abī Talīb*, Tehran, WOFIS, 1981/1401.

Ayatollah Morteza MOTAHARI, *Stellung der Frau im Islam*, Bonn, Botschaft der islamischen Republik Iran (Islamische Renaissance, 7), 1982.

Murtadā MUTAHHARI, *The Rights of Women in Islam*, Tehran, World Organization for Islamic Services (= WOFIS), 1981.

Ayatullah Murtaza MUTAHHARI, *Fundamentals of Islamic Thought: God, Man and the Universe*, trans. R. Campbell, Introduction by H. Algar, Berkeley, Mizan Press (Contemporary Islamic Thought, Persian Series), 1985.

Murtaza MUTAHHARI, *The Islamic Modest Dress*, trans. L. Bakhtiar, Albuquerque, Abjad, [1988?].

Ali SHARI'ATI, *On the Sociology of Islam*, trans. H. Algar, Berkeley, Mizan Press, 1979.

Ali SHARI'ATI, *Fatima is Fatima*, trans. L. Bakhtiar, Tehran, Shari'ati Foundation and Hamdami Publishers, 1980.

Ali SHARI'ATI, *Marxism and Other Western Fallacies: An Islamic Critique*, trans. R. Campbell, preface by H. Algar, Berkeley, Mizan Press, 1980.

Ali SHARI'ATI, *Man and Islam*, trans. F. Marjani, Houston, Filinc (= Free Islamic Lit., Inc.), 1981.

Ali SHARI'ATI, *What is to be Done*, trans. F. Rajaee, preface by J. Esposito, Houston, Institute for Research and Islamic Studies, 1986.

Sayyid Mahmud TALEGHANI, *Society and Economics in Islam: Writings and Declarations*, trans. R. Campbell, annotated and introduced by H. Algar Berkeley, Mizan Press, 1982.

Seyyed Mahmood TALEQANI, *Islam and Ownership*, trans. A. Jabbari and F. Rajaee, Lexington, Mazda, 1983.

Mahmud TALEQANI, Mortada MUTAHHARI, and Ali SHARI'ATI, *Jihād and Shahādat: Struggle and Martyrdom in Islam*, trans. M. Abedi and G. Legenhausen, preface by M. Ayoub, Houston, Institute for Research and Islamic Studies, 1986.

Women's Rights

See the list given at the beginning of chapter 6.

Index